PRAISE FOR *NAVIGATING INSURTECH*

T0293344

'*Navigating Insurtech* is a valuable source for anyone who wishes to find out more about insurtech. Written by a leading entrepreneur who has developed insurance products by utilising technology, the book illustrates how insurtech is shaping the future of the insurance industry. It is brilliantly written and offers an encyclopaedic information on the subject.'
Professor Baris Soyer, Director of Institute of International Shipping and Trade Law, Swansea University

'*Navigating Insurtech* is an essential guide for the insurance industry offering strategic insights and practical advice to navigate digital transformation. An invaluable resource for both seasoned professionals and newcomers, it sheds light on the route to innovation within the insurance sector. A much-needed prompt for this centuries-old sector.'
Dame Inga Beale, former CEO, Lloyd's of London

'Insurtech is transforming the global insurance landscape at breakneck speed. Yet navigating this complex terrain is not easy. *Navigating Insurtech* offers practical guidance to help insurance companies harness the power of technology. Whether you are an established player or a new entrant, this book is an invaluable guide to realising strategic goals amidst digital disruption. Janthana Kaenprakhamroy cuts through the noise, charting a clear path forward.'
Sabine VanderLinden, CEO and Venture Partner, Alchemy Crew Ventures

'Janthana Kaenprakhamroy's book provides a great overview of how insurtech has evolved over the years and provides some useful perspective of where it might go next. I am sure *Navigating Insurtech* will become a useful read not only for investors, but also for budding insurtech founders who will be able to better understand the complexities of business building in the insurtech space.'
Robert Lumley, Director and Co-Founder, Insurtech Gateway

'Janthana Kaenprakhamroy offers pragmatic counsel to assist insurance firms in leveraging technology's potential. Through astute analysis and tangible case studies, *Navigating Insurtech* delves into the opportunities and hurdles of adopting digital solutions. Whether you're a seasoned player or a fresh contender, this book serves as an invaluable compass for achieving strategic objectives amidst digital upheaval.'
Vanessa Vallely OBE, CEO, WeAreTechWomen

'*Navigating Insurtech* serves as an indispensable guide for both seasoned professionals and newcomers to the field, providing a detailed chronicle of the historical roots of insurtech and its transformative effects in the digital age. It offers a clear roadmap for navigating the opportunities and challenges presented by digital solutions in insurance. Janthana Kaenprakhamroy's expertise and experience shine through in every chapter, making this book an essential resource for anyone looking to stay ahead in the age of digital disruption.'
Megan Kuczynski, President, Insurtech Insights USA

'Amid such a fast-moving, complex and nuanced landscape, when so much is at stake, this *Navigating Insurtech* offers an invaluable guide to how the insurtech landscape is changing – and how insurtechs are changing insurance. While offering great context and explanation of what has gone before, more importantly, this book looks to the future. No insurance leader can ignore the impact of technology on their sector – every insurance leader would benefit from reading this book.'
Wyn Jenkins, Publishing Director, Intelligent Insurer

'Drawing on her vast experience as the founder of Tapoly and insights from industry thought leaders, Janthana Kaenprakhamroy offers invaluable perspectives on the insurance sector's transformation. Her exploration of the challenges and innovations shaping insurance technology are both timely and impactful. *Navigating Insurtech* is crucial for anyone looking to understand or influence the future of insurance.'
Susanne Chishti, Chair, FINTECH Circle

Navigating Insurtech

*Opportunities and challenges
in digital insurance*

Janthana Kaenprakhamroy

KoganPage

First published in Great Britain and the United States in 2024 by Kogan Page Limited

2nd Floor, 45 Gee Street
London
EC1V 3RS
United Kingdom

8 W 38th Street, Suite 902
New York, NY 10018
USA

www.koganpage.com

Kogan Page books are printed on paper from sustainable forests.

ISBNs

Hardback   978 1 3986 1534 2
Paperback   978 1 3986 1532 8
Ebook   978 1 3986 1533 5

British Library Cataloguing-in-Publication Data

A CIP record for this book is available from the British Library.

Library of Congress Cataloging-in-Publication Data
Names: Janthana Kaenprakhamroy, author.
Title: Navigating insurtech : opportunities and challenges in digital
   insurance / Janthana Kaenprakhamroy.
Description: London ; New York, NY : Kogan Page, 2024. | Includes
   bibliographical references and index.
Identifiers: LCCN 2024006263 (print) | LCCN 2024006264 (ebook) | ISBN
   9781398615328 (paperback) | ISBN 9781398615342 (hardback) | ISBN
   9781398615335 (ebook)
Subjects: LCSH: Insurance–Technological innovations.
Classification: LCC HG8051 .J36 2024 (print) | LCC HG8051 (ebook) | DDC
   368–dc23/eng/20240209
LC record available at https://lccn.loc.gov/2024006263
LC ebook record available at https://lccn.loc.gov/2024006264

Typeset by Integra Software Services, Pondicherry
Print production managed by Jellyfish
Printed and bound by CPI Group (UK) Ltd, Croydon, CR0 4YY

CONTENTS

PREFACE

Welcome to *Navigating Insurtech*, your indispensable guide to the rapidly evolving world of insurance technology, commonly known as 'insurtech'. I hope this book offers a deep understanding of the sector, providing insights and lessons directly from the core of the insurtech revolution as technology rapidly transforms the industry.

In the narrative, I trace the development of insurtech from its inceptions. The insurance sector, a field traditionally resistant to change, is now rapidly adopting technological advancements. This shift has been notably influenced by the industry's response to various challenges, such as market fluctuations, the Covid-19 pandemic and geopolitical shifts.

My goal is for *Navigating Insurtech* to serve as a manifesto for this change, offering a comprehensive guide for both seasoned professionals and those new to the field. I delve into the complexities of insurtech, exploring customer experiences, technological progression and the critical role of insurtech in shaping the future of the industry.

I also draw from personal experiences as the founder of Tapoly to provide unique insights into this evolving industry.

As the book unfolds, I discuss the essential metrics and tools necessary to understand and excel in the insurtech space, including an analysis of the key players in the insurance industry and the various lines of business.

In many ways, the *Navigating Insurtech* is aimed to be more than a mere book. I hope it represents a significant shift in the insurance industry. I extend my sincere gratitude to the multitude of industry experts and pioneers for their invaluable insights and contributions that have greatly enriched this book.

1

Insurtech: An overview

Introduction

The rise of insurtech, the marriage of insurance and technology, has significantly reshaped the insurance industry, ushering in innovative approaches and improving the overall insurance experience. This chapter takes a deep dive into the historical context of insurtech, providing insights into the key players in the insurance market and the various lines of insurance business that exist today.

My personal journey in the insurtech industry took an unconventional path. Unlike many insurance experts who have traditional insurance backgrounds, my introduction to the world of insurance began as a customer. I was an Airbnb host looking for insurance coverage in 2016 when I discovered a significant gap in the market. At the time, there was a lack of insurance options for individuals participating in the sharing economy, especially those who rented out their homes through platforms like Airbnb. Traditional insurance companies didn't understand the risks associated with the sharing economy, resulting in limited coverage options and exorbitant premiums. I faced challenges finding affordable insurance that would adequately protect my property and my guests. This experience led me to realize the insurance gap that existed for individuals like me who were part of the sharing economy.

Motivated by the desire to address this gap and serve the sharing economy's underserved customers, I embarked on a mission to create a solution. This mission eventually gave birth to Tapoly, a pioneering insurtech company that specializes in providing on-demand and personalized insurance solutions tailored explicitly for gig workers and sharing economy participants.

But why do I care so deeply about the sharing economy? The sharing economy represents a transformative force with the potential to address some of our world's most pressing challenges. It challenges the traditional ownership model by promoting the sharing and utilization of existing assets, reducing waste and minimizing the environmental footprint. In this model, people can access and utilize resources without the need to accumulate or purchase them outright. It encourages community engagement and supports local economies by enabling individuals to work and stay in their local areas without the need for extensive relocations.

The sharing economy's significance extends beyond environmental and economic benefits. It has the power to enhance social connections, foster a sense of trust among participants and promote inclusivity. By facilitating resource sharing and collaboration, the sharing economy encourages a more communal and interconnected way of life.

Recognizing the importance of the sharing economy and its potential to bring about positive change, I became dedicated to supporting its growth. But, you might wonder, what can a former internal audit director and chartered accountant, with a career predominantly in investment banking, contribute to the insurance industry and the sharing economy?

My background and expertise proved invaluable in navigating the intricacies of the insurance landscape, particularly in the context of regulatory compliance and operational risk management. Insurance is a highly regulated industry, and my comprehensive understanding of regulatory requirements, supervisory oversight and technological advancements allowed me to lead Tapoly as its CEO effectively. My experience equipped me with a multifaceted perspective, enabling me to blend regulated practices with innovative solutions to tackle industry challenges.

Over seven years, I led the establishment and growth of Tapoly, an insurtech venture recognized for its ground-breaking contributions to the UK's insurance sector. Our company emerged as a pioneer in

Europe's insurtech landscape, introducing revolutionary on-demand and personalized insurance solutions tailored specifically to the needs of over 1 billion gig workers worldwide.

In this book, I have the privilege of sharing insights and experiences from my journey as an insurtech founder and industry thought leader. Through my experiences, I've gathered valuable lessons on how to build, operate and scale an insurtech business. I've witnessed the evolution of the insurtech industry and observed first hand how technology is reshaping the insurance landscape, both in the present and the future.

Early roots of insurtech

With over a decade of existence, the term 'insurtech' has become firmly rooted in the industry lexicon. Remarkably, not long ago, insurtech was a term that sparked debates over its very spelling and nomenclature, with some favouring 'Instech' as a complement to 'Fintech'. Yet, what began as an exploratory concept has now matured into a potent force, instigating a transformation within an industry steeped in tradition.

The growth of insurtech has unfolded at a breath-taking pace, transcending its initial status as a subset of fintech to establish itself as a distinct and influential domain. This evolution has been marked by the creation of innovative solutions, novel business models and a collaborative ecosystem that spans established insurance players and dynamic start-ups alike. Insurtech's impact permeates various aspects of the insurance landscape, spanning customer engagement, underwriting practices, claims processing and risk assessment.

As we navigate through the chapters of this book, it becomes evident that insurtech is not solely a technological advancement; it signifies a shift in the insurance industry's mindset. It ushers in the possibility of tailored experiences, streamlined processes and fresh value propositions that cater to the evolving preferences of modern consumers. Through the integration of emerging technologies such as artificial intelligence, IoT and blockchain, insurtech has paved the way for a new breed of insurance solutions characterized by agility, efficiency and responsiveness to the demands of the digital age.

Exploring the rich history of insurance

Insurance, a practice dating back millennia, serves as a crucial tool for mitigating and hedging against uncertainty and future risks. This concept has roots in the ancient civilizations of Babylon and China, with evidence of early insurance practices emerging around 4000–3000 BC. These pioneering risk management techniques laid the foundation for the insurance industry we know today.

Around 1750 BC, the Code of Hammurabi included some of the earliest documented insurance laws. These laws encompassed various principles, covering areas such as loan repayment, liability for theft and responsibilities of shipbuilders and ship managers. They set the stage for the development of insurance practices in ancient Babylon.

In 1901 and 1902, archaeologists unearthed a tablet from the Temple of Antinous in Egypt, shedding light on rules and membership dues of a burial society collegium established in Italia during the reign of Hadrian in AD 133. This early form of life insurance demonstrates the enduring human need to hedge against life's uncertainties.

As history unfolded, diverse forms of insurance emerged worldwide. In ancient Greece and Rome, individuals could pay fees to safeguard themselves against financial losses during sea voyages. The Middle Ages witnessed the rise of guilds, where members collectively contributed to a shared fund, offering compensation for fellow members' losses.

The 14th-century city of Genoa, Italy, witnessed the emergence of separate insurance contracts and insurance pools supported by landed estates. In 1347, the first known insurance contract in Genoa marked the birth of modern insurance practices.

By the late 17th century, London had become a hub for various insurance schemes, including property insurance. The Hamburg Fire Office, founded in 1676 in response to the Great Fire of London in 1666, played a pivotal role in mitigating property losses.

Life insurance found its roots in London in 1706 with the establishment of the Amicable Society for a Perpetual Assurance Office. This innovative society introduced a system where members paid annual contributions, and benefits were distributed to heirs upon a member's demise.

Lloyd's Coffeehouse, an influential marine insurance marketplace in 18th-century London, served as the epicentre of modern insurance. European and American traders frequented this establishment to secure insurance coverage for their shipments.

In the late 19th century, accident insurance emerged, with the Railway Passengers Assurance Company leading the way by offering coverage against railway accidents in 1848.

National insurance programmes began to emerge in the late 19th century in countries like Germany and the United Kingdom. These programmes provided protection against sickness, old age and unemployment, setting the stage for the development of modern welfare states.

The Social Security Act of 1935 in the United States marked a significant milestone in promoting insurance as a means of financial security. It paved the way for programmes like VA Home Loans and GI life insurance policies post-Second World War.

Throughout its remarkable journey, insurance has continually adapted to the unique needs of diverse cultures and historical periods. Today, insurance stands as a vital pillar of financial security, offering protection against unforeseen risks and events. Its historical evolution is a testament to humanity's enduring quest to mitigate uncertainty and secure its future.

Lloyd's of London

Lloyd's of London holds the distinction of being one of the world's most ancient and expansive insurance markets. This venerable market is steeped in history and encompasses numerous syndicates, insurers, brokers and other insurance intermediaries, making it not only one of the most diverse but also one of the most resilient insurance markets. It serves as the go-to destination for addressing risks that are deemed uninsurable elsewhere, often crafting bespoke insurance solutions.

In the realm of the insurance industry, Lloyd's of London is a key player. Lloyd's operates as a market where insurance underwriters and brokers converge to provide coverage for a broad spectrum of risks. Its origins can be traced back to a London coffee house owned by Edward Lloyd in the late 17th century. Over centuries, Lloyd's has ascended to a prominent position in the global insurance arena, earning a reputation for its exceptional proficiency in offering coverage for intricate and unconventional risks.

Lloyd's, renowned as the world's specialist insurance and reinsurance market, boasts an unmatched legacy of expertise that has been meticulously honed over centuries. It not only serves as the bedrock of the insurance industry but also charts a course for its future. Guided by seasoned underwriters and brokers spanning over 200 territories, the Lloyd's market plays a pivotal role in fashioning the indispensable, intricate and vital insurance solutions that underpin human progress.[1]

Backed by a robust foundation of diverse global capital resources and holding exceptional financial ratings, Lloyd's collaborates with a vast network of over 4,000 insurance professionals worldwide. Together, they cultivate and expand the realm of insured possibilities, bolstering resilience for businesses and local communities while fortifying economic growth across the globe.

Lloyd's caters to a diverse clientele, ranging from agile start-ups to small and medium-sized enterprises, from national governments to multinational corporations. These esteemed clients entrust their protection needs to the Lloyd's market, placing reliance on its specialized knowledge, robustness and unwavering security.

A glimpse into Lloyd's market, as evidenced by the 2023 Annual Report:[2]

Syndicates: 77

Coverholders: 3,434

Brokers: 380+

Lines of business: 200+

Leading insurance companies: 50+

Gross written premium: £46.7 billion

This snapshot underscores the formidable presence of Lloyd's market, an entity that not only treasures its rich historical legacy but also stands at the vanguard of shaping the future of insurance.

As of 2023, Lloyd's of London commands a gross written premium of £46.7 billion, solidifying its stature as one of the world's premier insurance markets. Within this market, underwriters provide coverage for a wide gamut of risks, spanning from major commercial disasters to high-profile celebrity body parts. While Lloyd's enjoys a storied history and a reputation for delivering specialized insurance solutions, it has confronted recent challenges stemming from the increasingly competitive landscape of the insurance industry and the transformative influence of new technologies on traditional business models.

Lloyd's of London functions as a bustling marketplace where insurers, reinsurers and brokers converge to offer comprehensive insurance solutions to their discerning clientele. Over the course of its illustrious history, the Lloyd's market has consistently played a pivotal role in shaping the insurance industry as it exists today. Through myriad trials, including the momentous Great Fire of London in 1666 and the profound losses incurred from the Titanic disaster in 1912, Lloyd's has steadfastly maintained its standing as one of the world's pre-eminent and most influential insurance markets.

Significant events in the 20th century

Insurance fundamentally serves as a risk-hedging tool, born out of the need to mitigate uncertainty and unforeseen risks. Consequently, various types of insurance have emerged in response to significant and unexpected catastrophes, shaping the history of the insurance industry.

The last decade has witnessed a series of significant events that have left their mark on the insurance landscape. Among these, the global financial crisis of 2008 stands out prominently. This crisis triggered a substantial decline in premium income and investment returns for many insurers, compelling them to re-evaluate their risk management strategies and fortify their business models for greater resilience.

Another momentous event was the enactment of the Affordable Care Act (ACA) in the United States in 2010. This legislation brought sweeping changes to the health insurance sector, mandating insurers to offer a minimum level of coverage irrespective of an individual's health status or pre-existing conditions. This shift brought both challenges and opportunities to insurers operating in this space.

The insurance industry has also grappled with the impacts of climate change and political instability, resulting in increased insurance claims and shifts in pricing structures that affect profitability. Hurricane Ida, for instance, triggered billions of dollars in insurance claims in the United States, while Lloyd's of London paid out over £21 billion for claims related to the war in Ukraine, Hurricane Ian and other events, leading to a pre-tax loss of £769 million in 2022.

Beginning in 2020, the Covid-19 pandemic has left an indelible mark on the insurance sector. It ushered in a surge in claims related to business interruption, event cancellation, travel insurance and more. The pandemic's economic fallout is estimated to have caused a global decrease in economic output exceeding £7 trillion ($8.5 trillion) between 2020 and 2022. In 2020, Lloyd's of London grappled with an estimated loss of £6.2 billion, with the loss ratio surging from 110.4 per cent to 129.8 per cent due to the pandemic.

In addition to contending with these challenges, the insurance industry faces a dual threat in the form of the rising influence of insurtech and the growing spectre of cybersecurity threats. These factors have the potential to disrupt traditional insurance models and introduce new forms of risks.

Moreover, as the industry increasingly relies on technology for risk management and claims processing, its susceptibility to cyberattacks and data breaches has grown significantly. This vulnerability is underscored by alarming statistics, including Lloyd's estimate that cybercrime imposes an annual cost of $400 billion on US businesses, and Allianz's projection that the European cyber insurance market will reach $20 billion by 2025. Traditional risk assessment and pricing models are no longer adequate, posing greater challenges in accurately evaluating and pricing risks.

Changes in regulations, including Solvency II, have wielded significant influence over the insurance sector. New laws and guidelines have impacted various facets of the industry, spanning underwriting to claims handling. Solvency II, specifically designed for insurance companies within the European Union, has introduced fresh requirements related to risk management, capital sufficiency and transparency. These mandates have compelled insurance companies to re-evaluate their risk profiles and financial positions, while also drawing increased scrutiny from regulators. As a result, some insurance firms have undergone restructuring or exited certain markets to align with these new regulations.

The new age post-pandemic

The Covid-19 pandemic has introduced a mixture of challenges and opportunities to the insurance sector. Established insurers are facing pressure to expedite their digitization efforts due to the pandemic's impact on their operations and the widespread adoption of remote work by both customers and employees. Simultaneously, this situation has opened doors for new entrants with robust technological capabilities to assist established insurers on their digitalization journey.

The pandemic has highlighted gaps in technology, systems, products and processes for both traditional insurers and insurtech companies. The unpredictability of 2020 has prompted the industry to rethink its products and processes to ensure resilience in the face of future crises.

One of the lasting impacts of Covid-19 is the growing emphasis on digital business models that prioritize exceptional customer experiences. The adoption of digital and remote sales channels is accelerating, driven by customer expectations for fast and hassle-free service.

Customers now expect real-time responses from insurers, whether it's speedy claims processing or immediate answers about coverage details. Any delays or lack of responsiveness can erode their confidence.

The concept of 'insurance-as-a-utility' is gaining traction, with policyholders seeking flexible coverage options that align with their actual usage. They also want incentives for positive behaviours that reduce the frequency and severity of claims. This has led to the emergence of pay-per-use insurance products, traditionally associated with property and casualty carriers, but now expanding into life and health insurance.

During times of crisis, customers rely on insurance firms the most. They expect reassurance that they are covered and access to essential services like claims processing. Insurance companies must ensure business continuity and maintain regular communication with policyholders during such situations.

Empathy plays a crucial role in customer expectations. Insurers are expected to show understanding and take proactive initiatives to demonstrate care for customers, especially when they are dealing with policy-related concerns or facing distress due to a crisis. Building an emotional connection with customers is essential.

The digital experience (DX) is becoming paramount in today's rapidly changing business landscape. Policyholders want access to insurance offerings anytime, anywhere and through various channels. Customer-centric insurers are meeting these expectations by providing intuitive self-service options that enable access at any time and from any location.

The rise of insurtech: Transforming the insurance landscape

In response to shifting customer demands and market expectations, the insurance sector has experienced a significant paradigm shift aimed at enhancing efficiency, transparency and accessibility. This transformative wave is commonly referred to as 'insurtech', a portmanteau of insurance and technology, signifying the convergence of the insurance industry with cutting-edge technological innovations. The overarching objective of insurtech is to drive multifaceted enhancements across various dimensions of insurance operations, thereby elevating customer experiences and advancing risk management practices.

The rise of insurtech represents a dynamic metamorphosis within the insurance sector, as it harnesses the capabilities of technology to revolutionize and augment various facets of the industry. Insurtech confronts several pressing challenges confronting traditional insurers, which include:

Meeting evolving customer expectations: In today's digital age, customers expect insurance services to be swift, convenient and tailored to their individual needs. This translates into a demand for access to policies, claims processing and customer support via digital channels such as mobile applications, chatbots and web portals. Insurtech firms leverage advanced technologies, such as artificial intelligence and big data analytics, to automate processes, enhance customer experiences and elevate overall satisfaction levels, thereby aligning insurers with these contemporary customer expectations.

Enhancing operational efficiency: Traditional insurers often grapple with elevated operational costs attributable to outdated manual processes and legacy systems that impede their operational performance and profitability. To remain competitive in the modern landscape, insurers must streamline their operations, reduce expenditures and bolster their agility. Insurtech solutions, which encompass technologies such as robotic process automation (RPA), cloud computing, artificial intelligence (AI) and machine learning (ML), and application programming interfaces (APIs), offer avenues for simplifying and optimizing workflows and systems. This results in heightened operational efficiency and cost-effectiveness.

Driving product innovation: The insurance sector faces dynamic shifts characterized by heightened competition, evolving regulatory frameworks and the emergence of novel risks that challenge traditional insurance products and business models. Insurers must innovate their product offerings, introduce new lines of coverage and adapt pricing and underwriting strategies to cater to diverse customer segments and their evolving requirements. Insurtech entities leverage telematics, the Internet of Things (IoT) and ML to craft customized and flexible insurance policies that align with real-time customer behaviours and risk profiles, fostering innovation within the industry.

Streamlining claims processing: Traditional claims processing methods often exhibit sluggishness, complexity and susceptibility to errors, posing challenges for insurers and policyholders alike. Insurtech solutions introduce efficiency into claims management through automation and data analytics. Technologies such as AI and computer vision enable swift and accurate claims assessments, thereby reducing processing times and enhancing customer satisfaction.

Advanced risk management: As the insurance landscape contends with increasingly complex insurance and regulatory risks, risk assessment and mitigation assume pivotal roles within the industry. Insurtech leverages data analytics and predictive modelling to elevate risk management practices. Insurers can better evaluate risks, competitively price policies and detect fraudulent claims through the application of advanced technologies.

These challenges represent critical pain points for insurers in the contemporary environment, and insurtech emerges as a pivotal force in their resolution. Insurtech not only fuels innovation but also reshapes the insurance sector, ushering in an era of enhanced efficiency, customer-centricity and technological sophistication in insurance services. In essence, insurtech aspires to modernize and disrupt the traditional insurance landscape by harnessing the transformative potential of technology.

While insurtech is a relatively recent concept, its growth has been remarkable in recent years. According to a 2021 McKinsey report, global investments in insurtech surpassed $11 billion in 2021,[3] doubling the previous year's figures. This trend underscores the enduring impact of insurtech on the insurance industry, hinting at the persistence of new opportunities and challenges for insurers and policyholders alike.

The early days: Pre-2000s

Before the term 'insurtech' gained widespread recognition, the seeds of innovation were already being sown within the insurance industry. The early adoption of computers in the mid-20th century marked the initial steps towards digitizing insurance processes. However, it wasn't until the late 20th century that the insurance industry truly began to embrace technology.

1980s: The use of computers for actuarial and underwriting purposes became more common. Insurance companies started to store policyholder information digitally, improving data management.

1990s: The internet began to play a role in insurance, with some companies offering online quotes and policy purchasing. Still, the industry remained largely paper-based.

Growth: 2000s–2010s

The new millennium marked a significant turning point for insurtech. Technological advancements, coupled with changing consumer behaviours, pushed the insurance industry to explore innovative solutions more aggressively.

Early 2000s: Online insurance comparison websites began to emerge. These platforms allowed consumers to compare quotes from multiple insurers, introducing a new level of transparency and choice.

Mid-2000s: The proliferation of mobile devices led to the development of mobile apps for insurance. Policyholders could now manage their policies, file claims and receive assistance through their smartphones.

Late 2000s: Telematics devices, capable of monitoring driver behaviour, were introduced, particularly in motor insurance. These devices paved the way for usage-based insurance (UBI) and pay-as-you-go policies.

2010s: The insurance industry saw a surge in insurtech start-ups. These companies focused on various aspects of insurance, from distribution and underwriting to claims processing and customer service.

Modern era: 2010s–present

The modern era of Insurtech is characterized by rapid innovation, data-driven decision-making, and increased collaboration between traditional insurers and start-ups.

2010s: Peer-to-peer (P2P) insurance models gained attention. P2P platforms allowed groups of individuals to pool their resources and share risk collectively, eliminating the need for traditional insurers.

2014: Lemonade, a well-known insurtech start-up, was founded. Lemonade introduced a digital, P2P insurance model that utilized AI and chatbots to streamline the claims process.

2016: Blockchain technology made its way into insurance. It was explored for its potential to improve transparency, reduce fraud and streamline processes like policy issuance and claims management.

2018: Insurtech investments reached record levels, with venture capital pouring into start-ups. This influx of funding further fuelled innovation and expansion.

Insurtech has become an integral part of the insurance ecosystem. It continues to influence customer experiences, pricing models, risk assessment and the development of entirely new insurance products.

Driving factors behind insurtech's rise

The rise of insurtech can be attributed to a combination of factors and converging trends that provided fertile ground for technological innovation within the insurance sector.

Technological advancements: The rapid advancement of technology, including the proliferation of smartphones, increased internet connectivity and the growth of big data analytics, provided the infrastructure and tools for disrupting traditional insurance processes.

Consumer expectations: Consumers increasingly demanded more convenient, transparent and personalized services across various industries, including insurance. They expected the same level of digital engagement and ease of use they found in other areas of their lives.

Regulatory changes: Regulatory changes and initiatives in different regions encouraged innovation and competition within the insurance sector. Regulatory bodies recognized the potential benefits of insurtech in improving customer outcomes and market efficiency.

Start-up ecosystem: A thriving start-up ecosystem, particularly in financial technology (fintech), attracted entrepreneurs and investors to explore opportunities in insurance technology. This ecosystem provided the necessary support and capital for insurtech ventures.

Data availability: The availability of vast amounts of data, including social media data, IoT-generated data and historical insurance data, enabled insurers to make more data-driven decisions, leading to better risk assessment and pricing.

Disruptive business models: As explored in Chapter 2, insurtech start-ups introduced new business models that challenged traditional insurance companies. Additionally, Chapter 4 delves into the transformation of distribution channels. These innovative models aim to provide customers with more customized and cost-effective insurance options in areas where traditional insurers either couldn't or didn't offer solutions.

Customer-centricity: Evolving customer preferences inspire innovation in both insurtech's product offerings and operational aspects, leveraging technology as a key component. The aim is to elevate the customer experience by offering digital platforms for policy purchase, claims management and access to insurance services, streamlining the entire process for greater user-friendliness.

Investment interest: As insurtech gained momentum and demonstrated its potential for transformation, it attracted significant investments from venture capital firms and corporate investors, further fuelling its growth. This, in turn, has encouraged talented entrepreneurs to flock into the insurtech industry.

Insurtech is important

Insurtech holds significant importance due to the pressing challenges and inefficiencies that have long plagued the insurance industry. Traditional insurance has often been viewed as an old, cumbersome and inefficient industry where the cost of operations frequently consumes a substantial portion of profits. This is precisely where insurtech steps in to drive change and innovation.

Elevating customer experiences: One of the primary reasons insurtech matters is its ability to enhance the customer experience. By harnessing technology, insurtech companies engage customers in selecting coverage, comprehending their insurance needs and delivering personalized services. This shift towards self-service, online interactions empowers customers to choose how they engage with insurers, reducing the need for time-consuming in-person or phone-based interactions.

Promoting efficiency: Insurtech significantly improves the efficiency of insurance processes. Policy-seekers and policyholders can now independently research and explore insurance options using digital platforms and apps. This eliminates the need to wait for business hours or an available representative, allowing users to access the information they need swiftly and without unnecessary bureaucracy.

Emphasizing individuality: Insurtech goes beyond one-size-fits-all insurance policies. It leverages innovative data gathering and processing tools to better understand each individual's unique needs and risk profile. This not only improves the accuracy of pricing but also results in more reliable and consistent coverage based on historical data and individual requirements.

Improving flexibility: Modern insurtech offerings are marked by flexibility. They often include customizable, short-term or transferable insurance plans, allowing individuals to tailor their coverage to specific needs and durations. This flexibility provides a level of adaptability that traditional insurance models struggle to match.

Reducing operating costs: Insurtech operates on a leaner, more cost-efficient model compared to traditional insurance companies. By eliminating the need for brick-and-mortar locations and reducing manual labour through automation, insurtech companies can offer competitive pricing while maintaining profitability.

Decreasing fraud: Insurtech utilizes data analytics, trend analysis and ML to detect and prevent fraudulent activities. This not only safeguards insurance providers but also ensures that honest policyholders are less likely to bear the burden of fraud-related costs.

Solving insurance challenges: Insurtech addresses longstanding challenges within the insurance industry. This includes streamlining claims management, enhancing underwriting accuracy, automating contract execution and bolstering risk mitigation. These innovations result in more efficient and cost-effective insurance processes.

Insurtech matters because it addresses the inherent inefficiencies of the traditional insurance industry. It responds to the widening gap between customer needs and the limitations of conventional insurance models. By leveraging cutting-edge technologies, insurtech enhances the customer experience, promotes operational efficiency and offers more individualized and flexible insurance solutions. As we delve into the insurtech landscape in Chapter 2, 'The insurtech landscape', we'll dive deeper into this transformation.

Key insurtech metrics

The convergence of these factors led to the emergence of insurtech, which has since become a driving force in reshaping the insurance industry. Insurtech companies continue to innovate, offering a wide range of digital solutions that aim to make insurance more accessible, affordable and responsive to the evolving needs of consumers and businesses. The insurtech industry is dynamic and rapidly evolving, and new statistics and trends may have emerged since publication.

Global funding: Insurtech companies attracted significant funding. In 2021, insurtech start-ups raised approximately $11 billion in funding globally.[4]

Market growth: The global insurtech market was expected to grow by $3.729 billion at a compound annual growth rate (CAGR) of over 39 per cent from 2020 to 2027.[5,6]

Start-ups: Currently, the global insurtech landscape is home to more than 1,000 start-ups. These innovative companies specialize in different aspects of the insurance value chain, spanning distribution, underwriting and claims processing. Notably, platforms like CrunchBase catalogue between 1,100 and 3,475 insurtech firms, underscoring the sector's remarkable diversity and dynamism.

Usage-based insurance (UBI): UBI, which utilizes telematics and IoT devices to determine premiums based on individual behaviour, was gaining traction. It was predicted that UBI policies would account for 20 per cent of all motor insurance premiums by 2025.

Digital transformation: Traditional insurance companies were increasingly adopting digital technologies. For example, around 74 per cent of insurance companies had either already implemented or were planning to implement digital transformation strategies.

Customer experience: Customer-centricity remained a focus. Over 90 per cent of insurers identified improving the customer experience as a top strategic priority.

AI: AI and ML were being used for various applications in insurtech, including fraud detection, underwriting automation, and chatbot-driven customer service.

Blockchain: Blockchain technology was explored for enhancing transparency and security in insurance processes, especially in areas like claims management and record-keeping.

Health and wellness: Insurtech was expanding into health and wellness, with companies offering innovative health insurance and wellness programmes that reward policyholders for healthy behaviour.

Regulatory environment: The regulatory environment was evolving to accommodate insurtech innovations. Regulatory sandboxes and partnerships between regulators and insurtech start-ups were becoming more common.

Inside the insurtech toolbox

The insurtech toolbox is a treasure trove of cutting-edge technologies, both established and emerging, that are revolutionizing the insurance industry. It's a fusion of traditional insurance practices and the relentless march of technology, including the latest advancements and emerging innovations. Let's take a closer look at what's inside this toolbox:

1 **AI and ML:** AI and ML are the dynamic duo reshaping insurance. These technologies enable insurers to automate underwriting, assess risks with pinpoint accuracy, and optimize pricing based on vast datasets. Claims processing is expedited, fraud detection becomes more robust, and customer interactions are personalized like never before. More use cases will be discussed in Chapter 3 on 'Emerging technologies in insurtech'.

2 **Advanced data analytics:** Data analytics forms the backbone of insurtech. It involves the sophisticated analysis of large volumes of data to extract valuable insights. Insurers can make data-driven decisions, assess customer behaviour and enhance risk assessment models for better pricing and underwriting.

3 **Blockchain:** Blockchain technology is making insurance transactions more secure and transparent. Smart contracts, executed automatically when predefined conditions are met, streamline processes like claims management and policy execution like smart contracts that are used in various insurance types, such as travel and parametric insurance.[7] This not only reduces the potential for disputes but also enhances trust within the insurance ecosystem.

4 **IoT and telematics:** The proliferation of IoT devices, including telematics systems installed in vehicles, offers insurers invaluable real-time data streams. Connected vehicles equipped with

telematics allow motor insurers to closely track driving behaviours, enabling a more precise risk assessment. Similarly, smart home sensors empower home insurers to identify potential hazards promptly. These IoT-driven insights pave the way for personalized coverage options and, subsequently, reduced premiums for policyholders.

5 **Cloud computing:** Cloud technology facilitates seamless data storage, access and scalability. Insurers can leverage cloud-based platforms to enhance customer experiences, enable remote work and process data-intensive tasks with ease.

6 **Robot automation:** Robot automation brings efficiency and accuracy to insurance processes. Robots can be deployed for tasks like data entry, document processing and customer service, streamlining operations and reducing costs.

7 **Emerging technologies:** Insurtech is not limited to established technologies; it also embraces emerging innovations like quantum computing, virtual reality (VR), augmented reality (AR), the metaverse and 5G. While these technologies are still evolving, they hold the potential to further transform insurance processes and customer interactions.

The insurtech toolbox represents a dynamic fusion of cutting-edge technologies, such as AI, ML, advanced data analytics, blockchain, IoT (including telematics), cloud computing and emerging innovations. This fusion is reshaping various facets of insurance operations, including underwriting, claims processing, customer engagement and risk assessment.

In the upcoming chapters, we will closely examine these technologies and their practical applications. Starting with Chapter 3, titled 'Emerging technologies in insurtech', and continuing through Chapter 6, we will explore how industry stakeholders harness these tools to enhance customer experiences, streamline underwriting and optimize claims processes. Moreover, we will conduct a thorough assessment of their substantial impact on the continually evolving insurance sector.

New era in insurtech

At the heart of the insurtech revolution lies the harnessing of data. The proliferation of digital interactions and interconnected devices has generated an unprecedented reservoir of data that insurers can leverage to glean insights into customer behaviour, preferences and risk profiles. This data-driven approach empowers insurance companies to craft bespoke insurance solutions that align precisely with each customer's distinct needs.

Historically, the insurance industry was perceived as intricate, laden with paperwork and plagued by sluggish processing times, obscure policies and minimal customer engagement. Yet, the emergence of insurtech has disrupted these notions, ushering in a fresh era of customer-centricity to an industry that was once deemed detached from its policyholders.

Personalization stands as a cornerstone of insurtech-fuelled customer experiences. Today's customers anticipate insurance products that mirror their lifestyles, aspirations and risk landscapes. Whether it involves calibrating premium rates based on driving patterns or tailoring coverage choices for specific life stages, insurtech empowers a degree of personalization that was previously inconceivable.

In summary, insurance has a rich history spanning cultures and centuries, from ancient Babylon to modern times. It has overcome various challenges, adapted to technological advancements, and grown into a £4 trillion (€5 trillion) premium industry. Lloyd's of London continues to be a major player, known for its diverse risk coverage.

Insurance remains vital for financial security, evolving to meet current needs and future challenges.

Key participants in the insurance industry

In the insurance industry, there are three main categories of key participants: insurance intermediaries (such as brokers, agents and managing general agents (MGAs)), risk takers (including insurers and reinsurers) and supporting entities like claim handlers and service providers. Here's a brief overview of each:

Insurance intermediaries:

- Insurance brokers: Independent intermediaries who help clients find insurance coverage from various insurers.
- Insurance agents: Professionals who work for specific insurance companies and sell their products.
- MGAs: Intermediaries with specialized underwriting authority, often involved in underwriting and policy administration.
- Insurance associations: Industry organizations that promote best practices.
- Insurtech firms: Tech companies providing digital solutions to insurers.

Risk-takers:

- Insurers: Companies providing insurance coverage to policyholders.
- Reinsurers: Companies that offer insurance to primary insurers, spreading risk.
- Underwriters: Experts who assess risk and set policy terms.

Supporting entities:

- Actuaries: Statisticians who analyse data to calculate risks.
- Claims adjusters: Professionals who investigate and evaluate insurance claims.
- Policyholders: Individuals or businesses purchasing insurance.
- Regulators: Government agencies overseeing insurance operations.

In summary, insurance intermediaries like brokers and agents connect insurers and policyholders, while MGAs have broader responsibilities, including underwriting authority and, in some cases, claims management. Understanding these roles is essential in navigating the insurance industry effectively. For more detailed descriptions, refer to the glossary section.

Main lines of insurance businesses

The main lines of insurance businesses are categorized into four broad categories, or lines:

Property insurance: Property insurance provides coverage for the loss or damage of property due to various perils, including fire, theft, natural disasters and more. It can be further divided into:

- Personal lines: This includes insurance for individuals, such as home insurance and motor insurance.

- Commercial lines: Commercial property insurance offers coverage for businesses and includes policies like business or farm insurance.

Casualty insurance: Casualty insurance covers the legal liability of the insured for bodily injury or property damage to others. It can also encompass other types of coverage, such as:

- Workers' compensation: Providing benefits to employees injured on the job.

- Professional liability: Protecting professionals from claims of negligence or errors in their services.

- Cyber liability: Offering coverage against losses resulting from data breaches and cyberattacks.

Life insurance: Life insurance provides a lump-sum payment to the beneficiaries of the insured in the event of their death or terminal illness. It may also include other benefits such as:

- Annuities: Providing periodic payments to the policyholder.

- Pensions: Offering retirement income to policyholders.

- Savings plans: Combining insurance with a savings or investment component.

Health and disability insurance: Health and disability insurance cover medical expenses and income loss of the insured due to illness or injury. This category can also encompass other types of benefits, including:

- Dental insurance: Providing coverage for dental care services.

- Vision insurance: Offering coverage for eye care and vision-related expenses.
- Long-term care insurance: Addressing the costs associated with long-term care services.

Insurance companies may specialize in one or more of these lines of insurance, depending on their expertise and market focus.

Key global insurance players in 2023

As of 2023, the global insurance landscape is dominated by several key players. According to Forbes report 2023,[8] here are the top insurance companies in the world in terms of total assets and market value:

Top five insurance companies by total assets ($ billion):

Allianz (Germany) – $2,163 billion

Ping An Insurance (China) – $1,650 billion[9]

Prudential Financial (United States) – $1,361 billion[10]

ING Group (Netherlands) – $1,081.81 billion[11]

Axa (France) – $933 billion[12]

Top five insurance companies by market value ($ billion):

UnitedHealth Group (United States) – $490.15 billion

Ping An Insurance (China) – $121.69 billion

AIA Group (Hong Kong) – $120.19 billion

Allianz (Germany) – $96.42 billion

Chubb (United States) – $87.31 billion

These insurance giants operate on a global scale, providing a wide range of insurance products and services to customers around the world. Their substantial assets and net premiums written reflect their significant presence in the global insurance industry.

Conclusion

This chapter serves as an introduction to various aspects of the insurtech landscape. It begins by defining insurtech and explaining its emergence. The chapter also provides key metrics to gauge the significance of insurtech within the insurance industry and explores the insurtech toolbox, highlighting the tools and technologies employed in this sector.

We ventured into the historical development of insurance, with a particular focus on notable events such as the emergence of Lloyd's of London Market and other significant milestones.

With this foundational understanding in place, we will now transition to Chapter 2, 'The insurtech landscape', where we will delve deeper into the evolving insurtech landscape and its various facets. In the chapters that follow, we will explore the technologies, trends and innovations reshaping the insurance industry in the 21st century.

Notes

1 'Key Facts and Figures', Lloyd's. www.lloyds.com/about-lloyds/media-centre/key-facts-and-figures (archived at https://perma.cc/LPX3-EJAU)

2 'Key Facts and Figures', Lloyd's. www.lloyds.com/about-lloyds/media-centre/key-facts-and-figures (archived at https://perma.cc/7M2Y-SRK3)

3 'How Insurtechs Can Accelerate the Next Wave of Growth', McKinsey, 5 May 2022. www.mckinsey.com/industries/financial-services/our-insights/insurance-blog/how-insurtechs-can-accelerate-the-next-wave-of-growth (archived at https://perma.cc/78UY-C99K)

4 'How Insurtechs Can Accelerate the Next Wave of Growth', McKinsey, 5 May 2022. www.mckinsey.com/industries/financial-services/our-insights/insurance-blog/how-insurtechs-can-accelerate-the-next-wave-of-growth (archived at https://perma.cc/PDA6-WRAX)

5 'Global InsurTech Market Report 2020–2024', PR Newswire, 30 Mar. 2021. www.prnewswire.com/news-releases/global-insurtech-market-report-2020-2024---influence-of-digitization-will-drive-the-market-301257608.html (archived at https://perma.cc/MQ4V-DVL5)

6 'Insurtech Market Opportunities & Forecast 2020–2027', GMI Research. www.gmiresearch.com/report/insurtech-market/ (archived at https://perma.cc/ E9MC-R76V)

7 'Blockchain Technology and the Future of the Global Insurance …'. www.clydeco.com/en/insights/2021/11/blockchain-technology-and-the-future-of-the-global (archived at https://perma.cc/CC4P-6AUN)

8 'TOP 20 Largest Insurance Companies', Forbes Global 2023, 18 Aug. 2023. beinsure.com/ranking/top-20-largest-insurance-companies-forbes-global/ (archived at https://perma.cc/HW74-5K2E)

9 'Ping An Insurance of China Total Assets 2010–2023', PNGAY. www. macrotrends.net/stocks/charts/PNGAY/ping-an-insurance-of-china/total-assets (archived at https://perma.cc/EWL2-8GQM)

10 'Prudential Financial, Inc. Announces Third Quarter 2023 Results', 1 Nov. 2023. www.nasdaq.com/press-release/prudential-financial-inc.-announces-third-quarter-2023-results-2023-11-01 (archived at https://perma.cc/ KF7V-JTEE)

11 'Allianz Earnings Release: 2Q & 6M 2023', 10 Aug. 2023. www.allianz.com/ en/press/news/financials/business_results/230810_Allianz-2Q-2023-earnings-release.html (archived at https://perma.cc/9FFU-RH3T)

12 '2023-05-15 – AXA – Press Release – 1Q23 Activity Indicators', 15 May 2023. www-axa-com.cdn.axa-contento-118412.eu/www-axa-com/bc18de41-0b2e-469d-bce3-60c92818c601_axa_pr_20230515.pdf (archived at https://perma. cc/H3XR-WDDH)

2

The insurtech landscape

Introduction

In this chapter, we delve deeper into the evolving insurtech landscape and its various facets. We'll explore the transformative journey that insurtech has embarked upon, tracing its path from its early roots to its current state as a thriving and distinct industry. As we investigate the evolution of insurtech, we'll uncover the significant milestones, shifts and trends that have shaped its trajectory. From its initial emergence as a subset of fintech to its recognition as a powerful standalone force, we'll witness how insurtech has rewritten the rules of the insurance game.

Types of insurtech and their value proposition

Insurtech companies are at the forefront of leveraging technology, data analytics and digital platforms to innovate and enhance various aspects of the insurance industry. These companies offer solutions for customer engagement, underwriting, claims processing and more. The insurtech domain can be further subdivided into distinct categories, each with its own value proposition.

Insurtech companies: These firms often focus on distribution, obtaining licences and, at times, establishing themselves as managing general agents (MGAs) to create specialized insurance products.

Enablers: Enablers exclusively refer to technology providers. While they typically don't fall under the regulatory oversight of financial authorities, many choose to self-regulate to build trust and gain a competitive edge. The number of service providers entering this segment has seen a significant surge.

Full carriers: Full carriers represent insurers equipped with the capability to issue their own policies, stepping into the role of the insurer and assuming associated risks. It's noteworthy that the line between enablers and distributors can sometimes blur, leading many insurtech firms to adopt both roles, creating complexities in managing dual business models and revenue streams.

The global insurtech revolution

The global insurtech revolution is reshaping the insurance industry on a global scale. The inception of insurtech can be traced back to around 2010, and since then it has experienced remarkable growth. Currently, there are over 3,000 insurtech companies operating worldwide, with venture capital funding raised exceeding $7 billion in 2022. The global insurtech market, valued at $5.45 billion in 2022, is on an exponential growth trajectory, projected to achieve a staggering compound annual growth rate (CAGR) of 52.7 per cent from 2023 to 2030. By 2030, it is anticipated to reach a substantial revenue of $152.43 billion.

The global landscape of insurtech innovation is marked by several prominent hubs that lead the charge in revolutionizing the insurance industry. According to Insurtech Digital, three standout countries in this domain are the United States, the UK and Germany.

The United States is undeniably the largest and most dynamic hub for insurtech innovation globally, with a staggering 1,370 insurtech companies, reflecting the competitive marketplace and entrepreneurial spirit. Holding an impressive 44 per cent share of the global insurtech market, the United States is home to industry titans like Lemonade and Hippo Insurance, known for their pioneering approaches to insurance. The UK stands as the second major hotspot for insurtech innovation, with 313 established insurance firms, concentrated mainly in London. London is home to the highest number of insurtech businesses globally. Innovators like Zego and Bought by Many lead the way by leveraging cutting-edge technology to provide personalized and actionable insurance products. Finally, Germany has rapidly ascended as a hub of insurtech innovation, thanks to its highly educated workforce and unwavering technological commitment. Notable insurtech brands like Wefox and Getsafe are making substantial impacts in Germany's competitive insurance market.

These global insurtech hubs encompass a diverse spectrum of innovation and investment opportunities within the insurance technology space. With each hub offering unique strengths and a commitment to technological progress, the insurtech sector is poised for further growth and transformation.

Trends that shaped the evolution of insurtech

Birth of peer-to-peer (P2P) insurance

The emergence of peer-to-peer (P2P) insurance models marked a significant turning point in the trajectory of insurtech. P2P insurance disrupted the established insurance landscape by introducing a collaborative framework, shifting away from reliance on centralized insurance providers. Instead, P2P models empowered individuals to collectively manage risks, emphasizing shared responsibility and transparency.

Notable players within this movement introduced distinctive value propositions. For instance, Friendsurance focused on empowering policyholders by forming small affinity groups, fostering a sense of community and trust. This community-driven approach enabled policyholders to actively shape their insurance coverage, collaboratively assessing risks and establishing equitable premium rates. This approach stood in stark contrast to the distant and standardized methods found in traditional insurance paradigms.

An innovative aspect of the P2P model was the introduction of a claims-free bonus system. It rewarded safer driving behaviour and responsible actions with lower insurance rates, creating a mutually beneficial scenario for policyholders and the broader community. This approach not only aligned incentives toward safer practices but also promoted a culture of risk prevention. By emphasizing collaboration, transparency and active participation, P2P insurance introduced a refreshing chapter in insurtech's evolution, opening doors to more personalized and community-driven insurance solutions.

Rise of digital distribution platforms

One of the pivotal shifts brought about by insurtech was the rise of digital distribution platforms, encompassing marketplaces and price comparison sites. These platforms redefined how insurance products were not only purchased but also accessed and experienced, transforming the customer journey. In the pre-insurtech era, insurance purchases were often seen as tedious and time-consuming. Customers had to navigate through complex paperwork, terminology and limited information sources, resulting in a lack of transparency and clarity. Insurtech recognized this pain point and sought to revolutionize the distribution process.

Digital distribution platforms, powered by cutting-edge technology, emerged as the solution to these long-standing challenges. They acted as virtual marketplaces, seamlessly connecting insurance providers and consumers in a user-friendly digital environment. Through intuitive interfaces, users could effortlessly browse, compare and select insurance policies tailored to their specific needs.

The rise of digital distribution platforms has been closely linked with the flourishing gig and sharing economy. As services like ride-sharing (Uber, Lyft, BlaBla Car) and home-sharing platforms such as Airbnb gained traction, new insurance dimensions emerged, requiring innovative coverage solutions to address the evolving landscape. The gig economy, characterized by rapid growth, necessitates tailored insurance solutions to support responsible operations.

Millennials have played a pivotal role in shaping the intersection of insurance and the sharing economy. As one of the largest age cohorts, their preference for digital transactions has prompted insurers to reconsider distribution and claim management strategies. Millennials often seek more modern and user-centric insurance approaches, emphasizing the need for personalized services.

The sharing economy reflects a willingness, particularly among millennials, to engage in P2P transactions and a certain scepticism toward established business processes such as insurance. This trend presents an opportunity for insurers to adapt and offer more personalized services, leveraging data analytics and robo-advice to provide tailored solutions. However, the rise of the gig economy also poses unique challenges to insurance underwriting, which insurers address with innovative solutions, adapting to the dynamic nature of these activities.

Insurtech-driven digital distribution platforms, integrated into the gig economy, have given rise to tailor-made insurance solutions that cater to the requirements of emerging service platforms. As the sharing economy continues to reshape traditional industries, insurers must remain adaptable, harnessing technology to offer seamlessly integrated coverage aligned with evolving consumer preferences.

Rise of digital ecosystems

The extensive integration of digital technologies into daily life has redefined the norm. Engaging in Airbnb accommodations, hailing Uber rides via smartphones and ordering meals through platforms like GrubHub or Seamless have become commonplace. Apple and Facebook transcend being mere technology providers, having assumed the status of lifestyle essentials. This reality has made it apparent that consumers can address their diverse needs through smartphones. Placing customers at the core of digital activities has not only spurred adoption but also unlocked previously unforeseen value. Of the 10 largest companies based on market capitalization, seven are ecosystem players – Alibaba, Alphabet, Amazon, Apple, Facebook, Microsoft and Tencent. This trend only begins to illustrate the potency of digital power. Uber, founded in 2009, now operates in over 630 cities across 80 countries, Airbnb accumulated a million rooms quicker than Marriott by a remarkable 50 years and WeWork has globally sublet 10 million square feet of office space since 2010.[1]

Via digital ecosystems, companies are seizing significant opportunities capable of reconfiguring global markets and ushering in a 'sectors without borders' era. However, the benefits of these digital ecosystems won't be evenly distributed. McKinsey's research unveils a divide where digital technology propels some companies to resounding market triumph while eroding corporate earnings and overall value for others.

Ecosystems: A new paradigm for value creation

By 2025, McKinsey forecasts the emergence of twelve major ecosystems focused on essential human and organizational needs. These ecosystems are poised to generate $60 trillion in revenue, accounting for roughly 30 per cent of the world's global revenues. The composition of these ecosystems will vary across countries and regions due to regulatory influences, cultural customs and preferences. While insurance could feature as a risk-mitigation service within these ecosystems, insurance companies can also carve out their sub-ecosystems catering to individuals and institutions.[2]

Furthermore, insurtech-powered digital distribution platforms have wholeheartedly embraced a customer-centric approach. Leveraging the power of data analytics, these platforms delve into customer preferences, enabling them to offer personalized recommendations. Consequently, users find themselves more immersed in their insurance journey, as these platforms present tailor-made options that perfectly align with their individual circumstances.

To illustrate the profound impact of these platforms, let's consider the case of John, a young professional in search of health insurance coverage. In a traditional setting, John would have grappled with the daunting task of contacting multiple insurance agents, deciphering intricate policy documents and struggling to find an optimal fit.

However, with the empowerment of insurtech-driven digital distribution platforms, John seamlessly inputs his preferences and needs. Almost instantaneously, the platform presented him with a carefully curated array of policies tailored to his requirements, complete with transparent comparisons of coverage and pricing. With confidence, John selected a policy that aligned with his lifestyle and financial circumstances, all within a matter of minutes.

This proliferation of digital distribution platforms has ignited healthy competition among insurance providers. In a landscape characterized by enhanced transparency and accessibility, insurers are motivated to elevate their offerings, amplify customer experiences and remain competitive within an ever-evolving market.

Through the embrace of technology, personalization and convenience, insurtech has not only streamlined the distribution process but has also fundamentally transformed the way consumers perceive and engage with insurance. In summary, the synergy between insurtech and the rise of distribution platforms, as well as ecosystem players, has paved the way for bespoke insurance solutions meticulously designed to cater to the unique demands of emerging service platforms. As the sharing economy continues to expand and reshape traditional industries, insurers must demonstrate adaptability by harnessing technology to provide seamless coverage that perfectly aligns with the evolving preferences and behaviours of the dynamic consumer landscape.

The ascent of insurtech-powered digital distribution platforms intertwined with the dynamics of the gig economy has given rise to a new era of tailored insurance solutions designed to meet the evolving needs of emerging service platforms. As the sharing economy continues to reshape conventional industries, insurers must remain agile and leverage technology to offer uncomplicated coverage that seamlessly aligns with the ever-changing preferences of consumers.

Telematics and usage-based insurance

The fusion of telematics and IoT (Internet of Things) technology with insurance practices has ignited a remarkable transformation across various sectors. In the realm of home insurance, the incorporation of simple devices capable of detecting burst pipes has emerged as a proactive measure to prevent water damage. This innovative approach benefits both policyholders and insurers by averting potential losses.

In the domain of motor insurance, the introduction of telematic devices such as sensors and GPS trackers within vehicles has revolutionized the collection of real-time data concerning driving behaviour and vehicle performance. This data-driven approach has paved the way for ground-breaking usage-based insurance (UBI) models.

UBI disrupts the conventional uniform premium structure by harnessing the intricate insights gleaned from telematics to tailor insurance offerings. This personalized approach empowers insurers to adjust premiums based on actual driving habits, ushering in a dynamic and equitable pricing paradigm. The implications of telematics-driven UBI extend beyond financial savings. It serves as a catalyst for safer driving habits, fostering a proactive stance toward risk mitigation. As policyholders recognize the direct correlation between their driving behaviour and insurance costs, they are incentivized to adopt safer practices on the road. This alignment of incentives results in a mutually beneficial scenario: insurers curtail claims costs through reduced accidents, while policyholders reap financial rewards through responsible driving habits.

USE CASE: TELEMATICS-BASED UBI

To illustrate the potential of telematics-based UBI programmes, consider a strategic partnership between an established insurance company and an automobile manufacturer. This collaboration tran-scends mere driving behaviour tracking, encompassing comprehensive benefits such as enhanced accident response through detailed driving data analysis, efficient vehicle tracking and recovery from theft, and proactive driver safety monitoring to minimize accident risks.

UBI's early beginnings and evolution The inception of UBI programmes in the United States over a decade ago, spearheaded by Progressive Insurance Company and General Motors Assurance

Company (GMAC), marked a significant turning point. These pioneers introduced mileage-linked discounts by combining GPS technology and cellular systems to track miles driven. These discounts often included supplementary benefits such as roadside assistance and vehicle theft recovery.[3]

Nonetheless, the integration of telematics and UBI programmes presents its unique set of challenges. Privacy concerns come to the forefront as mileage and behaviour monitoring become more prevalent, leading some countries to enforce tracking transparency regulations. Moreover, the successful implementation of these programmes requires substantial technological investments to accurately capture and analyse driving data, placing significant resource demands on insurers.

However, it's essential to recognize that the rise of telematics-based UBI signifies a profound shift in the insurance landscape. These programmes offer precise risk assessment, personalized pricing structures and incentives for safer driving practices. As a result, insurance becomes more accessible to low-risk drivers, and road safety as a whole is significantly improved. With technology advancing and consumer interest growing, telematics-based UBI is positioned to reshape the future of motor insurance. It not only revolutionizes the industry but also enhances the overall driving experience.

Moreover, the influence of technology-driven insurance innovations extends beyond the realm of vehicles. P2P home sharing platforms like Airbnb have sparked transformative shifts in insurance paradigms. The unique nature of home sharing necessitates additional coverage beyond traditional homeowner policies. While existing policies may partially cover single-occasion rentals, ongoing home-sharing arrangements call for supplementary or commercial insurance, particularly to address liability concerns related to guest damage.

Insurers are responding to this shift by offering monthly coverage tailored to these scenarios. Airbnb itself initiated a substantial move in this direction by introducing a 'Host Protection Insurance' plan in 2015, offering up to $1 million in coverage for hosts and landlords to address liability concerns arising from P2P rentals. It's important to note that this coverage excludes intentional acts and certain property issues.

The convergence of telematics and IoT technology not only show-cases insurtech's capacity to reshape norms but also its potential to cultivate risk awareness and prevention among policyholders. This heralds a significant shift in how individuals engage with and perceive their insurance coverage, marking a significant stride toward the future of motor insurance and beyond.

Technological advancements in insurtech

Technological advancements have been at the heart of insurtech's remarkable growth, reshaping the insurance landscape and transforming how insurers interact with their customers. As discussed in the previous section, innovations in artificial intelligence (AI), machine learning (ML), blockchain, smart contracts, data analytics and predictive modelling have been instrumental in the evolution of insurtech.

Cognitive and neurotic technologies, such as AI and deep learning (DL), exemplified by convolutional neural networks and deep learning, are evolving to efficiently process complex data streams. These technologies, inspired by the human brain's learning capabilities, are poised to become the standard for handling the vast and intricate data generated by 'active' insurance products tied to individual behaviour. Insurers will gain access to continuously learning models that adapt to changing risks and behaviours in real time, thus open-ing doors to new product categories and engagement methods.[4]

The proliferation of connected consumer devices, encompassing vehicles, fitness trackers, home assistants, smartphones and smartwatches, has unleashed an unprecedented data deluge. Experts predict that by 2025 there could be up to 1 trillion connected devices. This influx of data provides insurers with deeper insights into their clients' behaviours, paving the way for new product categories, personalized pricing structures and real-time service delivery.

Advancements in robotics, including additive manufacturing (3D printing), autonomous drones, farming equipment and surgical robots, are rapidly becoming commercially viable. For instance, by

2025, we can expect 3D-printed buildings to be commonplace. These innovations arc reshaping how insurers assess risks and necessitate a re-evaluation of risk pools, customer expectations and product development strategies.

The impact of these technological strides on both insurtech and the broader insurance industry has been profound. With AI and ML capabilities at their disposal, insurtech companies are poised to deliver highly personalized and efficient services. These technologies not only enhance the precision of risk assessments but also expedite claims processing, resulting in a seamless experience for policyholders. Furthermore, data analytics and predictive modelling have revolutionized insurers' understanding of customer preferences. This newfound knowledge empowers insurers to craft tailor-made products and services that align precisely with customer expectations. Consequently, the entire insurance sector is undergoing a transformation, becoming increasingly customer-centric and responsive to the ever-evolving trends in the market. Further exploration of this topic will be undertaken in Chapter 4.

The insurtech ecosystem

Insurtech start-ups

Insurtech encompasses a diverse ecosystem comprising start-ups, incumbent insurers, investors, venture capitalists, technology providers and regulators – all collaborating to enhance customer experiences, streamline operations and drive industry growth. Each participant plays a crucial role in developing innovative solutions, new business models and transformative changes.

Start-ups are pivotal in shaping the insurtech landscape by injecting innovation and fresh perspectives. These dynamic and agile companies introduce new technologies, novel business models and customer-centric approaches that disrupt traditional norms. Their distinctive value propositions significantly influence the evolution of both insurtech and the broader insurance industry.

Identifying unmet needs within insurance, start-ups pinpoint gaps and pain points in the value chain. They develop targeted solutions that address these challenges, offering products and services tailored to evolving customer demands. Focusing on niche areas or underserved segments, start-ups introduce innovative offerings that resonate with specific audiences.

Disruptive business models are another hallmark of start-ups, challenging established norms and inspiring industry-wide transformation. Their agility allows them to experiment with novel ways of delivering insurance, such as P2P insurance, on-demand coverage and micro-insurance. These innovative models reshape the traditional insurance value proposition, making it more adaptable and accessible.

Customer experience is at the core of start-up-driven innovation. They prioritize customer needs and preferences, designing user-friendly interfaces and personalized solutions. By placing customers at the centre, start-ups enhance engagement, increase customer satisfaction and foster lasting relationships – a paradigm shift in the insurance industry's approach. Start-ups also collaborate with incumbents, investors and technology providers to amplify their impact. Partnerships with established insurers enable start-ups to leverage industry expertise, distribution channels and customer trust, resulting in hybrid models that combine start-up agility with incumbent resources, driving comprehensive innovation.

Start-ups are the vanguard of change in the insurtech ecosystem, propelling innovation, creating novel solutions and challenging conventional practices. With their focus on technology, market gaps, disruptive models and customer-centricity, start-ups are instrumental in shaping the trajectory of insurtech and influencing the broader landscape of insurance innovation.

Incumbent insurers

At the heart of the insurtech landscape, established insurance companies, known as incumbents, hold a central role that profoundly influences the industry's evolution. Drawing upon their extensive industry experience and the foundation of customer trust, incumbents contribute a unique set of value propositions that reshape the trajectory of insurance innovation.

Incumbents possess a wealth of industry expertise and legacy knowledge stemming from their enduring presence in the insurance arena. This deep familiarity with insurance operations and customer preferences provides them with a vantage point to drive transformative changes that resonate with their customer base. Moreover, the reservoir of customer trust they've cultivated over the years serves as a foundation for new ventures and technological explorations.

As the insurtech landscape evolves, incumbents must navigate the dual imperative of leveraging their legacy strengths while adapting to rapid technological shifts. The emergence of new paradigms, such as artificial intelligence, blockchain and data analytics, necessitates the integration of digital advancements into their existing operations. This modernization streamlines processes and enhances customer experiences, ultimately fortifying their competitive stance within the industry.

To remain at the forefront of innovation, many incumbents actively engage with insurtech start-ups, fostering an exchange of ideas, technologies and perspectives. This collaboration leads to a symbiotic relationship that drives industry-wide progress. By tapping into the agility and fresh perspectives of start-ups, incumbents infuse innovation into their traditional operations, creating a dynamic ecosystem that blends tradition with innovation.

Understanding the profound impact of technology, established insurers initiate strategic investments to accelerate digital transformation. This frequently entails allocating resources towards research and development, fortifying technology infrastructure and adopting cutting-edge tools. Through this embrace of technology-driven evolution, incumbents enhance their capacity to withstand disruption, assume leadership roles in innovation and navigate a path towards enduring growth. By harmonizing their well-established strengths with the dynamism of emerging technologies, incumbents create an environment where tradition and innovation seamlessly converge, propelling the insurance industry into an era of unparalleled progress.

Investors and venture capitalists

Investors and venture capitalists play pivotal roles in shaping the insurtech landscape and propelling insurance innovation forward. Recognizing the vast potential of insurtech, these financial backers assume crucial positions by injecting funds into start-ups and emerging ventures within the industry. Their financial contributions serve as powerful catalysts, enabling insurtech entities to expand their operations, accelerate growth and transform visionary concepts into tangible solutions.

Their financial backing empowers insurtech ventures to scale their operations, enhance their technological offerings and establish a formidable presence in the competitive market landscape. This support enables insurtech start-ups to allocate resources towards research and development, leading to the creation of innovative technologies.

By fostering an environment conducive to entrepreneurial pursuits within the insurtech domain, and by providing not only financial resources but also mentorship and expertise, investors and venture capitalists nurture start-ups and guide them towards success. This supportive ecosystem encourages creative thinking and problem-solving, resulting in the generation of novel solutions to long-standing industry challenges.

Empowered by the financial backing of investors, start-ups introduce fresh business models, customer-centric approaches and technology-driven services that reshape the insurance landscape. This disruptive influence compels established insurers to adapt and evolve, ultimately benefiting the entire industry. Moreover, investors and venture capitalists act as bridges between start-ups and incumbent insurers, facilitating collaborations and partnerships that drive comprehensive innovation. These synergistic efforts leverage the strengths of both parties, paving the way for the creation of hybrid models that hold the promise of future success.

In the quest to redefine insurance through technology, investors and venture capitalists emerge as pioneers who not only provide financial resources but also ignite innovation and fuel growth. Their unwavering support empowers insurtech start-ups to push boundaries, challenge conventions and shape the future of insurance, thereby contributing to the evolution of the entire insurtech ecosystem.

Regulatory oversight

Regulatory authorities assume a pivotal role in maintaining integrity and stability within the insurtech landscape. Their essential function shapes the path of insurtech and insurance innovation by striking a delicate balance between promoting innovation and safeguarding consumer interests. These entities bear the responsibility of establishing and upholding a regulatory framework that fosters growth while ensuring adherence to legal and ethical standards. They actively contribute to the evolution of insurtech by providing a structured environment for responsible innovation. Through the definition of guidelines and standards, they furnish a roadmap for start-ups and established players to develop and deploy novel technologies that align with industry requirements and ethical considerations.

The primary role of regulatory authorities hinges on maintaining a delicate equilibrium between nurturing innovation and protecting consumer rights. These bodies oversee insurtech advancements, ensuring they do not compromise consumer data security or privacy or create systemic risks. By delineating clear boundaries, they establish a framework in which innovation can thrive without compromising the industry's core integrity.

Functioning as facilitators of collaboration between insurtech start-ups, incumbents and other stakeholders, regulatory authorities offer a common ground for discussions and encourage dialogue on emerging technologies, business models and industry challenges. This collaborative approach aids in the formulation of regulations that encompass the diverse perspectives of the insurtech ecosystem.

At the heart of the regulatory authorities' role lies the prioritization of consumer interests. Through the evaluation of the impact of insurtech innovations on consumers, they ensure that products and services adhere to ethical standards and deliver genuine value. This vigilance prevents potential pitfalls and upholds consumer trust in the insurtech sector.

As insurtech continues its evolution, regulatory authorities adapt their frameworks to accommodate emerging technologies and trends. Their agility in comprehending the nuances of evolving insurtech models, such as P2P insurance and blockchain-based contracts, is crucial for maintaining regulatory relevance and effectiveness.

In the interconnected world of insurtech, regulatory authorities also foster international cooperation. They collaborate with counterparts from different regions to establish a harmonized regulatory approach that facilitates cross-border innovation and ensures a consistent experience for consumers and industry players alike. Guided by their ethical compass and oversight, regulatory authorities ensure that advancements align with societal values, creating an environment where innovation and progress coexist within a framework of responsibility, accountability and trust.

Technology enablers in the insurtech realm

In the dynamic landscape of insurtech, technology providers assume a multifaceted role as enablers of innovation and essential infrastructure. They provide the fundamental tools and platforms that propel progress within the insurance industry. These companies specialize in a diverse range of solutions, spanning from software development and data analytics to cloud computing and artificial intelligence. Their mission is to empower both insurtech start-ups and established insurers in designing, developing and delivering state-of-the-art products and services.

Technology providers serve as catalysts for insurtech innovation by equipping industry players with cutting-edge solutions. Their comprehensive toolkit, encompassing software, data analytics, cloud-based architecture and AI, empowers insurtech start-ups and established insurers to embrace transformative technologies. It's worth noting that while technology providers are integral to the insurtech landscape, not all insurtech entities exclusively fulfil this role. Many insurtech companies themselves serve as technology providers, contributing innovative solutions that shape the industry's future. Conversely, some insurtech ventures may primarily focus on distribution strategies and may not licence their proprietary technology to others.

For insurtech start-ups, technology providers offer the vital resources needed to bring imaginative ideas to fruition. By leveraging these solutions, these start-ups can create tailored products, stream-line operations and optimize customer experiences. Established insurers also stand to gain significantly from technology providers. They can harness advanced solutions to modernize legacy systems, enhance customer engagement and respond swiftly to changing market demands. Collaboration between technology providers and insurtech entities fosters a virtuous cycle of innovation. Many insurtech start-ups, while utilizing the services of technology provid-ers, also contribute to the broader insurtech ecosystem by providing their proprietary technology and solutions to enhance distribution strategies.

Ultimately, technology providers redefine the boundaries of what is achievable within the insurance industry. By offering a vast array of tools, they empower insurtech and insurance entities to reimagine insurance processes, refine customer interactions and chart a course toward a digitally transformed future.

Customers: The driving force of insurtech transformation

Customers wield a profound influence within the insurtech ecosystem, serving as the ultimate catalyst for innovation and transformation. This includes both individual consumers and businesses, each playing distinct roles in shaping the evolution of insurance solutions.

The dynamic and ever-evolving preferences of customers act as navigational beacons that chart the course of insurtech innovation. Customers' expectations for convenient and personalized experiences have compelled the industry to embrace technological advancements and reimagine traditional insurance offerings. Customer needs and pain points serve as wellsprings of inspiration for insurtech start-ups and established insurers to craft novel insurance products and services. By identifying gaps in coverage, addressing customer dissatisfaction or meeting unmet demands, insurtech entities customize their offerings to cater to these specific requirements.

The ascendancy of insurtech is tightly interwoven with the burgeoning demand for personalized and bespoke products, available at competitive prices, and accessible through the most convenient means. Customers' growing reliance on digital platforms has accelerated the quest for seamless and user-friendly experiences. Insurtech companies concentrate on simplifying complex processes, from policy purchase to claims filing, ensuring that interactions with insurance services are as intuitive and efficient as possible, accessible via desktop computers or smartphones.

As customers articulate their preferences for modernized insurance experiences, insurtech start-ups and incumbents are compelled to adapt and innovate. This customer-centric approach reshapes the industry's landscape, revolutionizing traditional insurance models and propelling the evolution of the insurtech ecosystem. The symbiotic relationship between customers and insurtech is reciprocal – customers benefit from enhanced convenience, tailored solutions and improved experiences, while insurtech companies gain valuable insights from customer interactions to refine and develop future offerings.

The interconnected nexus between customers and insurtech propels an ongoing cycle of innovation. As customer preferences evolve and technology advances, the insurtech landscape responds with ever-evolving solutions that continually redefine the insurance industry.

The shift in customer expectations: From transactional to personalized Historically, insurance transactions were often viewed as impersonal and transactional. Customers would purchase policies and hope to avoid interactions with their insurers unless a claim arose. However, the ascent of insurtech has upended this narrative by placing customers at the centre of the insurance journey. Today's customers demand more than mere coverage. Insurtech empowers insurers to utilize data analytics and artificial intelligence to gain profound insights into customer behaviour, enabling them to deliver additional value that aligns with customer needs and preferences. This transformation has shifted insurance from being a reactive service to a proactive partnership, where insurers anticipate customer needs and offer solutions that harmonize with their lifestyles.

The role of customer-centric insurtech solutions

Numerous insurtech innovations exemplify the industry's unwavering commitment to customer-centricity, fundamentally reshaping the way customers engage with insurance. One prime example, as discussed earlier in this chapter, is usage-based insurance (UBI), which has revolutionized the dynamics of the customer–insurer relationship.

In addition to UBI, insurtech has ushered in the concept of on-demand insurance, granting customers the ability to activate coverage for specific activities or items as needed. Whether it's securing travel insurance for a vacation or obtaining coverage for a one-day event, this flexible approach aligns with customers' ever-changing requirements and eliminates the necessity for long-term commitments.

Traditionally, the process of filing an insurance claim was laden with complexity. Insurtech has streamlined this experience by empowering customers to digitally submit claims, often through mobile applications. This not only expedites the claims procedure but also enhances transparency and customer satisfaction. Insurers have also embraced AI-driven chatbots and virtual assistants to deliver immediate customer support. Through these digital channels, customers can pose enquiries, access policy information and even initiate claims, ensuring a convenient and round-the-clock service experience. Specifically in the domain of cyber insurance, providers frequently bundle supplementary features like domain analysis and threat assessments, offering customers recommendations for bolstering their website security against intrusions or malware infestations. By addressing vulnerabilities at the source, these solutions yield direct benefits for all stakeholders involved.

Tailoring insurance for every individual

As insurtech continues to evolve, the focus on customer-centricity is only intensifying. The integration of emerging technologies like blockchain, ML and IoT will further enable insurers to craft hyper-personalized insurance solutions. These will not only cater to customers' specific needs but also seamlessly integrate into their daily lives.

The transformation of customer dynamics is an ongoing journey – one where insurtech serves as both the vehicle and the destination. With every innovation that enhances engagement, simplifies processes and anticipates needs, insurtech propels the industry towards a future where insurance is no longer a distant transaction, but a personalized, accessible and integral part of customers' lives.

Transforming insurance processes: Real-world insurtech cases

Simplifying policy purchase through digitalization

CASE STUDY: LEMONADE'S INSTANT INSURANCE

Lemonade, a digital insurance company, has revolutionized the policy purchase process. Leveraging AI and ML, Lemonade's platform enables customers to secure the homeowner's or renter's insurance within minutes. Through a conversational interface, customers answer questions, and Lemonade's AI system generates personalized policies tailored to their needs. This eliminates complex forms and provides immediate coverage, showcasing how digitalization simplifies and expedites policy purchases.

Traditionally, initiating an insurance claim involved forms, documents and lengthy processing. In contrast, Lemonade uses statistics and digitalization to automate much of the claims process. In 2017, they famously approved and paid out a claim for a stolen jacket in just three seconds. Despite accusations of a publicity stunt, this incident prompted insurers to reconsider the efficiency and cost trade-offs of their claims processing pipelines.

CASE STUDY: METROMILE'S PAY-PER-MILE MOTOR INSURANCE
Metromile, a pioneer in usage-based motor insurance, employs digitalization to streamline claims differently. Their pay-per-mile model utilizes a device tracking customers' mileage. In case of an accident, the technology detects the impact and triggers a claims process. Customers can then submit images and details through a mobile app, eliminating extensive paperwork. This demonstrates how digitalization enhances efficiency while minimizing customer effort.

Empowering policy management with digital solutions

CASE STUDY: POLICYGENIUS'S POLICY MANAGEMENT PLATFORM
Policygenius, an insurtech company, offers a comprehensive platform for effortless policy management. Through their digital dashboard, customers can access policy details, initiate changes and compare insurance options. This transparency and control engage policyholders actively with their coverage, highlighting insurtech's role in enhancing policy management through user-friendly interfaces.

CASE STUDY: TAPOLY'S END-TO-END FULFILMENT SYSTEM
Tapoly, a digital insurance provider, specializes in flexible insurance solutions for the gig economy. Beyond policy management, Tapoly's platform provides an end-to-end fulfilment system encompassing distribution, policy administration, claims processing, pricing and risk management. By offering a comprehensive solution directly to customers, Tapoly demonstrates how insurtech meets the unique needs of modern workers through an integrated digital ecosystem.

The path forward: Embracing digital transformation

The insurtech-driven transformation is just the beginning. As technology continues to advance, the insurance industry will integrate emerging technologies such as blockchain for enhanced security, AI for predictive analytics and IoT for data-driven insights. The focus remains on streamlining processes, boosting efficiency and providing customers with seamless experiences that meet their evolving expectations.

Through companies like Lemonade, Metromile, Policygenius and Tapoly, we witness the tangible benefits of insurtech for customers. As the industry embraces digital transformation, insurance processes become more customer-centric, transparent and adaptable – a testament to innovation reshaping the insurance landscape.

The rise of insurtech: Regulatory challenges and solutions

As insurtech reshapes the insurance landscape, the intricate interplay between innovation and regulation takes centre stage. Regulatory frameworks are essential to ensure that insurtech operations align with ethical standards, data protection requirements and financial stability. The delicate balance between encouraging new entrants and upholding industry integrity is central to effective regulation.

In response to the regulatory challenges faced by insurtech start-ups, various jurisdictions have introduced innovation hubs and regulatory sandboxes. These platforms allow start-ups to test their innovative solutions under controlled environments, providing them with an opportunity to demonstrate their capabilities while regulators assess their impact. Notable examples of this approach include the UK's Financial Conduct Authority (FCA) Innovation Hub and Singapore's Monetary Authority of Singapore (MAS) regulatory sandbox.

One of the key challenges for insurtech start-ups is navigating the licensing and capital requirements necessary for insurance underwriting. Traditional requirements can be prohibitive, leading many start-ups to focus on broker licence instead. These requirements, while essential for policyholder protection, can also act as barriers to market entry for new players. Regulators are exploring ways to strike a balance between prudent regulation and enabling innovation.

The integration of big data, analytics and AI into insurtech processes raises privacy and data protection concerns. Insurtech companies must adhere to data protection regulations and ensure transparent handling of customer data. Regulations like the European Union's General Data Protection Regulation (GDPR) require insurtech firms to demonstrate responsible data use, security measures and compliance protocols.

Regulatory technology, or RegTech, is emerging as a critical tool in managing compliance challenges in the insurtech landscape. RegTech solutions utilize technologies such as AI and ML to streamline compliance processes, monitor transactions and ensure adherence to regulations. By automating these functions, insurtech companies can reduce human error and enhance efficiency.

Given the global nature of insurtech, cooperation between regulatory bodies is essential. Bilateral agreements between regulatory authorities allow innovative businesses to enter new markets more seamlessly. These agreements facilitate cross-border expansion for start-ups, ensuring a smoother path to growth and scalability. As insurtech continues to evolve, the regulatory landscape will play a pivotal role in shaping its trajectory. Striking the right balance between promoting innovation and maintaining consumer protection requires constant dialogue between regulators and industry players. With ongoing collaboration, insurtech can thrive within a regulatory framework that encourages transformative advancements while upholding ethical standards and industry stability.

Global insurtech: Regional dynamics and regulatory challenges

The global insurtech revolution has set in motion a wave of transformation that transcends borders, yet its influence is intricately shaped by the regional intricacies of insurance markets. This section delves into the profound impact of insurtech on insurance markets worldwide, considering the nuanced regional variations in adoption, growth trajectories and the complex interplay of regulatory frameworks that define this evolution. From North America to Asia, Europe to Africa, insurtech is instigating innovations that challenge established norms and bring forth novel business models.

Insurance, as a business, is inherently regional, shaped by intricate regulatory frameworks, localized consumer behaviours, varying risk profiles and distinct market conditions. Each country's unique regulatory landscape poses both opportunities and challenges for insurtech's global diffusion.

Regulatory differences often render it intricate to harmonize regulations, data standards and insurance products. The distinct policy and terms of insurance can vary vastly from one insurer to another, reflecting the nuances of their underwriting appetites. The result is a fragmented landscape where the vision of standardized global regulations remains a complex puzzle.

Attempting to globalize and standardize insurtech regulations becomes a formidable task. The diversity in regulatory frameworks and cultural dynamics necessitates a granular approach, one that appreciates the intricacies of each jurisdiction. The ambitious goal of standardizing insurtech regulations grapples with the reality of the insurance industry's deeply rooted regionalism. Naturally, this challenging problem is an area where insurtech itself is exploring and proposing solutions, closely aligned with its ally RegTech.

The evolution of insurtech within regions highlights its ability to navigate intricate regulatory landscapes while addressing local challenges. Collaborative efforts between start-ups, established insurers and regulators are shaping a regulatory environment that facilitates innovation while protecting consumer interests. Despite regional variations, certain themes resonate universally. Data privacy, cybersecurity and consumer protection emerge as shared concerns. The safeguarding of sensitive consumer data, the prevention of cyber threats and ensuring transparent practices unite regulators globally in their pursuit of responsible insurtech advancement.

As insurtech defies geographical confines, collaboration emerges as the linchpin for a harmonious global insurtech ecosystem. Cross-border investments, international regulatory dialogues and knowledge-sharing platforms foster a sense of unity amidst diversity, bridging the regional divide.

Conclusion

In this chapter, we have navigated through the intricate landscape of insurtech, uncovering its multifaceted nature and the transformative trends that have driven its evolution. We witnessed the birth of disruptive models like P2P insurance, which brought about a shift from traditional centralized systems to collaborative community-driven approaches. Additionally, we explored the rise of digital distribution platforms, which have redefined how insurance products are accessed and experienced.

Throughout this journey, we recognized the pivotal roles played by various stakeholders in the insurtech ecosystem. Insurtech start-ups injected innovation and fresh perspectives, while incumbent insurers leveraged their industry knowledge to instigate transformative changes. Investors and venture capitalists provided vital financial support, while regulatory bodies maintained a delicate balance between fostering innovation and protecting consumer interests. Technology providers equipped insurtech entities with cutting-edge tools, and customers, with their evolving needs, acted as the driving force behind insurtech's evolution.

Real-world insurtech case studies, including Lemonade, Metromile, Policygenius and Tapoly, underscored how technology is reshaping insurance processes and enhancing customer experiences. We also delved into the regulatory challenges and solutions facing the insurtech industry, emphasizing the importance of global cooperation in this interconnected landscape.

As we move forward, Chapter 3 will delve into the cutting-edge tech reshaping the insurance industry on a global scale and in regional dynamics.

Notes

1 'Insurance Beyond Digital: The Rise of Ecosystems and Platforms', 10 Jan. 2018. www.mckinsey.com/industries/financial-services/our-insights/insurance-beyond-digital-the-rise-of-ecosystems-and-platforms (archived at https://perma.cc/K6ZR-T4EW).

2 'Insurance Beyond Digital: The Rise of Ecosystems and Platforms', 10 Jan. 2018. www.mckinsey.com/industries/financial-services/our-insights/insurance-beyond-digital-the-rise-of-ecosystems-and-platforms (archived at https://perma.cc/XE3K-EZ82).

3 'CIPR Study – NAIC'. content.naic.org/sites/default/files/inline-files/cipr_study_150324_usage_based_insurance_and_vehicle_telematics_study_series_1.pdf (archived at https://perma.cc/DV5F-PXKZ).

4 'Insurance 2030 – The Impact of AI on the Future of Insurance', 12 Mar. 2021. www.mckinsey.com/industries/financial-services/our-insights/insurance-2030-the-impact-of-ai-on-the-future-of-insurance (archived at https://perma.cc/ETE3-ZH74).

3

Emerging technologies in insurtech

Introduction

The insurtech landscape is undergoing a profound transformation, driven by a wave of emerging technologies that are reshaping traditional insurance practices. This chapter delves into the intricate web of innovation, exploring how technologies like blockchain, Internet of Things (IoT), artificial intelligence (AI), machine learning (ML), big data analytics, augmented reality (AR), virtual reality (VR), robotic process automation (RPA), biometrics, identity verification and cloud computing are redefining the insurance industry. We will navigate through each technology's features, benefits and real-world use cases, highlighting how they contribute to enhancing customer experiences, improving risk management strategies and revolutionizing the insurance ecosystem.

Insurtech denotes the application of technological innovations to enhance the efficiency and effectiveness of the insurance industry. Insurtechs are tech-driven insurance companies or start-ups that harness technologies like artificial intelligence, big data, cloud computing, blockchain and IoT to introduce ground-breaking products, services and business models. These innovations challenge the traditional methods of conducting insurance.

Blockchain technology: Revolutionizing trust and transparency

Blockchain technology stands as a transformative force within the insurance landscape, leveraging its decentralized and unchangeable characteristics to reshape the way things work. By upholding data integrity and security, it brings an elevated level of trust and transparency to the table. In the realm of insurance, blockchain's influence spans a wide range of areas, from making claims smoother to detecting fraud and even improving underwriting processes.

At its core, blockchain is a digital marvel that operates as a secure and decentralized ledger or system for keeping records. What sets it apart is that it enables multiple parties to record transactions in a way that's both transparent and resistant to tampering, all without needing a central authority to oversee it. Imagine it as a series of connected blocks, with each block holding a bunch of transactions. As these blocks link together, they create an unbroken chain of information. Once something is added to a block and joins the chain, changing it becomes almost impossible.

This technology isn't just theoretical; it's already making waves in the insurance world. From ensuring that claims are genuine to making sure nobody's pulling a fast one with fraudulent activity, blockchain is becoming a go-to tool for enhancing the insurance experience. It's like a digital guardian that keeps everything secure and honest, all while helping the insurance industry become more efficient and transparent than ever before.

Here's a simplified breakdown of how blockchain works:

Decentralization: Unlike traditional centralized systems, where a single entity controls the data, blockchain operates on a distributed network of computers, often referred to as nodes. Each participant in the network has access to the entire blockchain and helps maintain its integrity.

Transactions: When a new transaction occurs, it is bundled together with other transactions in a block. For instance, in the context of insurance, a transaction could represent a policy purchase, a claim submission or a payment.

Cryptography: Each block contains a unique code, called a hash, generated based on the data within that block. This hash acts like a digital fingerprint and is used to distinguish one block from another.

Linking blocks: The magic of blockchain lies in how blocks are linked together. Each block contains not only its own data but also the hash of the previous block. This creates a chain of blocks, hence the name 'blockchain'.

Consensus mechanism: Before a new block is added to the chain, network participants must agree that the information within it is accurate. This consensus is achieved through various mechanisms, such as proof-of-work (used in bitcoin) or proof-of-stake. These mechanisms ensure that malicious actors cannot alter the chain's history.

Immutability: Once a block is added to the blockchain, changing any information within it is extremely difficult due to the cryptographic links between blocks. If someone attempts to alter the data in one block, the hashes of subsequent blocks would need to be changed as well, requiring an impractical amount of computational power.

Key characteristics:

- Transparency: All participants can see the same data, enhancing trust.
- Security: Data is stored across the network, making it difficult to alter.
- Decentralization: No single entity has complete control over the data.
- Tamper-resistance: The design makes it extremely hard to modify past transactions.
- Efficiency: It eliminates intermediaries, reducing costs and delays.

Applications in insurance

In the insurance industry, blockchain has various applications, such as:

- Claims processing: Streamlining claims verification and settlement processes.

- Fraud detection: Detecting fraudulent claims through transparent and auditable records.
- Smart contracts: Self-executing contracts that automatically trigger actions based on predefined conditions.
- Proof of insurance: Providing instant and verifiable proof of insurance coverage.
- Data sharing: Securely sharing sensitive information among insurers, reinsurers and regulators.

Overall, blockchain technology has the potential to transform the industry by introducing a new level of transparency, security and efficiency in record-keeping and transaction management.

Use case: B3i (Blockchain Insurance Industry Initiative)[1] is a collaborative effort by a consortium of renowned insurance companies, including Aegon, Allianz, Munich Re, Swiss Re and Zurich. They joined hands in 2016 to streamline and enhance the reinsurance process using blockchain. By sharing data on a common ledger, insurers can reduce discrepancies, enhance transparency and expedite claims settlement.

Limitations of blockchain in the insurance industry

Although blockchain technology offers numerous benefits to the insurance industry, it is not without its limitations. Understanding these limitations is crucial for insurers and stakeholders as they navigate the integration of blockchain into their operations. Here are some key points to bear in mind:

1 **Scalability:** Blockchain's distributed nature requires all participants to store and verify every transaction, which can lead to scalability challenges as the network grows. In the insurance industry, where massive volumes of transactions occur, scaling up the blockchain network to accommodate these demands can be technically complex and resource-intensive.

2 **Speed and performance:** The consensus mechanisms used in blockchain networks can impact transaction processing speed. In

some cases, this may result in slower transaction times compared to traditional centralized systems, which could be a concern in time-sensitive insurance processes such as claims processing.

3 **Data privacy and GDPR compliance:** While blockchain enhances data security through encryption, it can pose challenges related to data privacy and compliance with regulations like the General Data Protection Regulation (GDPR). Immutable records on the blockchain may conflict with the right to be forgotten and other privacy requirements.

4 **Integration complexity:** Integrating blockchain with existing legacy systems and processes can be complex and require significant investment in terms of time, resources and expertise. Ensuring seamless interoperability between blockchain networks and legacy systems is a critical challenge.

5 **Energy consumption:** Many blockchain networks rely on resource-intensive consensus mechanisms, leading to high energy consumption. As environmental concerns grow, insurers may face scrutiny for adopting energy-intensive technologies.

6 **Regulatory uncertainty:** The regulatory landscape for blockchain in the insurance industry is still evolving. Regulatory authorities may need to address issues related to smart contracts, liability and cross-border transactions, among others.

7 **Smart contract reliability:** While smart contracts automate processes and enhance transparency, they are not immune to bugs, vulnerabilities or legal ambiguities. Errors in smart contracts can lead to unexpected outcomes and disputes.

8 **Initial investment:** Implementing blockchain requires an initial investment in terms of technology, development and training. The upfront costs can be substantial, particularly for smaller insurance companies.

9 **Governance and standards:** The lack of standardized protocols and governance frameworks can lead to fragmentation within the industry. Consensus on protocols, data formats and interoperability standards is essential to realizing the full potential of blockchain.

10 **Human factors:** Blockchain technology may require a shift in mindset and skill set for employees. Training and education are necessary to help employees understand and navigate the complexities of blockchain adoption.

11 **Immutability challenges:** While immutability is a core feature of blockchain, it can pose challenges in scenarios where errors or inaccuracies need to be corrected. Making changes to data on the blockchain requires consensus from network participants, which can be difficult to achieve.

12 **Network security:** While blockchain is known for its security features, it is not impervious to cyberattacks. Attacks on the underlying infrastructure, smart contract vulnerabilities and user errors can still compromise the security of blockchain networks.

13 **Adoption barriers:** Convincing all stakeholders in the insurance ecosystem to adopt blockchain can be challenging due to resistance to change, lack of awareness and concerns about disruption.

In conclusion, while blockchain holds immense promise for the insurance industry, these limitations underscore the importance of careful planning, thorough evaluation and strategic implementation. Addressing these challenges will be pivotal in harnessing the true potential of blockchain to revolutionize the insurance landscape.

Internet of Things (IoT): Data-driven insights

IoT encompasses a network of interconnected physical devices, sensors, machines and objects embedded with technology to gather, exchange and transmit data over the internet. These devices range from everyday items like household appliances, vehicles and wearables to industrial equipment and infrastructure components. The data collected by IoT devices can encompass details about their surroundings, usage patterns, performance and more.

IoT technology enables seamless communication between these devices and centralized systems, enabling real-time data analysis and informed decision-making. This interconnectedness and data sharing facilitate automation, remote monitoring and the creation of intelligent systems capable of responding to environmental changes and user behaviour.

The ubiquity of IoT devices has triggered a transformation in various industries and has created novel avenues for innovation. Insurers, in particular, have a unique opportunity to develop innovative products, explore new distribution channels and expand their scope to include predictive, preventive and assistance services.

Impact of IoT in the insurance domain

The imminent revolution of IoT is centred around interconnected devices. In 2010, approximately 12.5 billion such devices were operational, a figure predicted to exceed 1 trillion by 2025.[2] These devices, often equipped with sensors and automated functionalities, seamlessly integrate into various facets of individuals' lives, spanning both work and leisure. Their user-friendly set-up and portability generate substantial real-time data for analysis or automated functions, prompting transformations in traditional business models across diverse sectors.

While insurers have primarily harnessed IoT capabilities to enhance customer interactions and streamline insurance processes, a fresh wave of IoT-based service and business models is surfacing, grabbing insurers' attention. Within these evolving models, IoT-powered digital networks stand as crucial underpinnings for insurers. Through collaborations with other companies, insurers can foster enhanced cross-industry products and services that leverage IoT technologies and nascent ecosystems.

IoT technologies empower insurers to fine-tune risk assessment with remarkable precision. In the past, auto insurers relied on indirect indicators such as driver age, location and credit history for premium calculations. Now, data on driving behaviour and vehicle usage, including speed and night-time driving frequency, is readily available. Experience in mature IoT markets demonstrates insurers' elevated capacity to assess risks with heightened accuracy.

Connected devices also pave the way for insurers to engage customers more frequently and introduce innovative services based on the amassed data. In the realm of insurance, where interactions frequently occur through agents or brokers, IoT has the potential to significantly enhance customer relationships, forging deeper and more individualized connections.

IoT has unlocked a wealth of real-time data that insurers can harness for personalized risk assessment, dynamic pricing and proactive risk management. Connected devices amass data that empowers insurers to provide usage-based insurance premiums and mitigate risks.

Essential aspects

At the heart of IoT's influence lies its ability to sustain an uninterrupted flow of data, delivering real-time insights into user behaviours, environmental intricacies and device functionalities. This perpetual data stream, coupled with sophisticated analytics, empowers insurers to make informed decisions, optimize operations and elevate the quality of their services.

While IoT has already become an integral part of consumers' daily lives, its potential within the insurance sector is only recently being explored. As the realm of connected devices expands, opportunities for insurers also grow, encompassing the development of personalized products, improved cost management and enhanced risk prediction and prevention.

As the competition in the insurance market intensifies, IoT offers real-time data and analysis that can prove crucial for sustained success. The understanding of IoT technology is rooted in the network of physical objects – such as smartphones, medical sensors and security systems – embedded with sensors, software and technologies. These devices continually exchange data via the internet, facilitating real-time communication and information sharing.

The abundant data available through IoT-enabled devices allows industries, including insurance, to redefine business models and create new value. For insurers, IoT grants access to continuous, real-time data, transcending the reliance on historical data, policyholder-reported information or external sources. By harnessing IoT device data, insurers can uncover greater value, enhancing customer experiences and strengthening their own financial standings.

USE CASE: PROGRESSIVE'S SNAPSHOT PROGRAM[3]

A prime example of IoT's prowess unfolds within Progressive's Snapshot program. Through the integration of IoT devices, this initiative orchestrates the real-time monitoring of drivers' behaviours. The multifaceted data accrued – ranging from driving patterns to vehicular metrics – constructs a holistic depiction of each policyholder's risk exposure. This repository of insights emboldens Progressive to reimagine the traditional motor insurance premium structure. Conscientious drivers, as discerned through IoT data, enjoy the privilege of reduced insurance rates – a transformative shift in premium assessment reverberating throughout the industry.

The integration of IoT's real-time insights into the fabric of insurance amplifies the precision of risk assessment, enhances customer engagement and paves the way for a paradigm shift in the customization and provision of insurance solutions.

Within the insurance sector, IoT offers several specific opportunities:

Safer homes: IoT devices can monitor home security and safety, enabling insurers to detect anomalies and intervene to prevent damage. This fosters safer homes for customers and reduces risk for insurers.

Optimized risk assessment and prevention: IoT data empowers insurers to predict events rather than react to them, improving customer loyalty and trust. For instance, IoT devices can anticipate issues like boiler malfunctions and notify policyholders and insurers to take preventative action.

Enhanced claim cost management: Insurers can analyse IoT data to optimize risk prediction, reducing claims and costs. Lower IoT device prices further make this technology cost-effective for both insurers and customers.

Improved customer experience: IoT data identifies coverage gaps and allows customized products for different customer segments. External data sources streamline processes and enhance user experiences.

Challenges of adopting IoT in insurance include:[4]

Data security: Vulnerability to cyberattacks and phishing threats challenges IoT data security, making customers reluctant to provide constant data access.

Data management: Handling massive IoT data influx while adhering to data privacy regulations is complex. Insurers need quick yet careful data management solutions.

Resistance to change: The insurance industry's historical slow adaptation hampers IoT integration. Overcoming resistance and communicating benefits are crucial.

To maximize IoT investments, insurers must prioritize data accountability. Security measures for customer data, awareness programmes and training are vital. A well-established enterprise data management strategy ensures customer data protection while harnessing IoT's potential.

In conclusion, IoT-driven solutions provide a competitive edge for insurers seeking innovative ways to add value to customers and manage risk. However, overcoming challenges through robust data management and cultural shifts is essential to realizing IoT's full potential in the insurance industry.

AI and ML: Powering automation, insight and predictive precision

Artificial Intelligence and Machine Learning (AI and ML) are two closely linked technologies. AI involves replicating human intelligence in machines, enabling them to analyse data, make judgements and handle tasks that usually require human thinking. Machine learning, a subset of AI, focuses on training algorithms to learn from data patterns and improve their performance without explicit programming.

In the realm of insurance, AI and ML algorithms play a pivotal role in processing vast volumes of data, identifying intricate patterns and deriving meaningful insights that guide decision-making. However, it's important to note that the effectiveness of these technologies depends greatly on the quality and quantity of the data they're fed. These advanced tools empower insurance providers to automate operations, enhance precision and uncover valuable insights that conventional methods might overlook. This symbiotic relationship between AI, ML and high-quality data reshapes the insurance landscape by fostering efficiency and customer-centric solutions.

Important to note that AI, big data and predictive analytics are three interrelated concepts that have different meanings and applications. Here is a brief comparison of them:

AI is a broad branch of computer science that aims to create systems and machines that can perform tasks that would normally require human intelligence, such as reasoning, learning, decision making and problem solving. AI can use various techniques and methods, such as machine learning, natural language processing computer vision and robotics.[5]

ML falls within the realm of AI and leverages statistical methods and data to develop algorithms and models for the purpose of learning.[6]

Big data encompasses the vast volume, variety, velocity and veracity of data originating from diverse sources, including sensors, devices, applications and social media. Handling, processing, analysing and leveraging such data presents both challenges and opportunities.[7,8] Essentially, if AI and predictive analytics serve as the engine, data serves as the fuel powering them.

Predictive analytics is a form of data analysis that uses historical data and statistical techniques to make predictions about future events or behaviours. Predictive analytics can use methods such as data mining, modelling, machine learning, artificial intelligence and statistics. Predictive analytics can help organizations identify trends, patterns, risks and opportunities from the data. Predictive analytics can also be a subset of AI or a tool for AI to achieve its goals.[9,10]

When we consider these emerging technologies within the insurance realm – AI, ML, big data and predictive analytics – we find both commonalities and distinctions. ML and predictive technologies operate as subsets of AI, with big data acting as the pivotal resource fuelling these advancements. Collaboration between these technologies and the quality of data at hand is paramount for effective modelling and model enhancement in the insurance sector. While they intersect and offer mutual benefits across various insurance domains and applications, it's vital to acknowledge that each possesses its own unique definitions, scopes and specific challenges. Recognizing and addressing these distinctions is crucial for unlocking their full potential within the ever-evolving landscape of the insurance industry, where data-driven insights hold immense value.

Applications in insurance

AI and ML have found extensive applications in the insurance landscape due to their ability to address complex challenges and improve operational efficiency. Some key applications include:

Claims processing and fraud detection: AI and ML algorithms can expedite claims processing by automatically reviewing and categorizing claims, thus reducing manual efforts. Additionally, these technologies can detect anomalies and patterns indicative of fraud, ensuring a more robust claims validation process.

Underwriting and risk assessment: Insurers utilize AI and ML to analyse vast amounts of data, including historical claims data, credit scores and external sources, to accurately assess risks and determine appropriate premiums for policyholders.

Customer support: Chatbots powered by AI provide customers with instant responses to enquiries, offer guidance and facilitate policy-related interactions, thereby enhancing customer experiences and reducing response times.

Predictive analytics: AI and ML models can predict future trends and behaviours based on historical data, enabling insurers to anticipate risks and make informed decisions.

Personalized policies and pricing: AI enables insurers to offer personalized insurance policies and pricing based on individual characteristics and behaviours, fostering customer satisfaction and loyalty.

Widespread adoption in insurance

AI and ML's extensive adoption in insurance is attributed to their capacity to handle the industry's data-intensive nature and complex decision-making processes. The vast amount of data generated by insurance transactions, claims and customer interactions can be efficiently processed and analysed by AI and ML algorithms, yielding valuable insights for insurers. This technology transcends traditional limitations, enabling insurers to optimize operations, enhance customer engagement and mitigate risks effectively.

In essence, AI and ML are the cornerstones of a smarter, more efficient and customer-centric insurance ecosystem, driving the industry towards a future marked by innovation and heightened performance.

USE CASE: JAPANESE INSURANCE FIRM REPLACES STAFF WITH AI

In January 2017, Fukoku Mutual Life Insurance, a Japanese insurance company, replaced 34 employees with an AI system. The AI, based on IBM's Watson technology, is designed to calculate insurance pay-outs and gather information for policyholders' claims by reading medical certificates and data related to surgeries or hospital stays. This move is expected to increase productivity by 30 per cent and result in annual savings of about 140 million yen. It reflects a growing trend as other Japanese insurers also consider adopting AI systems for tasks such as optimizing coverage plans for customers. This shift towards AI-based automation aligns with a broader global prediction of job displacement due to AI and robotics.[11]

Limitations of AI in the insurance domain   AI has ushered in a new era of possibilities in the insurance sector, but it is imperative to recognize that this technology is not without its limitations. As insurers and insurtech companies increasingly integrate AI into their operations, they must also be mindful of the challenges and constraints that AI presents. Here are some key limitations to consider:

1 **Lack of human judgement and common sense:** AI systems are proficient in analysing data and patterns, but they lack human judgement and common sense. They may struggle to understand nuanced situations, context and emotions that humans easily grasp. In complex insurance scenarios, such as assessing liability in unique claims, AI may struggle to make accurate decisions.

2 **Data quality and bias:** The effectiveness of AI relies heavily on the quality of the data it is trained on. If the training data is biased or incomplete, the AI system can perpetuate those biases or make inaccurate predictions. In insurance, biased data can lead to discriminatory outcomes, such as unfairly denying coverage to certain demographics.

3 **Lack of transparency:** AI algorithms often operate as 'black boxes', meaning their decision-making processes are not easily understandable by humans. This lack of transparency can be a challenge in the insurance industry, where regulatory compliance and ethical considerations are paramount. Insurers need to ensure that AI-driven decisions are explainable and justifiable.

4 **Limited adaptability to novel scenarios:** AI systems are trained on historical data, which means they may struggle to adapt to unprecedented situations or sudden changes in the environment. For instance, a new type of insurance claim that hasn't been seen before may confound AI algorithms that lack relevant training data.

5 **Security and privacy concerns:** The increased reliance on AI introduces security and privacy concerns. Storing and processing sensitive customer data for AI analysis can become a vulnerability if not properly secured. Additionally, there's a risk that AI-generated insights could be used maliciously or lead to unintended disclosure of private information.

6 **High implementation and maintenance costs:** Integrating AI into existing insurance systems requires substantial investments in terms of technology, infrastructure and personnel. Moreover, maintaining and updating AI systems to keep up with evolving technology can also be costly. These costs may exceed the savings provided by such AI systems.

7 **Ethical and moral dilemmas:** AI systems may confront insurers with ethical and moral dilemmas. For instance, determining liability in accidents involving autonomous vehicles or deciding whether to prioritize cost-cutting over policyholders' well-being can be complex decisions that AI may not be equipped to handle.

8 **Job displacement concerns:** While AI can streamline processes and improve efficiency, it also raises concerns about job displacement. Routine tasks that were previously handled by humans, such as data entry and basic customer interactions, may be automated, potentially leading to job losses in the industry.

9 **Overreliance and decision-making autonomy:** Over reliance on AI can lead to a reduced role for human expertise. Relying solely on AI-driven decisions without human oversight can be risky, as AI systems may fail to account for exceptional or unforeseen circumstances.

10 **Resistance to adoption:** Introducing AI into an organization requires a cultural shift and changes in workflows. Resistance to change from employees and stakeholders can hinder the successful adoption of AI technologies.

While AI offers transformative potential for the insurance industry, it is essential to approach its adoption with a clear understanding of its limitations and challenges. Balancing the advantages of AI with its constraints will be crucial for insurers seeking to harness its power effectively while upholding ethical and regulatory standards.

Big data: Extracting insights and fuelling AI advancements

The connection between big data and the advancement of AI technology is notably profound. Big data constitutes extensive volumes of both structured and unstructured information that is rapidly produced from a wide array of sources including digital platforms, sensors, social media, transactions and various other channels. This data possesses three fundamental attributes that define its nature: volume, reflecting its substantial quantity; velocity, capturing the speed at which it is generated; and variety, encompassing its diverse range of data types.

The surge in data generation is fuelling a revolution in the insurance sector through the prowess of big data analytics. This dynamic process involves scrutinizing data to extract meaningful insights that drive pivotal decisions. Its applications span diverse fronts, from predictive analytics to fraud detection, policy calculation and leveraging data from sources like open networks, IoT and social media.

However, the true power of big data becomes most apparent when intertwined with the evolving capabilities of AI. As we explored earlier, AI relies on copious amounts of high-quality data to refine its intelligence. The connection between big data and AI is a symbiotic one. Big data provides the fuel that powers AI algorithms to perform complex tasks, while AI, in return, augments big data's analysis capabilities.

Statistics from 2019 by insurance business advisor Willis Towers Watson underline this connection. Over two-thirds of surveyed executives in the Americas believed that predictive analytics, enabled by big data, significantly cut costs. Moreover, 60 per cent of respondents recognized the invaluable role of this extra insight in expanding sales and bolstering profitability.[12]

The insurance landscape is witnessing an unprecedented metamorphosis where the combination of big data and AI is unlocking new dimensions. From fine-tuned risk assessment to personalized customer interactions, this synergy is propelling the industry into a realm of innovation and optimization. As the data-empowered AI journey continues, the insurance sector is poised to navigate uncharted territories with confidence and agility.

Big data's impact on insurance

Within the insurance realm, big data stands as a game-changing technological advancement. Insurers harness sophisticated analytical tools to process and decipher the vast reservoirs of data available, unveiling meaningful insights, patterns and trends. These revelations empower insurers to make informed decisions, optimize their operations and elevate their services.

Highlighted below are key domains where big data is reshaping the landscape of insurance:

- **Risk evaluation and underwriting:** Big data empowers insurers to assess risks with greater precision through comprehensive data analysis. This encompasses historical claims records, policyholder particulars, external data like weather patterns and economic indicators, among others. By delving into these data streams, insurers can tailor underwriting protocols and pricing strategies to specific risk profiles, fostering equitable and personalized premium structures.

- **Customer grouping and personalization:** Big data facilitates more effective customer segmentation for insurers. By dissecting data on customer behaviours, preferences and demographics, insurers can craft targeted marketing initiatives, provide customized insurance products and offer personalized customer interactions.

- **Fraud detection and prevention:** Big data analytics act as a guardian against potential fraudulent activities by identifying discernible patterns. By scrutinizing historical claims data and monitoring real-time transactions, insurers can flag suspicious occurrences and mitigate losses arising from fraud.

- **Insights into customers and retention:** Big data analytics yield profound insights into customer behaviours and inclinations. Armed with this knowledge, insurers can enhance customer engagement, formulate loyalty programmes and furnish tailored solutions to boost customer retention.

- **Telematics and usage-based insurance:** Telematics devices, which capture data on driving behaviours, epitomize big data's role in insurance. Insurers leverage this data to provide usage-based insurance premiums, where rates correspond to actual driving practices. This promotes safer driving habits and fosters fairer premium structures.

- **Predictive analytics:** Big data facilitates predictive modelling, enabling insurers to foresee trends, risks and customer behaviours. This proactive foresight supports agile decision-making and strategy optimization.

USE CASE: BIG DATA AND IOT COLLABORATION IN INSURANCE

Progressive has introduced a program named Snapshot, which seamlessly integrates big data and telematics technology to gather comprehensive insights into drivers' behaviours and driving patterns. Customers have the option to install a compact device in their vehicles, which diligently collects data on various aspects like speed, mileage, time of day and braking tendencies. The amassed data is subsequently subjected to analysis, allowing for a detailed evaluation of individual driving conduct.

Usage-based insurance: Capitalizing on the data garnered through the Snapshot initiative, Progressive pioneers usage-based insurance policies. Customers showcasing responsible and secure driving practices through the accumulated data become eligible for discounts on their insurance premiums. This personalized strategy, rooted in tangible driving habits, delivers advantages to both policyholders by enabling cost savings and to the insurance company by facilitating more precise risk assessment.[13]

By harnessing the synergy between big data and telematics technology, Progressive elevates its ability to provide customers with finely tailored insurance alternatives and pricing structures based on their distinct driving tendencies. This twofold effect not only encourages safer driving habits but also empowers the company to make well-informed decisions pertaining to underwriting and pricing strategies.

Challenges encountered in implementing big data in insurance

- **Data precision and quality:** Ensuring data accuracy and quality is paramount for generating dependable insights. Inaccurate or incomplete data can lead to erroneous conclusions and decisions.

- **Data confidentiality and security:** Safeguarding sensitive customer data mandates adherence to privacy regulations and robust security measures to fend off breaches and unauthorized access.

- **Data fusion:** Integrating data from diverse sources, both internal and external, is intricate and necessitates streamlined data integration procedures.

- **Skill and resource gap:** Executing big data analytics necessitates proficient data scientists, analysts and IT experts familiar with the technology and its applications.

- **Ethical considerations:** The collection and utilization of personal data raise ethical questions surrounding privacy, consent and the potential for bias in decision-making processes.

In summation, big data's potential to reshape the insurance industry is formidable, furnishing insurers with crucial insights for risk appraisal, customer interaction and operational optimization. However, tackling challenges linked to data quality, privacy and talent is pivotal to fully unlock its potential.

Augmented reality (AR) and virtual reality (VR): Immersive experiences

The use of augmented reality (AR) and virtual reality (VR) is changing the insurance industry. These technologies bring new challenges and opportunities, affecting areas like personal health and business security. As AR and VR become more popular, insurance companies need to quickly take advantage of this new market while dealing with the complexities of using these technologies. The use of AR and VR in insurance has been growing recently. But the ideas behind these technologies go back to the 1950s when early versions like the Sensorama and Telesphere Mask were created.[14]

AR and VR exert a notable influence on the insurance trade. They find utility in diverse domains such as the military, healthcare, education and entertainment. In the realm of insurance, when leveraged effectively, these technologies possess the potential to heighten customer satisfaction, ultimately leading to increased profitability.[15]

Impact on insurance

The impact of AR and VR on insurance is twofold. On one hand, they provide opportunities to enhance risk assessment accuracy, expedite processes and elevate customer engagement. On the other hand, they necessitate substantial investments in technology, skilled personnel and data security measures. Successfully integrating AR and VR can position insurers as innovators, but a misstep could lead to negative customer experiences and reputational damage.

- **Enhancing risk visualization:** AR and VR hold the potential to revolutionize risk visualization by overlaying computer-generated images onto real-world views. This empowers insurers to offer clients a heightened understanding of potential risks associated with specific locations. However, ensuring the accuracy of the data overlay and avoiding misinterpretations become a critical challenge.

- **Virtual property inspections:** The application of VR for property inspections offers notable advantages in terms of efficiency and cost reduction. Insurers can remotely assess properties, reducing the need for physical site visits. Yet, challenges arise in ensuring the accuracy of virtual inspections, potential limitations of capturing intricate details and addressing concerns related to data privacy.

- **Training and risk management:** AR and VR provide immersive training platforms, enabling insurance professionals to simulate real-life scenarios. This enhances their expertise in claims processing, risk assessment and customer interactions. However, the challenge lies in creating high-quality, realistic simulations that effectively mimic real-world complexities.

- **Elevating customer experiences:** By integrating AR and VR, insurers can deliver interactive experiences that facilitate customer understanding of insurance offerings and claims processes. This leads to improved customer engagement and satisfaction. However, challenges include creating user-friendly interfaces, ensuring compatibility with various devices, and maintaining a seamless experience.

USE CASE: INSURANCE TRAINING

Zurich Insurance demonstrates a practical application of AR and VR. They utilize VR to provide staff training, enabling employees to navigate real-world scenarios in a controlled virtual environment. While this enhances their decision-making capabilities, the challenge lies in ensuring that the virtual scenarios accurately reflect the complexities of actual insurance scenarios.[16]

Challenges encountered[17]   The integration of AR and VR technologies into the insurance industry presents a range of challenges that require strategic solutions to overcome. These obstacles are multifaceted and require careful consideration to navigate effectively:

- **Technical complexities:** The implementation of AR and VR in insurance involves intricate technical elements, from developing immersive content to ensuring seamless user experiences across various devices. Creating lifelike simulations demands a profound grasp of hardware capabilities, software integration and user interface design.
- **High initial costs:** The adoption of AR and VR technologies demands a substantial financial investment. Procuring advanced hardware, developing software and maintaining these technologies contribute to significant initial expenses. This financial hurdle may dissuade certain insurers from embracing these technologies.

- **Skilled content creation:** Crafting captivating AR and VR experiences necessitates a pool of adept content creators proficient in 3D modelling, animation and interactive design. Attracting and retaining such talent can be challenging, potentially leading to delays or compromised content quality.

- **Data privacy and security:** The interactive nature of AR and VR experiences raises concerns about data privacy and security. Insurers must ensure that user data collected during these experiences remains shielded against unauthorized access, breaches and misuse. Adhering to data protection regulations becomes of utmost importance.

- **User comfort and well-being:** A notable challenge tied to VR is the possibility of motion sickness, discomfort or adverse physical reactions among users. Insurers must take precautions to minimize these issues, as negative experiences could deter users and influence perceptions of AR and VR applications.[18]

- **Integration with existing processes:** Seamlessly integrating AR and VR into established insurance processes and workflows necessitates meticulous planning. Ensuring these technologies enhance rather than disrupt operations can be intricate, particularly within larger organizations with well-established practices.

- **User adoption and training:** AR and VR experiences might be novel to many users, requiring orientation and training to ensure optimal engagement. Educating both employees and customers on effective navigation of these technologies is pivotal for achieving desired outcomes.

- **Content quality and relevance:** The success of AR and VR applications hinges on the quality and relevance of the content offered. Crafting content that accurately mirrors real-world scenarios while delivering value to users necessitates a profound understanding of insurance processes and customer needs.

By addressing these challenges head-on, insurers can position themselves to harness the potential benefits of AR and VR while mitigating possible risks. Through investments in technology, talent, security measures and user experience design, insurers can ensure a seamless incorporation of AR and VR into their operations, providing augmented value to customers and stakeholders alike.

In conclusion, the incorporation of AR and VR into the insurance field holds immense potential, even though it comes with its set of challenges. Insurers need to navigate technical complexities, address privacy concerns and allocate financial resources while aiming to provide improved customer experiences and more accurate risk assessment. Successfully embracing these technologies can pave the way for a more efficient, captivating and innovative insurance industry.

Robotic Process Automation (RPA): Efficiency and accuracy

Robotic Process Automation (RPA) is a mature technology that utilizes software robots or 'bots' to automate repetitive and rule-based tasks within business processes. These bots mimic human actions by interacting with digital systems, applications and data sources. RPA aims to enhance efficiency, accuracy and consistency by reducing the need for manual intervention in routine tasks.

Applications of RPA in the insurance industry

RPA has found significant application in the insurance sector due to its ability to streamline various processes, including:

Claims processing: RPA can automate data extraction from claims forms, verification of policy details and even generate claim settlement calculations, leading to faster and more accurate claims processing.

Policy administration: RPA can handle policy issuance, renewals and updates by automatically updating customer information across systems, reducing errors and processing time.

Underwriting: RPA can assist in gathering and analysing data for risk assessment, helping underwriters make informed decisions more quickly.

Data entry and validation: RPA can automate data entry tasks like transferring customer details from emails to CRM systems and validating data for accuracy.

Compliance and reporting: RPA can assist in generating compliance reports by extracting relevant information from different databases and systems.

Impact on the insurance industry

RPA offers several benefits to the insurance industry:

- **Efficiency:** By automating repetitive tasks, RPA reduces manual effort and frees up employees to focus on more complex and strategic activities.

- **Accuracy:** RPA minimizes the risk of human errors, leading to improved data accuracy and reduced inconsistencies.

- **Speed:** Tasks that would take hours or days to complete manually can be done by bots in minutes, accelerating processes like claims settlement and policy issuance.

- **Cost savings:** RPA reduces operational costs by optimizing resource utilization and decreasing the need for additional human resources.

USE CASE: IMPLEMENTATION OF RPA BY ZURICH
Zurich Insurance employs RPA to automate underwriting processes. This technology-driven automation expedites the underwriting process and ensures consistency in decision making.[19]

Challenges of Implementing RPA   While RPA offers many advantages, there are challenges to consider:

- **Complex processes:** RPA is most effective for well-defined, rule-based processes. Complex tasks that involve decision making based on context might not be suitable for automation.

- **Integration:** Integrating RPA with existing systems and legacy software can be challenging and require significant effort.

- **Change management:** Employees might be resistant to change, especially if they fear job displacement due to automation. Effective change management is crucial.

- **Maintenance:** RPA systems require regular monitoring, updates and maintenance to ensure they function correctly.

- **Data security:** RPA involves the handling of sensitive data, and ensuring data security and compliance with regulations is essential.

In conclusion, RPA is revolutionizing the insurance industry by automating routine tasks, improving efficiency, accuracy and customer experiences. While its implementation comes with challenges, successful integration can lead to significant improvements in operational processes and overall business performance.

Biometrics and identity verification: Secure authentication

Biometrics technology is a method of identifying and verifying individuals based on their unique physical or behavioural characteristics. It involves the use of distinctive traits, such as fingerprints, facial features, iris patterns, voice tones or even behavioural patterns like typing style or walking gait, to accurately establish someone's identity. Biometric technology transforms these traits into digital data and uses advanced algorithms to match and authenticate individuals.

The core principle behind biometrics is that each person possesses characteristics that are highly unlikely to be replicated by others. This uniqueness makes biometrics a secure and reliable method for identification and authentication in various applications, including security systems, access control, digital transactions and customer verification.

Biometrics technology involves several steps:

- **Enrolment:** During enrolment, an individual's biometric traits are captured and converted into digital templates. These templates serve as reference points for future comparisons.

- **Storage:** The digital templates are securely stored in a database, often in an encrypted form, to protect the individual's privacy.

- **Matching:** When authentication is required, the person provides their biometric trait, such as a fingerprint or facial scan. The system then compares this biometric data with the stored template to determine if there's a match.

- **Decision:** Based on the degree of similarity between the provided biometric data and the stored template, the system either grants or denies access.

Benefits of biometrics technology include enhanced security, convenience, accuracy and a reduced likelihood of identity fraud. However, it's important to address privacy concerns and implement proper security measures when collecting and storing biometric data.

Biometrics and identity verification technologies play a crucial role in establishing and confirming the identity of individuals. These technologies utilize unique physical or behavioural traits, such as fingerprints, facial features, voice patterns or even retinal scans, to verify a person's identity. This ensures that only authorized individuals gain access to sensitive systems or perform certain actions.

Benefits and applications in insurance

In response to the rising challenge of online crime in the insurance sector, insurers are turning to biometric face verification technology as a robust solution. Biometric face verification utilizes unique facial characteristics to authenticate users and ensure secure transactions. This technology is being employed to protect against various forms of digital crime, including account takeover fraud and money laundering.

USE CASES: DETECTING AND PREVENTING FRAUD WITH BIOMETRIC FACE VERIFICATION

Proof of life verification: Insurers often face the daunting task of confirming the existence of policyholders, especially in the case of pension and annuity claims. Biometric face verification technology, such as iProov's Genuine Presence Assurance, enables insurers to validate the authenticity of remote users. By analysing live facial scans, insurers can verify that the claimant is not only the correct person but also a real individual. This verification process ensures that only genuine policyholders are granted access to their accounts and claims.

Account takeover prevention: Biometric face verification serves as a powerful deterrent against account takeover fraud. This type of fraud occurs when malicious actors gain unauthorized access to a policyholder's account and manipulate sensitive information. Insurers can implement biometric authentication during login attempts, requiring users to provide a live facial scan in addition to traditional credentials. This ensures that even if login credentials are compromised, fraudsters cannot gain access without a valid biometric match.

Money laundering detection: Criminal networks often exploit insurance policies to launder illicit funds. Biometric face verification can play a pivotal role in thwarting these attempts. Insurers can use this technology to verify the identity of individuals purchasing insurance policies. By confirming the identity of the policyholder and cross-referencing it with international databases, insurers can reduce the risk of money laundering schemes.

Benefits and impacts   Biometric face verification technology offers a range of advantages and significant impacts on the insurance industry:[20]

- **Enhanced online security:** Biometric face verification technology adds an extra layer of security to online insurance services. By relying on unique facial features, insurers can significantly reduce the risk of unauthorized access and fraudulent activities.

- **Effortless user experience:** Customers can access their insurance accounts and submit claims with ease, as biometric verification eliminates the need for complex passwords or PINs.

- **Regulatory compliance:** Biometric verification aids insurers in adhering to Know Your Customer (KYC) and anti-money laundering (AML) regulations, further strengthening their reputation and regulatory standing.

- **Reputational trust:** Implementing biometric technology demonstrates insurers' commitment to safeguarding customer information, fostering trust and loyalty among policyholders.

- **Policy purchases:** Insurance companies can employ biometrics to ensure that the right individuals are purchasing policies, minimizing the risk of fraudulent transactions.

- **Claims submissions:** Biometric authentication can be used to validate the identity of customers when submitting insurance claims, reducing the possibility of false claims.

- **Fraud prevention:** By using biometrics, insurers can better detect and prevent fraudulent activities, as it is significantly harder to impersonate someone's unique biometric traits.

Challenges in developing biometric solutions   Developing biometric solutions comes with its share of challenges:

- **Privacy concerns:** Collecting and storing biometric data raises privacy issues, as this data is highly personal and sensitive.

- **Accuracy and reliability:** Biometric systems must be accurate and reliable, ensuring that legitimate individuals are not denied access while unauthorized individuals are still prevented from entry.

- **Data security:** Biometric data needs to be stored and transmitted securely to prevent breaches that could expose sensitive information.

- **Technological evolution:** As technology evolves, biometric systems can become outdated quickly, necessitating frequent updates and adaptations.

- **User acceptance:** Some users might be uncomfortable with providing their biometric data, raising concerns about user acceptance and adoption.

In summary, biometrics and identity verification technologies offer a secure and efficient way to authenticate individuals in the insurance industry. These technologies find utility across tasks like policy purchases, claims submissions and fraud prevention. However, challenges such as privacy concerns, data security and technological evolution must be carefully addressed when developing and deploying biometric solutions.

Cloud computing: Scalability and accessibility

Cloud computing is a transformative technology that enables businesses, including the insurance sector, to access information and applications over the internet. This guide delves into the significance of cloud computing in the insurance industry, highlighting its advantages and disadvantages, while incorporating insights from industry experts.

Advantages of cloud computing for the insurance industry

Cloud computing entails the provision of computing assets, such as data storage, computational capabilities and software applications, via the internet. These assets are hosted on external servers managed by cloud service providers. Insurers can readily access and utilize these resources, eliminating the requirement for physical hardware and infrastructure on their premises.

Cloud computing transforms data management practices, offering insurers an array of advantages:[21]

- **Enhanced efficiency:** Insurers can access information and applications from various devices, promoting remote work and increasing overall efficiency.

- **Cost savings:** Cloud storage is more cost-effective than traditional methods, and its scalability allows businesses to adjust computing resources according to demand, leading to reduced costs.

- **Technological advancements:** Cloud adoption enables insurers to utilize cutting-edge technology platforms, resulting in faster product and service development and deployment.

- **Improved customer service:** Cloud computing empowers insurers to provide prompt customer service, respond quickly to enquiries, offer real-time quotes and facilitate online policy management.

- **Scalability:** Cloud platforms can handle high traffic volumes, making them suitable for insurers experiencing fluctuations in activity due to events like natural disasters or marketing campaigns.

- **Quick time-to-market:** Insurers can swiftly launch new applications and services in the cloud, speeding up the introduction of new products to the market.

- **Accessibility:** Cloud-based systems enable remote access to data and applications, facilitating collaboration among remote teams and supporting work-from-home arrangements.

- **Business continuity:** Cloud services often include built-in disaster recovery and back-up solutions, ensuring that critical data is protected even in the event of hardware failures or natural disasters.

Applications and use cases of cloud computing in the insurance industry

Cloud computing technology has become a transformative force in the insurance sector, offering diverse applications that enhance efficiency, data management and customer engagement. Insurance companies are leveraging cloud-based solutions in various ways to streamline their operations and provide better services. Some prominent applications and use cases of cloud computing in the insurance industry include:[22]

- **Data storage:** One of the fundamental applications of cloud computing in insurance is data storage. Insurance companies deal with vast amounts of policyholder information, claims data and historical records. Storing this data in the cloud provides several benefits. Cloud platforms offer secure and reliable storage solutions, ensuring that sensitive customer information is protected. Furthermore, the cloud's scalability ensures that insurers can easily accommodate growing data volumes without investing heavily in on-premises infrastructure.

- **Claims processing:** Cloud-based systems have revolutionized the way insurance claims are processed. Cloud technology enables real-time access to relevant data for claims adjusters, facilitating more efficient claims processing. Adjusters can access policy information, customer data and relevant documents from any location with an internet connection. This results in faster and more accurate claims assessments, reducing the processing time and enhancing customer satisfaction.

- **Customer engagement:** Cloud computing supports the implementation of customer relationship management (CRM) systems, which are pivotal for enhancing customer engagement. Insurers can use cloud-based CRM platforms to manage customer interactions, track communication history and personalize service delivery. Cloud-based CRM systems enable insurance companies to respond promptly to customer enquiries, offer tailored solutions and provide a seamless experience across various touchpoints.

- **Underwriting and risk assessment:** Cloud-based data analytics tools have transformed underwriting and risk assessment processes in the insurance industry. Insurers can harness the power of cloud computing to analyse vast datasets efficiently. Cloud platforms offer the computational resources required for processing and analysing complex data, leading to more accurate risk assessments. By leveraging cloud-based data analytics, insurance companies can identify trends, patterns and correlations in data, ultimately improving the precision of underwriting decisions.

USE CASE: METLIFE'S ADOPTION OF CLOUD COMPUTING

MetLife leverages cloud computing to enhance customer interactions through its mobile app. Policyholders can access information, file claims and manage policies seamlessly.[23]

Challenges of adopting cloud computing in the insurance industry While cloud computing offers numerous advantages to the insurance sector, its adoption comes with several challenges that insurance companies need to address. These challenges can impact data security, privacy, operations and reliability. Some of the key challenges of adopting cloud computing in the insurance industry include:

- **Data security:** Storing sensitive customer information, including personal and financial data, in the cloud requires robust security measures. Insurance companies must implement strong encryption, access controls and multi-factor authentication to prevent data breaches and unauthorized access. Ensuring the confidentiality, integrity and availability of data (known as the CIA triad) is crucial to maintaining customer trust and regulatory compliance.

- **Data privacy:** Insurance companies handle a vast amount of customer data, and ensuring compliance with data protection regulations is paramount. Cloud providers must adhere to strict data privacy standards, especially in regions with stringent data protection laws such as GDPR. Insurers need to address concerns about the potential exposure of customer data to unauthorized parties and implement mechanisms for data anonymization and pseudonymization.

- **Integration complexity:** Migrating existing systems and applications to the cloud and integrating them seamlessly can be a complex process. Inadequate planning and execution can lead to disruptions in operations and services. Insurance companies need to carefully assess their current infrastructure, design a comprehensive migration plan and ensure that data and applications are compatible with the cloud environment. Poorly executed migrations can result in downtime and lost business opportunities.

- **Vendor reliability:** Relying on third-party cloud service providers introduces a level of dependency on their reliability and security practices. Insurance companies need to thoroughly evaluate potential cloud vendors based on their track record, reputation and adherence to industry security standards. They should also consider factors such as uptime guarantees, disaster recovery plans and data back-up procedures to ensure that their business operations are not compromised by vendor-related issues.

In conclusion, cloud computing offers insurers scalable data storage and remote accessibility advantages. It supports efficient data management, analytics and collaboration, transforming traditional insurance processes. However, adopting this technology requires addressing challenges related to security, privacy, integration and vendor reliability. Proper planning and strategic implementation can enable insurers to harness the full potential of cloud computing while minimizing risks.

Conclusion

In this chapter, we embarked on an enlightening journey through the established and emerging technologies that shape the insurtech landscape. We explored a wide array of ground-breaking innovations and their far-reaching implications for the insurance industry. These technologies included blockchain's transformative impact on trust and transparency, the data-driven insights harnessed by IoT, the automation and precision achieved through AI and ML, the wealth of insights extracted from big data, the efficiency gains enabled by RPA, the secure authentication capabilities delivered by biometrics and the scalability advantages presented by cloud computing.

Throughout this journey, we examined real-world use cases that vividly demonstrated how these technologies are reshaping the insurance landscape. From Progressive's Snapshot program showcasing the potential of IoT to Japanese insurers implementing AI for operational efficiency, we witnessed tangible examples of insurtech's capabilities in action.

As we wrap up this chapter, we've gained a comprehensive understanding of how these emerging technologies are revolutionizing insurance. Their transformative potential stands ready to redefine customer experiences, optimize operational processes and enhance risk management practices.

Our voyage now leads us into Chapter 4 where we delve into how insurtech is revolutionizing the way customers engage with insurance, ushering in a more personalized and customer-centric era.

Notes

1 'Insurers and Reinsurers Launch Blockchain Initiative B3i', Allianz.com, 19 Oct. 2016. www.allianz.com/en/press/news/commitment/sponsorship/ 161018-insurers-and-reinsurers-launch-blockchain-initiative-b3i.html (archived at https://perma.cc/2SMM-KP5Z).

2 'Insurance 2030 – The Impact of AI on the Future of Insurance', McKinsey, 12 Mar. 2021. www.mckinsey.com/industries/financial-services/our-insights/ insurance-2030-the-impact-of-ai-on-the-future-of-insurance (archived at https://perma.cc/CV44-3TGH).

3 'Progressive Snapshot, Reviewed by Experts – Insurance', Bankrate, 8 Dec. 2023. www.bankrate.com/insurance/car/progressive-snapshot/ (archived at https://perma.cc/KC26-W954).

4 '5 Challenges for IoT in the Insurance Industry – SAS Institute'. www.sas.com/ en_in/insights/articles/big-data/5-challenges-for-iot-in-insurance-industry.html (archived at https://perma.cc/9M8P-ZMQG).

5 'Predictive Analytics vs. AI: Why the Difference Matters', TechBeacon. techbeacon.com/enterprise-it/predictive-analytics-vs-ai-why-difference-matters (archived at https://perma.cc/5J8U-KN3Q).

6 'AI versus ML versus Predictive Analytics', Tableau. www.tableau.com/ data-insights/ai/AI-ML-predictive-analytics (archived at https://perma.cc/ PS2J-LX9L).

7 'What Are Big Data & Predictive Analytics? How Do They Relate?', 17 Nov. 2022. www.weka.io/learn/ai-ml/big-data-predictive-analytics/ (archived at https://perma.cc/UEA8-23SJ).

8 'How Big Data and AI Work Together: Synergies & Benefits' - Qlik.

9 'Predictive Analytics vs. AI: Why the Difference matters ', TechBeacon. techbeacon.com/enterprise-it/predictive-analytics-vs-ai-why-difference-matters (archived at https://perma.cc/R9UW-9TYX).

10 'What's the Difference Between AI & Predictive Analytics?', 29 Mar. 2021. www.techadv.com/blog/whats-difference-between-ai-predictive-analytics (archived at https://perma.cc/5NTD-SYKK).

11 'Japanese Insurance Firm Replaces 34 Staff with AI', BBC News, 5 Jan. 2017. www.bbc.com/news/world-asia-38521403?source=Snapzu (archived at https://perma.cc/U8XM-5LT8).

12 'How Big Data Is Transforming the Insurance Sector', Plain Concepts, 7 Mar. 2023. www.plainconcepts.com/big-data-insurance/ (archived at https://perma.cc/S78P-L6CK).

13 'Snapshot Rewards You for Good Driving', Progressive.

14 'How Will AR and VR Reform the Insurance Industry?', Acko, 1 Mar. 2023. www.acko.com/articles/general-info/how-will-augmented-and-virtual-reality-reform-the-insurance-industry/ (archived at https://perma.cc/K9BT-599U).

15 'How Augmented and Virtual Reality Are Changing the Insurance Landscape', KPMG. assets.kpmg.com/content/dam/kpmg/xx/pdf/2016/10/how-augmented-and-virtual-reality-changing-insurance-landscape.pdf (archived at https://perma.cc/QYB5-TNJ9).

16 'Zurich Insurance Turns to Augmented Reality to Train 10000 Managers', Computer Weekly, 22 Apr. 2015.www.computerweekly.com/news/4500244733/Zurich-Insurance-turns-to-augmented-reality-to-train-10000-managers (archived at https://perma.cc/QM4P-9P9Y).

17 'Developing AR/VR Solutions: Challenges & Opportunities', A3logics 3 May 2023. www.a3logics.com/blog/explore-the-challenges-and-opportunities-of-developing-ar-vr-solutions (archived at https://perma.cc/Q3R4-VMQE).

18 'Virtual Reality Sickness: A Review of Causes and Measurements' *International Journal of Human-Computer Interaction,* 2 Jul. 2020. www.tandfonline.com/doi/full/10.1080/10447318.2020.1778351 (archived at https://perma.cc/76GJ-TVX9).

19 'Robotics Take the Tedium from Policy Administration – and Give Back Efficiency', Zurich, 13 Dec. 2021. www.zurich.com/en/commercial-insurance/sustainability-and-insights/commercial-insurance-risk-insights/robotics-take-the-tedium-from-policy-administration-and-give-back-efficiency (archived at https://perma.cc/39ZM-BGL5).

20 'Biometrics in Insurance: How to Use Face Verification to Protect Against Online Crime', iProov, 18 Aug. 2021. www.iproov.com/blog/biometrics-insurance-online-crime (archived at https://perma.cc/74HA-ERQU).

21 'Cloud Computing in the Insurance Sector: The Ultimate Guide', InsurTech, 21 Jan. 2022 insurtechdigital.com/digital-strategy/cloud-computing-insurance-sector-ultimate-guide (archived at https://perma.cc/2X8C-SBM6).

22 'All You Need to Know about Insurance Cloud Computing', SotaTek, 18 Jul. 2023. www.sotatek.com/all-you-need-to-know-about-insurance-cloud-computing/ (archived at https://perma.cc/Y7LG-5Z49).

23 'MetLife Renovates Legacy IT for the Cloud Era', CIO, 18 Dec. 2017. www.cio.com/article/228110/metlife-renovates-legacy-it-for-the-cloud-era.html (archived at https://perma.cc/F9NZ-H96Y).

4

Insurtech and customer experience

Introduction

In this chapter, we delve into the exciting intersection of insurtech and customer experience within the insurance industry. As we explore this multifaceted landscape, we will uncover the innovative ways in which technology-driven advancements are transforming the relationship between insurers and their customers.

Building upon the foundation laid in Chapter 3, we further examine how these emerging technologies are not just reshaping internal processes but also the external dynamics of customer interactions.

The insurance industry, historically perceived as traditional and often plagued by complex processes, is undergoing a significant metamorphosis. Insurtech, a fusion of insurance and technology, is driving this change. It is revolutionizing how insurance companies operate, and more importantly, how they interact with their customers.

We have structured this chapter into five key sections, each addressing a critical aspect of how insurtech is enhancing the customer experience through streamlining processes and communication, personalization and transparency.

Here, we dive into the realm of personalized insurance solutions, where insurtech leverages data and analytics to tailor coverage to individual needs. And we learn how transparency in pricing and policy terms is fostering trust and customer loyalty.

We also uncover the power of data analytics in revolutionizing risk assessment and management. We examine how insurtech's data-driven insights are leading to more accurate underwriting decisions and proactive risk mitigation. We explore the digital tools and platforms that are making insurance more accessible to customers. From mobile apps to online portals, we show how insurtech is putting policy management and claims reporting at customers' fingertips. Finally, we delve into the ways insurtech empowers customers to take control of their insurance journey. We also discuss how digital self-service options, real-time information and interactive engagement strategies are reshaping the customer experience.

Throughout this chapter, we will illustrate real-world examples and case studies that demonstrate the tangible benefits of insurtech in elevating customer satisfaction and loyalty. As technology continues to evolve, insurers are presented with unprecedented opportunities to create more seamless, personalized and engaging experiences for their policyholders.

Streamlining processes and communication

In this section, we will discover how insurtech is simplifying and expediting insurance processes, from policy issuance to claims settlement. We will explore how automation, streamlined operations and improved communication channels are reducing friction for customers and insurers alike, resulting in a win-win scenario for both parties.

Enhancing claims process speed and efficiency

The claims process stands as a pivotal element in customer satisfaction within the insurance industry. It's so vital that we'll explore it further in Chapter 6, 'Insurtech and Claims', which delves into the intricacies of claims in more detail. However, given its importance, it's worth discussing here as well. Customers often judge their insurance based on their claims experience, making a smooth and efficient process crucial. Insurtech significantly enhances this aspect by leveraging technology in various key areas to expedite and streamline the claims process.

Automation: Insurtech platforms implement automated workflows that significantly streamline the claims processing journey. By automating various tasks and processes, the need for labour-intensive manual data entry and paperwork is greatly reduced. This not only accelerates the overall claims process but also minimizes the chances of human error, resulting in more accurate and efficient claims handling. In fact, most insurtech companies offering Software as a Service (SaaS) solutions will look to increase automation to optimize insurers' operations.

Digital documentation: In the digital age, customers can conveniently submit their insurance claims electronically. Through user-friendly mobile apps or online platforms, policyholders can effortlessly upload essential documents, photos, videos and other evidence directly. This digital approach expedites both the quote and buy processes, as well as the claims submission process, and ensures that all necessary documentation is easily accessible to both insurers and customers.

Data analytics: Insurtech harnesses the power of data analytics to evaluate and process claims swiftly. By analysing a wide range of data points, including historical claims data and real-time information, insurers can make more informed decisions regarding claims approvals and settlements. This data-driven approach not only speeds up the assessment process but also enhances accuracy in determining the validity of claims. It's noteworthy that the data analytics is widely applied across various processes, extending beyond just claims handling.

AI and chatbots: Artificial intelligence (AI) and chatbots are increasingly integrated into the claims process. These intelligent virtual assistants play a vital role in assisting customers throughout the claims filing procedure. They offer immediate responses to customer enquiries, guide them through the necessary steps, and even aid in the initial assessment of claims. AI-driven chatbots contribute to a more user-friendly and efficient claims experience, reducing the time required for customers to receive assistance. It's worth noting that while AI and chatbots in insurance have not been universally adopted, many insurers and insurtech companies are actively developing and testing these technologies.

In summary, insurtech accelerates the claims process by capitalizing on technology's capabilities. Through automation, digital documentation, data analytics and the integration of AI and chatbots, insurtech not only expedites the claims journey but also enhances its overall efficiency, accuracy and customer-friendliness. This multifaceted approach results in a smoother and more responsive claims experience for policyholders and insurers alike.

Digital tools for policy management

When it comes to helping customers easily access and manage their insurance policies, insurtech offers an array of digital tools and platforms designed to simplify the insurance experience. Let's take a look at some of these solutions, and we'll also explore some real-world examples:

Web portals: Insurtech has ushered in user-friendly web portals designed to offer policyholders intuitive interfaces for managing their insurance-related tasks. These digital command centres serve as online hubs where customers can effortlessly access and update policy details, compare and purchase insurance products, and reach out to customer support when necessary. Within these portals, customers frequently encounter self-service tools, such as calculators, simulators and chatbots, providing personalized advice and immediate assistance. The emphasis on UI/UX design ensures that insurtech's web portals deliver a seamless experience for policyholders, enabling them to explore insurance options, calculate premiums and interact with AI-driven chatbots for instant support – all within a user-friendly interface, setting them apart from traditional insurance websites.

Mobile apps: In today's digital landscape, mobile applications stand as a cornerstone of customer-centric insurance. These apps empower policyholders by placing vital policy management functions at their fingertips. With these apps, customers can access their insurance information, conveniently make premium payments, initiate claims and receive critical notifications – all from the convenience of their smartphones. Many mobile apps also incorporate advanced security features like biometric authentication, geolocation services and push notifications to ensure secure interactions. For instance, Trōv, a leading digital insurance company based in San Francisco, utilizes advanced AI technology in its app to provide personalized motor and mobility insurance tailored to the specific requirements of vehicle owners. Another noteworthy example is Root Insurance, which has made a significant impact in the United States by pioneering motor insurance that relies solely on tracking driving behaviours through its smartphone app.[1]

Self-service portals: Insurtech has introduced user-friendly self-service portals, which serve as digital command centres for policyholders. These online hubs provide intuitive interfaces for policyholders to view and update policy information, compare and purchase insurance products and connect with customer support as needed. These portals often feature self-service tools such as calculators, simulators and chatbots, providing personalized advice and assistance. ABC Insurtech's self-service portal, for example, provides policyholders with a seamless experience, enabling them to explore insurance options, calculate premiums and engage with AI-driven chatbots for instant support – all within a user-friendly interface.

IoT devices: In addition to software solutions, insurtech introduces hardware innovations, notably Internet of Things (IoT) devices. Some insurers provide IoT-connected devices that furnish real-time data and policy-related insights. For instance, in motor insurance, telematics devices track driving behaviour, recording data such as speed, distance and braking patterns. This data enables insurers to assess risk more precisely, leading to personalized premiums based on policyholders' driving habits.

Progressive, a prominent US motor insurer, harnesses telematics and machine learning to monitor drivers' behaviour, enabling them to customize insurance premiums based on individual driving patterns, with a remarkable 1.7 trillion drives monitored.[2] IoT's applications extend to health and property insurance as well. For instance, John Hancock, a North American life insurer, monitors health and fitness data through devices like Fitbits and smartphones.[3] In the realm of property insurance, drones are employed by casualty insurers for efficient property inspections.

In conclusion, insurtech has introduced a wealth of digital tools and platforms aimed at simplifying policy access and management for customers. From web portals and mobile apps equipped with robust security features to intuitive self-service portals offering self-help options and AI-powered chatbots, insurtech is committed to enhancing accessibility and policy management. Additionally, the integration of IoT devices, such as telematics for motor insurance, contributes to more personalized and data-driven policy management, further improving the overall insurance experience for customers.

Facilitating customer-insurer communication via insurtech

Insurtech companies typically leverage one or more of the following communication technologies to enhance interactions with customers:

Live chat: The adoption of live chat support is on the rise among insurtech firms as a highly efficient means of facilitating communication between customers and insurance providers. Through this feature, customers can visit the insurer's website or app and engage in real-time conversations with trained representatives. For example, many insurtech websites integrate live chat or chatbot functionalities, allowing customers to swiftly ask questions, clarify doubts or seek immediate assistance. Whether it's enquiring about policy details or reporting a claim, live chat streamlines communication and enriches the customer experience by delivering rapid and responsive support.

Video calls: Video conferencing tools like Skype, GoToMeeting, Zoom or FaceTime have become integral components of insurtech applications, revolutionizing the way customers interact with insurance agents and adjusters. Insurers now offer video call capabilities, enabling policyholders to schedule remote assessments, consultations or claims inspections. Some insurtech providers have also embraced video calls for interactions between policyholders and claims adjusters. This feature empowers customers to visually convey information, showcase damage or accidents and receive expert guidance – all from the comfort of their own homes or within the realms of motor and health insurance. Video calls not only save time and reduce the need for in-person visits but also provide a more personalized and convenient communication channel. At Tapoly, we utilize video conferencing tools for customer enquiries and face-to-face interactions.

Social media integration: In today's digitally connected world, some insurtech solutions have harnessed the influence of social media to enhance communication. These platforms seamlessly integrate with popular social media channels, allowing customers to engage with insurance companies through familiar and accessible interfaces. While most insurers and insurtech companies maintain a social media presence across multiple channels, some opt for deeper integration with their insurtech CRM platforms or third-party solutions to create a consolidated and user-friendly hub for checking and responding to customer interactions. This approach empowers policyholders to reach out, ask questions and seek assistance via platforms like Facebook and Twitter. Leveraging the ubiquity of social media provides customers with a convenient and flexible means of communication, meeting them where they are most comfortable.

AI-powered chatbots: The integration of AI has given rise to AI-powered chatbots within the insurance domain. These chatbots leverage natural language processing and machine learning to interact with customers via text or voice, offering a versatile and responsive channel for customer engagement. They excel at addressing common queries, providing tailored recommendations and guiding customers through the intricacies of claims processes. Moreover, these chatbots seamlessly integrate with other digital channels, such as mobile apps and self-service portals, delivering a consistent and frictionless customer experience. For instance, Lemonade Insurance's AI-powered chatbot intelligently interacts with customers through various touchpoints, from answering policy enquiries to facilitating claims, ensuring rapid and efficient support.

Illustrating these technological advancements are insurtech projects such as Lemonade, a company that provides home and renters insurance leveraging AI and behavioural economics. Lemonade utilizes a chatbot for claims and policy management, delivering claims payouts within seconds. Moreover, Lemonade upholds a social impact mission by donating unclaimed funds to causes chosen by its customers.[4]

Email and notifications: In the dynamic world of insurtech, the utilization of various digital channels, including emails, push notifications, as well as popular messaging platforms like WhatsApp, Line and WeChat, assume a pivotal role in fostering customer engagement and facilitating seamless communication. Insurtech companies leverage these technologies to proactively keep policyholders informed about critical aspects of their insurance policies.

For instance, insurtech providers utilize emails and notifications to notify customers promptly about policy updates, share payment reminders and alert them to important deadlines. These automated communication methods are designed to ensure that policyholders remain well informed and connected with their insurance providers across multiple touchpoints. Whether it's a policy renewal notice delivered via email or a payment reminder sent through a WhatsApp or text messages, these digital interactions enhance the overall customer experience.

The beauty of these notifications lies in their ability to create a sense of transparency and trust between insurers and policyholders. Timely reminders and updates are appreciated by customers, as they contribute to a smoother and more efficient insurance experience. By automating these communication processes and extending them to popular messaging platforms like WhatsApp, Line and WeChat, insurtech companies efficiently manage interactions with their diverse customer base, leaving no room for important information to be overlooked or missed.

For example, a scenario where a policyholder receives a WhatsApp message from their insurtech provider reminding them of an upcoming premium payment. The convenience of receiving such notifications on a platform they regularly use for communication not only ensures that the policyholder remains aware of their obligations but also strengthens their relationship with the insurer. This integration of messaging apps into the insurtech communication ecosystem further enhances customer engagement and satisfaction.

Virtual assistants: In the rapidly evolving landscape of insurtech, some innovative applications utilize virtual assistants powered by AI. These virtual assistants are designed to enhance the customer experience by providing personalized assistance. While AI forms the foundation of these virtual assistants, it's important to note that AI and virtual assistants are not the same. AI is the underlying technology that enables machines to perform tasks that typically require human intelligence, such as understanding natural language, recognizing patterns and making decisions. Virtual assistants, on the other hand, are specific applications of AI designed for interacting with users in a conversational manner.[5]

Virtual assistants in insurtech leverage AI algorithms to analyse customer data and preferences, offering personalized policy recommendations, coverage options and pricing information. They serve as knowledgeable and attentive insurance advisors available around the clock. These virtual assistants can answer customer queries, provide real-time support and guide policyholders through complex insurance decisions.

By harnessing AI capabilities, insurtech companies aim to provide a highly personalized and seamless insurance journey tailored to each customer's unique needs. The integration of virtual assistants into insurtech applications represents a significant step forward in creating customer-centric insurance solutions. These digital companions empower policyholders with the information and guidance they need, ultimately enhancing their overall insurance experience. As technology continues to advance, virtual assistants are likely to become even more sophisticated and integral to the insurtech ecosystem, further revolutionizing how insurance is accessed and understood by customers.

In summary, insurtech applications have ushered in innovative features like emails and notifications, live chat support, video calls, social media integration and virtual assistants to revolutionize communication between customers and insurance companies. These technologies offer policyholders various channels for engaging with insurers, whether through automated email notifications, real-time text conversations with virtual assistants, face-to-face video consultations or the convenience of social media platforms. By providing flexible and convenient communication options, insurtech enhances the overall insurance experience, putting policyholders in control of how they interact with their insurers.

Elevating customer service in the insurtech era

Insurtech is a game-changer in the insurance industry when it comes to delivering better customer service throughout the policy life cycle. Here's how insurtech contributes to improving customer service and providing responsive support:

Personalization: Insurtech harnesses the power of data analytics to deeply understand individual customer profiles. By analysing factors like demographics, behaviour and previous interactions, insurtech tailors insurance offerings to meet the specific needs of each policyholder. This personalization ensures that customers receive more relevant coverage options and pricing, optimizing their overall experience.

Real-time communication: Digital channels and AI-driven chatbots are at the forefront of insurtech's approach to customer service. These tools enable insurers to provide instant responses to customer enquiries and issues. Policyholders can easily reach out through websites, mobile apps or social media platforms and receive timely assistance. Whether it's a question about policy details or a claim-related concern, insurtech ensures that customers are not kept waiting.

Claims transparency: One of the most stressful aspects of insurance for customers is the claims process. Insurtech solutions bring much-needed transparency to this stage of the policy life cycle. Customers can track the progress of their claims in real-time, from submission to approval and payment. This transparency reduces anxiety and frustration, as policyholders are kept informed every step of the way.

Predictive analytics: Insurtech doesn't just react to customer needs; it also anticipates them. Through the use of predictive analytics, insurtech helps insurers foresee potential issues or changes in a customer's circumstances. This enables proactive outreach to policyholders, offering solutions or adjustments to coverage before problems arise. This forward-thinking approach demonstrates a commitment to customer well-being.

Customer education: Insurtech platforms provide customers with valuable resources and educational materials. Mobile apps and online portals offer policyholders easy access to information about their policies, coverage details and benefits. This transparency empowers customers to make informed decisions at every stage of the policy life cycle, from initial purchase to policy renewals.

In conclusion, insurtech's innovative integration of technology and data-driven solutions is revolutionizing customer service in the insurance industry. By personalizing offerings, facilitating real-time communication, providing claims transparency, leveraging predictive analytics and offering customer education, insurtech ensures that customers receive responsive support and assistance throughout the policy life cycle. This customer-centric approach not only enhances the overall insurance experience but also builds trust and loyalty between insurers and policyholders.

Personalization and transparency

Insurtech (insurance technology) plays a crucial role in enabling more personalized insurance offerings that cater to individual customer needs in the following ways:

Advanced data analytics: Insurtech leverages advanced data analytics and machine learning algorithms to analyse vast amounts of data from various sources. This includes not only traditional demographic and historical data but also real-time data from IoT devices, social media and other unconventional sources. By analysing this data, insurtech companies gain insights into individual customer behaviour, preferences and risk profiles.

Telematics and IoT devices: Insurtech embraces telematics and IoT devices to collect real-time data from vehicles, homes or wearable devices. For example, in motor insurance, a telematics device can track driving habits such as speed, braking and mileage. In home insurance, smart sensors can monitor the condition of the property. This data is used to create personalized risk profiles and offer policies that align with a customer's specific circumstances.

Usage-based insurance: Insurtech has popularized usage-based insurance (UBI) models. These policies allow customers to pay premiums based on their actual usage or behaviour. For instance, pay-as-you-drive motor insurance calculates premiums based on the miles driven, while health insurance premiums can be adjusted based on fitness and wellness activities. This approach ensures that customers pay for what they use and encourages safer or healthier behaviour.

Dynamic pricing: Insurtech enables dynamic pricing models that adjust premiums in real-time based on changing circumstances. For example, motor insurance premiums can be influenced by real-time data such as traffic conditions or weather events. This dynamic pricing reflects the current risk exposure of the policyholder, leading to more accurate and fair pricing.

Personalized product bundles: Insurtech platforms often allow customers to tailor their insurance coverage by selecting only the specific protections they need. This customization ensures that customers are not paying for coverage they don't require and allows them to create insurance packages that cater to their unique needs.

Behavioural insights: Insurtech companies use behavioural economics principles to understand how customers make insurance-related decisions. By identifying patterns in customer behaviour, they can design policies and incentives that encourage desired actions. For example, customers who demonstrate safe driving behaviour may be offered discounts or rewards.

Instant underwriting and policy issuance: Insurtech streamlines the underwriting process through automation and data analysis. This allows for faster policy issuance, sometimes even within minutes. Customers can receive quotes and purchase coverage swiftly, eliminating the need for lengthy application processes and medical exams.

Risk mitigation services: Insurtech often goes beyond traditional insurance by offering risk mitigation services. For example, a home insurance provider may offer recommendations on improving home security, which could lead to lower premiums. This proactive approach helps customers manage and reduce their risks while potentially lowering their insurance costs.

Enhanced customer engagement: Insurtech platforms focus on improving customer engagement through digital channels. Customers can access their policy information, make changes and report claims conveniently online or through mobile apps. This accessibility encourages a more interactive relationship between insurers and policyholders, allowing for continuous adjustments to coverage as life circumstances change.

In summary, insurtech leverages data, technology and innovative approaches to create highly personalized insurance offerings that cater to individual customer needs. By analysing data, promoting dynamic pricing and offering customizable coverage options, insurtech companies ensure that insurance policies are not one-size-fits-all but are tailored to each customer's unique requirements and circumstances. This personalization enhances customer satisfaction and provides more relevant and cost-effective insurance solutions.

Enhancing policy and pricing transparency

Insurtech enhances transparency in insurance policies and pricing through several means:

Clear and simplified information: Insurtech companies strive to present insurance policies and pricing information in a straightforward and easily understandable manner. This clarity helps customers make informed decisions about their coverage. By simplifying complex insurance terminology and breaking down policy details, insurtech ensures that customers have a clear understanding of what they are purchasing.

Real-time updates: Customers can access policy information and updates in real-time through digital platforms and mobile apps. They receive immediate notifications about changes in coverage, policy terms or premium adjustments. This real-time communication keeps customers informed and empowers them to stay up-to-date with their insurance status.

Claims transparency: When it comes to claims, insurtech allows customers to track the status of their claims in real time. This visibility reduces anxiety and frustration, as customers can monitor the progress of their claims, from submission to settlement. They can easily check the status of their claims, view relevant documents and receive updates on any actions taken by the insurance company, promoting transparency and trust in the claims process.

Education and resources: Insurtech platforms often offer educational resources, such as articles, videos and FAQs, to help customers understand their coverage options better. These resources empower customers to make well-informed insurance decisions throughout their policy life cycle. By providing accessible information and guidance, insurtech fosters a more informed customer base, promoting transparency in the insurance industry. Customers can access these resources to clarify doubts, learn about different coverage options and make choices aligned with their specific needs and preferences.

Handling customer data and privacy in insurtech

Insurtech companies take data privacy and security seriously to ensure a secure and trustworthy customer experience. Here are some of the key measures they typically employ:

Data encryption: Insurtech companies use encryption protocols to protect customer data both during transmission and while it is stored. This ensures that sensitive information, such as personal details and financial data, remains confidential and secure.

Secure data storage: Customer data is stored in secure data centres or cloud environments that adhere to industry-leading security standards. These facilities implement advanced security measures, such as firewalls, intrusion detection systems and access controls, to safeguard stored data.

Access controls: Insurtech platforms implement strict access controls to ensure that only authorized personnel can access customer data. Role-based access control (RBAC) and multi-factor authentication (MFA) are commonly used to prevent unauthorized access.

Regular security audits and testing: Insurtech companies conduct regular security audits and penetration testing to identify vulnerabilities in their systems. These tests help them proactively address security weaknesses and protect customer data from potential threats.

Compliance with data protection regulations: Insurtech companies must comply with data protection regulations such as GDPR (General Data Protection Regulation) in Europe or HIPAA (Health Insurance Portability and Accountability Act) in the United States. Compliance involves strict adherence to data privacy principles, including obtaining informed consent, providing data access and notifying authorities of data breaches.

Data minimization: Insurtech companies collect and retain only the data that is necessary for their operations. They follow the principle of data minimization, which limits the amount of personal information collected to reduce potential privacy risks.

Customer consent and transparency: Insurtech platforms seek explicit consent from customers before collecting and processing their data. They also maintain transparency by informing customers about how their data will be used and providing clear privacy policies.

Anonymization and pseudonymization: To further protect customer privacy, insurtech companies often employ anonymization and pseudonymization techniques. These methods replace or mask personally identifiable information (PII) to ensure that customer data cannot be easily traced back to individuals.

Secure communication channels: Insurtech platforms use secure communication protocols (e.g. HTTPS) to protect data transmitted between customers and the platform. This prevents eavesdropping and data interception during online interactions.

Incident response plans: Insurtech companies develop comprehensive incident response plans to address potential data breaches or security incidents swiftly and effectively. These plans outline the steps to be taken in the event of a breach, including notifying affected customers and relevant authorities.

Data retention policies: Insurtech companies establish data retention policies to determine how long customer data will be stored. This helps minimize the risk associated with retaining data longer than necessary.

Employee training: Employees receive training on data privacy and security best practices. This ensures that everyone within the organization understands their responsibilities in protecting customer data.

Third-party vendors: When insurtech companies use third-party vendors or partners, they carefully assess their data security practices and ensure that they meet the same rigorous standards for data protection.

Regular updates and patch management: Insurtech platforms keep their software and systems up to date with the latest security patches and updates to mitigate vulnerabilities that could be exploited by attackers.

By implementing these comprehensive measures, insurtech companies aim to create a secure and trustworthy customer experience that respects customer privacy and safeguards their sensitive information. These efforts not only protect customers but also help insurtech companies comply with legal and regulatory requirements related to data security and privacy.

Empowering customers in insurance decision-making

Yes, there are insurtech solutions specifically designed to help customers better understand their coverage options and make informed insurance decisions. These solutions use technology and innovative approaches to simplify insurance information, provide educational resources and facilitate a more transparent decision-making process. Here are some ways in which insurtech enhances customer understanding of coverage options:

Interactive comparison tools: Insurtech platforms often offer interactive comparison tools that allow customers to compare different insurance policies side by side. These tools highlight key differences in coverage, deductibles, premiums and other policy features, making it easier for customers to evaluate their options.

Plain-language explanations: Insurtech companies aim to simplify complex insurance terminology and present policy information in plain language. They break down policy details into easily digestible explanations, helping customers understand what is covered, what is excluded and how the insurance works.

Online calculators: Some insurtech platforms provide online calculators that help customers estimate their insurance needs. For example, life insurance calculators can help customers determine the appropriate coverage amount based on their financial situation and goals.

Scenario analysis: Insurtech solutions may offer scenario analysis tools that allow customers to explore different coverage scenarios and their potential impact. Customers can adjust variables like coverage levels and deductibles to see how they affect premiums and coverage outcomes.

Educational content: Insurtech platforms often feature educational content such as articles, videos and FAQs. These resources help customers understand insurance concepts, policy types and best practices. By offering educational content, insurtech companies empower customers to make informed decisions.

Real-time quotes: Customers can obtain real-time insurance quotes through insurtech platforms. This immediate pricing information allows them to see how various factors, such as coverage levels and deductibles, influence premiums, enabling more informed decision-making.

Digital advisors: Some insurtech companies offer digital advisors or chatbots that guide customers through the insurance selection process. These virtual assistants ask questions and provide recommendations based on the customer's unique needs and circumstances.

Customization features: Insurtech platforms often allow customers to customize their insurance policies to fit their specific needs. Customers can add or remove coverage options, adjust deductibles and tailor their policies to align with their preferences.

Transparency in pricing: Insurtech promotes transparency in pricing by showing customers how various factors, such as their driving habits (for motor insurance) or health status (for health insurance), affect premiums. This information helps customers understand why their premiums are calculated the way they are.

Risk assessment tools: In the realm of insurance, there are innovative solutions that incorporate risk assessment tools to evaluate a customer's risk profile. These tools take into account various factors such as location, lifestyle and behaviour to recommend appropriate insurance coverage and pricing. A noteworthy use case of such risk assessment tools can be found in the domain of cyber insurance.

One prominent example is RSA Insurance, a company specializing in cyber insurance solutions. RSA Insurance offers comprehensive cyber insurance packages designed to safeguard businesses against the ever-evolving landscape of cyber threats. As part of their cyber insurance offering, RSA Insurance includes a detailed cyber risk assessment.[6] This assessment provides companies with valuable insights into the specific risks they face in the digital realm.

By clearly outlining potential vulnerabilities and suggesting effective countermeasures, the action plan enhances the client's ability to proactively protect their digital assets.

Customer reviews and ratings: Insurtech platforms often include customer reviews and ratings for insurance products and providers. These peer reviews can help customers gain insights into the experiences of others, contributing to their decision-making process.

In summary, insurtech solutions offer a range of tools and resources that empower customers to better understand their coverage options and make informed insurance decisions. These technologies aim to simplify the insurance process, enhance transparency and provide educational support to ensure that customers can choose insurance policies that align with their unique needs and preferences.

Data analytics and risk management

The power of data analytics stands out as a revolutionary force, reshaping the traditional paradigms of risk assessment and management. Insurtech, at the forefront of this transformation, harnesses data-driven insights to drive more accurate underwriting decisions and proactive risk mitigation. Let's delve into the role of data analytics in understanding customers. We will cover how insurtech contributes to fraud prevention and ensuring fairness in the claims process in Chapter 6.

Customer segmentation: Insurers use data analytics to segment their customer base according to various criteria, such as demographics, behaviours and preferences. This segmentation helps insurers tailor their products and marketing strategies to specific customer groups, ensuring that offerings are more relevant and appealing.

Risk assessment: Data analytics enables insurers to assess risk more accurately by analysing a wide range of data sources. For example, in motor insurance, telematics data from connected devices can provide insights into driving behaviour, helping insurers adjust premiums based on individual risk profiles.

Personalized pricing: Insurers can offer personalized pricing to customers by leveraging data analytics. By considering individual risk factors, such as health habits or driving history, insurers can provide pricing that reflects a customer's specific circumstances. This enhances fairness and competitiveness in the insurance market.

Product customization: Data analytics helps insurers develop and customize insurance products to meet the unique needs of different customer segments. Insurers can create modular policies that allow customers to select coverage options that align with their preferences and circumstances.

Fraud detection: Insurers use data analytics to detect fraudulent activities, such as false claims or identity theft. Advanced algorithms analyse patterns in claims data to identify suspicious behaviour, helping insurers mitigate losses and maintain fair premiums for honest customers.

Customer behaviour analysis: Data analytics provides insights into customer behaviour, such as the frequency of policy changes or interactions with digital platforms. This information helps insurers understand customer preferences and adjust their services to meet evolving expectations.

Customer lifetime value: Insurers use data analytics to calculate the lifetime value of a customer. By estimating how much revenue a customer is likely to generate over their relationship with the insurer, companies can prioritize customer retention efforts and provide superior service to high-value customers. However, it's essential for insurers to be aware of local regulations, such as 'Treat Your Client Fairly', to ensure that customer retention efforts don't inadvertently lead to unfair treatment of clients. Striking the right balance between prioritizing high-value customers and treating all clients fairly is crucial.

Claims processing efficiency: Data analytics streamlines claims processing by automating routine tasks and flagging claims that require closer scrutiny. This reduces processing time and improves the customer experience by expediting claims settlements.

Customer insights: Insurers can gain a deeper understanding of their customers' needs and pain points through data analytics. Customer feedback, online interactions and survey data are analysed to identify areas for improvement and inform strategic decisions.

Predictive analytics: Data analytics allows insurers to employ predictive models to anticipate customer behaviours, such as policy renewals or lapses. This enables proactive outreach to retain customers and optimize marketing strategies.

Marketing optimization: Data analytics informs marketing efforts by identifying the most effective channels, messaging and timing for customer outreach. Insurers can target potential customers with personalized and timely offers.

Compliance and risk management: Insurers use data analytics to ensure compliance with regulatory requirements. It helps monitor and manage risks associated with changing regulations, ensuring that customers are provided with compliant products and services.

In summary, data analytics is a cornerstone of modern insurance operations. It empowers insurers to gain valuable insights into customer behaviour, assess risk accurately, offer personalized products, streamline operations and enhance the overall customer experience. By leveraging data analytics, insurers can remain competitive, responsive to customer needs and well prepared to navigate an evolving insurance landscape.

Boosting customer retention and loyalty with insurtech

Insurtech has a significant impact on customer retention and loyalty within the insurance industry. It introduces various innovations and improvements that enhance the overall customer experience, making it more likely for customers to stay with their insurance providers. Here are some ways in which insurtech influences customer retention and loyalty:

Personalization: Insurtech enables insurers to offer more personalized insurance solutions. By tailoring coverage, pricing and policy options to individual customer needs, insurers can create a stronger bond with policyholders. Customers who feel their insurance is customized to their specific circumstances are more likely to remain loyal.

Transparency: Insurtech solutions promote transparency by simplifying policy information, providing real-time updates and offering clear pricing structures. When customers have a better understanding of their coverage and premiums, they are more likely to trust their insurance provider and stay loyal.

Convenience: Digital platforms and mobile apps offered by insurtech companies facilitate continuous customer engagement. Customers can easily access policy information, report claims and make changes to their coverage. This ongoing interaction keeps customers connected to their insurance provider, increasing loyalty.

Claims processing: Insurtech improves the claims experience by enabling digital claims reporting and providing real-time updates on claim status. Customers who have a smoother and more transparent claims process are more likely to stay with their insurer.

Value-added services: Many insurtech companies offer value-added services, such as risk mitigation advice or proactive alerts. These services help customers protect their assets and reduce risks, fostering a sense of loyalty and trust.

Price optimization: Insurtech allows insurers to offer more competitive and fair pricing through data-driven pricing models. When customers perceive that they are getting the best value for their money, they are more inclined to remain loyal.

Digital accessibility: Insurtech platforms provide customers with easy access to their policies and account information through digital channels. This accessibility enhances convenience and encourages customers to stay engaged with their insurance provider.

Data-driven insights: Insurtech leverages data analytics to gain insights into customer behaviour and preferences. This information helps insurers make data-driven decisions to enhance customer experiences and retention strategies.

In summary, insurtech positively impacts customer retention and loyalty within the insurance industry by improving personalization, transparency, efficiency and customer engagement. By offering value-added services and leveraging data-driven insights, insurtech helps insurers build stronger relationships with their customers, increasing the likelihood that policyholders will remain loyal and satisfied.

Adapting to evolving customer expectations

Insurtech companies adapt to changing customer expectations and continuously enhance their offerings to meet evolving needs using several strategies:

Experimenting and innovating: Insurtech firms are committed to experimentation and innovation. They leverage new technologies like blockchain, smart contracts and tokenization to create decentralized and transparent insurance platforms. Examples include companies like Etherisc, Nexus Mutual and Lemonade,[7] which pioneer new ways of delivering insurance services.

Learning and iterating: Insurtech companies embrace a culture of learning and iteration. They gather feedback, data and insights from customers and the market, using methodologies such as agile, lean and design thinking. This information helps them refine and optimize their solutions continually. Notable insurtech players like Trōv, Oscar and Policygenius use these methods to test and validate their assumptions and prototypes.

Collaborating and partnering: Insurtech companies recognize the importance of collaboration and partnerships within the insurance ecosystem. They work closely with incumbents, regulators, distributors and service providers to access new capabilities and resources. Strategic alliances, joint ventures and acquisitions are common approaches to leverage the strengths and expertise of partners, creating synergies and win-win outcomes. Companies like Zhong An, Cover Genius and Hippo have successfully utilized these strategies to expand their reach and offerings.

By following these strategies, insurtech companies stay responsive to changing customer needs, maintain a culture of innovation and leverage the broader insurance ecosystem to continually enhance their offerings and meet evolving customer expectations.

Digital tools and accessibility

Explore the digital tools and platforms that are making insurance more accessible to customers. From mobile apps to online portals, insurtech is putting policy management and claims reporting at customers' fingertips.

Simplifying insurance purchasing with insurtech innovations

Certainly, here are examples of insurtech innovations that simplify the process of comparing and purchasing insurance policies for customers:

AI-POWERED CHATBOTS AND VIRTUAL ASSISTANTS
Some insurtech firms deploy AI-powered chatbots and virtual assistants on their websites and mobile apps. These bots can answer customer queries, guide them through the insurance-buying process and provide instant quotes, making it easier for customers to get the information they need.

Lemonade use case: Lemonade is a digital insurance company that revolutionizes insurance through AI and chatbots.[8] They offer renters, homeowners, pet and life insurance products. Lemonade provides customers with instant quotes, quick answers to questions and a simplified claims process. What sets Lemonade apart is its commitment to social impact, allowing customers to choose a social cause to which their unused premiums are donated. This adds a unique and transparent dimension to the insurance process, making it fast, easy and socially conscious.

DIGITAL MARKETPLACES

Insurtech marketplaces serve as one-stop shops for insurance needs. Customers can browse, compare and purchase various insurance products, from motor and home insurance to travel and health insurance, all within a single platform. Examples include Policygenius and CoverHound.

Policygenius use case: Policygenius operates as an online insurance marketplace that empowers customers to compare and purchase insurance policies from a variety of insurers.[9] They offer a comprehensive range of insurance products, including life, home, motor, disability and pet insurance.[10] Policygenius simplifies the insurance process by providing customers with unbiased and personalized policy recommendations. They also offer expert financial advice and tools, making it easier for customers to make informed decisions about their insurance needs.

EMBEDDED INSURANCE

Insurtech companies, like Cover Genius, specialize in embedded insurance. This means that insurance is seamlessly bundled with the purchase of a product or service. For instance, when booking a flight or renting a car, customers can opt for insurance coverage during the same transaction. This simplifies the buying process, making it convenient and time-saving.

Cover Genius use case: Cover Genius is a global insurance distribution platform that collaborates with online businesses to offer insurance products to their customers. They specialize in embedded insurance, which means that insurance is bundled with the purchase of a product or service, such as a flight, car rental or online shopping item.[11] This approach ensures convenience and ease of purchase, as insurance is seamlessly integrated into the checkout process of the product or service provider.

TELEMATICS AND ON-DEMAND INSURANCE

In the realm of motor insurance, insurtech has introduced telematics and UBI. Customers can install devices or use mobile apps to monitor their driving behaviour. This real-time data is then utilized to offer personalized and often cost-effective insurance premiums based on actual driving habits.

Trōv use case: Trōv specializes in on-demand insurance for personal items. Customers can use their mobile app to insure individual belongings for specific durations, like a camera for a day or a laptop for a week. This flexibility simplifies the process of obtaining coverage for specific items when needed, without the need for long-term policies.

Another use case is Metromile: Metromile offers pay-per-mile motor insurance, particularly beneficial for low-mileage drivers. Their telematics device tracks mileage, and customers are charged based on the distance they drive. This innovation simplifies the process for infrequent drivers, making insurance more affordable and tailored to their usage.

These insurtech companies exemplify how technology and innovation simplify the traditionally complex world of insurance. They offer transparency, convenience and customization, making it easier for customers to navigate and select insurance policies that meet their specific needs.

Automating routine insurance tasks through insurtech

Insurtech can play a significant role in automating routine insurance tasks, reducing paperwork and streamlining administrative processes for both customers and insurance providers. Here's how:

Digital document management: Insurtech solutions enable the digitization and storage of insurance documents and policies. Customers can access their policy documents, certificates and receipts through online portals or mobile apps, reducing the need for physical paperwork.

Automated underwriting: Advanced algorithms and machine learning are used in automated underwriting to assess risk factors and determine policy eligibility. This speeds up the underwriting process, allowing customers to receive policy approvals and quotes more quickly.

Claims processing: Insurtech streamlines claims processing through automation. Customers can initiate claims through mobile apps, and AI-driven systems can analyse the claim details, assess damages and provide instant approvals for straightforward claims, expediting the payment process.

Chatbots and virtual assistants: AI-powered chatbots and virtual assistants can handle routine customer enquiries, policy enquiries and basic claims processing tasks. This reduces the need for customers to contact human representatives for common queries, saving time for both parties.

Telematics and IoT devices: In motor insurance, telematics and IoT devices monitor driving behaviour and collect data, which is then used to adjust premiums based on actual usage. This automation helps in providing fairer and more personalized pricing for customers.

Renewal reminders: Automated renewal reminders can be sent to customers through email, SMS or app notifications. This ensures that policyholders are informed about upcoming renewals and can take action without the need for paper-based reminders.

Data integration: Insurtech platforms often integrate with various data sources, such as government databases, medical records and weather data, to automate risk assessment and claims processing. This reduces the need for manual data entry and speeds up processes.

Blockchain for smart contracts: Blockchain technology is used to create transparent and self-executing smart contracts. These contracts can automate claims processing, releasing payments based on predefined conditions, without the need for extensive paperwork or manual approvals.

Machine learning for fraud detection: Machine learning models can analyse vast amounts of data to detect fraudulent claims. This automation not only reduces the administrative burden but also helps in preventing fraudulent activities, ultimately benefiting all policyholders.

Digital signatures: Digital signature solutions allow customers to sign policies and documents electronically. This eliminates the need for physical signatures, scanning and mailing of documents, making the process faster and more convenient.

By automating these routine tasks and administrative processes, insurtech improves efficiency, reduces human errors and enhances the overall customer experience by providing quicker responses, reducing paperwork and making insurance transactions more convenient and accessible.

Enhancing customer service in insurtech: Responsive support and assistance throughout the policy life cycle

Insurtech contributes to better customer service by enhancing responsiveness, providing support and offering assistance throughout the entire policy life cycle. Here's how insurtech achieves this:

Instant quotes and policy issuance: Insurtech platforms enable customers to receive instant insurance quotes and even purchase policies online. This eliminates the need for lengthy application processes and waiting for manual underwriting. Customers can get coverage quickly, which enhances their experience.

Self-service portals: Insurtech companies provide user-friendly self-service portals and mobile apps. Policyholders can access their policies, view documents, make changes and file claims without the need for extensive phone calls or paperwork. This self-service option empowers customers and saves time.

Chatbots and virtual assistants: AI-powered chatbots and virtual assistants are available 24/7 to answer customer queries and provide assistance. They can guide customers through the policy buying process, offer explanations and help with claims initiation. This ensures quick responses and support whenever needed.

Real-time updates: Insurtech platforms offer real-time updates to policyholders. Customers receive notifications about changes in coverage, policy terms, premium adjustments and claim status. This transparency keeps customers informed and reduces uncertainty.

Claims processing: Insurtech streamlines claims processing with automation. Customers can initiate claims through digital channels, and AI-driven systems can assess claims, provide instant approvals for straightforward cases and keep customers updated on the progress. This speeds up the claims settlement process.

Personalized recommendations: Insurtech leverages data analytics to offer personalized insurance recommendations. By understanding a customer's profile and needs, insurtech can suggest coverage options that are a better fit. This tailored approach improves customer satisfaction.

Flexible coverage options: Insurtech often offers flexible coverage options, allowing customers to customize their policies to match their specific needs. This flexibility ensures that customers get the coverage that matters most to them.

Education and resources: Many insurtech platforms provide educational resources such as articles, videos and FAQs. These resources help customers understand insurance concepts better and make informed decisions throughout the policy life cycle.

Renewal management: Insurtech platforms often send automated renewal reminders to customers. This ensures that policyholders are aware of upcoming renewals and can make necessary adjustments or payments on time.

Feedback loops: Insurtech companies actively seek and collect customer feedback. This feedback helps them improve their offerings and customer service continuously, ensuring that customer needs are met effectively.

Responsive customer support: While technology plays a significant role, insurtech companies also offer responsive human customer support. Customers can reach out to support teams through various channels, including phone, email, chat or social media.

Mobile apps for on-the-go assistance: Mobile apps provided by insurtech companies allow customers to access policy information, initiate claims and contact support while on the go. This convenience enhances the customer experience.

Overall, insurtech's use of technology, data analytics and automation ensures that customers receive responsive support and assistance throughout their policy life cycle. It simplifies interactions, reduces friction and fosters a more customer-centric approach in the insurance industry.

Customer empowerment and engagement

Delve into the ways insurtech empowers customers to take control of their insurance journey. We discuss how digital self-service options, real-time information and interactive engagement strategies are reshaping the customer experience.

Insurtech applications empower customers to play a more active role in managing their risk and insurance needs, particularly in the areas of life, health, assets and cyber risk. Here are some prominent examples:

IoT devices for health and wellness: Insurtech applications seamlessly integrate with IoT devices like fitness trackers and health monitors for health and wellness tracking. Customers can take an active role in monitoring their health metrics, including heart rate, physical activity and sleep patterns, using wearable IoT devices. This data serves as a foundation for personalized health and life insurance pricing and recommendations, potentially incentivizing healthier lifestyles and reducing health insurance premiums.

Personalized life and health insurance customization: Insurtech platforms offer customers the flexibility to tailor their life and health insurance policies based on their unique needs and preferences. Customers are actively involved in selecting coverage options, determining benefit amounts and participating in wellness programmes that align with their specific health and life insurance requirements. This customization is becoming increasingly reliable and dependable as insurers explore advanced pricing and underwriting models.

Health and wellness education: Insurtech companies provide customers with valuable educational resources related to health and wellness. These resources empower individuals to actively enhance their health, make well-informed decisions regarding wellness programmes and lead healthier lives.

IoT-based health monitoring: Insurtech applications seamlessly integrate with IoT devices designed to monitor individuals' health conditions. For instance, IoT-based remote patient monitoring delivers real-time health data to insurers, enabling proactive interventions and the creation of customized life and health insurance offerings.

Cyber risk assessment: Insurtech applications often include dedicated tools for assessing cyber risk. These tools assist customers in evaluating their cybersecurity posture by identifying vulnerabilities, suggesting improvements and guiding them in taking proactive measures to protect against cyber threats.

By incorporating life and health assessments, IoT integration and cyber risk assessment, insurtech applications empower customers to proactively manage their health, make informed decisions about insurance coverage, and actively participate in improving their overall well-being. This approach aligns with the evolving landscape of personalized and data-driven insurance solutions in the life, health and cyber insurance sectors.

Insurtech innovations simplifying insurance policy comparison and purchase for customers

Here are detailed examples of insurtech innovations that simplify the process of comparing and purchasing insurance policies for customers:

INSURANCE AGGREGATOR PLATFORMS

Insurtech has introduced insurance aggregator platforms that revolutionize the way customers compare and purchase insurance. These platforms act as virtual marketplaces where customers can easily and conveniently evaluate various insurance options from different providers. Here's a closer look at how they work:

Compare the Market: Compare the Market, for instance, is a prominent insurance aggregator platform. It allows customers to input their insurance needs and preferences, such as coverage type, coverage amount and budget. The platform then generates a list of insurance policies from multiple insurers, presenting them side by side. Customers can quickly see differences in coverage, premiums, deductibles and other policy details, making it simpler to identify the most suitable option.

PolicyBazaar: PolicyBazaar is another noteworthy aggregator platform, particularly popular in regions like India. Customers can input their insurance requirements, and the platform provides a comprehensive list of insurance policies from various companies. PolicyBazaar goes a step further by offering detailed policy comparisons, expert advice and a seamless purchasing process, ensuring customers have all the information they need to make an informed decision.

Confused.com: Confused.com, based in the UK, is yet another example. It specializes in motor insurance comparison but also offers comparisons for other types of insurance. Customers can quickly compare motor insurance quotes from different insurers, exploring coverage options, discounts and add-ons to find the best fit for their needs and budget.

DIGITAL MARKETPLACES

Insurtech digital marketplaces have transformed the way customers discover, evaluate and purchase insurance products. These one-stop shops simplify the insurance buying process, offering convenience and a wealth of choices. Here's more on how they function:

Policygenius: Policygenius is a well-known digital marketplace that caters to a wide range of insurance needs, including life, home, auto, disability and more. Customers can explore a variety of insurance options, all in one place, eliminating the need to visit multiple websites or contact numerous insurers individually. Policygenius provides personalized quotes, expert guidance and a user-friendly interface that empower customers to customize their insurance coverage based on their unique requirements.

CoverHound: CoverHound takes a similar approach, offering a centralized platform for customers to compare insurance plans across various categories, such as auto, home, renters and business insurance. Customers benefit from access to insurance advisors, who can assist in navigating the complexities of insurance policies. CoverHound's platform ensures customers can maximize available discounts, resulting in more cost-effective insurance solutions.

In summary, these insurtech innovations have redefined how customers engage with insurance providers and policies. Insurance aggregator platforms and digital marketplaces simplify the decision-making process, saving customers time and effort while providing transparency and choice. By leveraging technology, insurtech has reshaped the insurance landscape, making it more accessible, customer-centric and tailored to individual needs.

Tailoring communication and engagement strategies to customer preferences

Insurtech is a game-changer in how insurance companies tailor their communication and engagement strategies to individual customer preferences. Here's how it's done using various tools and techniques:

AI and chatbots: Insurtech harnesses AI and chatbots to provide rapid, personalized customer service. These AI-driven chatbots handle routine enquiries and tasks, such as generating quotes, addressing FAQs or making policy updates. By analysing customer interactions, they can gauge preferences, emotions and needs, ensuring more relevant and empathetic responses.[12]

Data analytics and predictive modelling: Data analytics and predictive modelling delve deep into customer behaviour, preferences and risk profiles. Insurtech leverages data from diverse sources, including social media, telematics, sensors and wearables, to segment customers, offer tailored pricing and recommend suitable products. These tools also help insurers detect and prevent fraud, optimize claims processing and enhance customer retention and loyalty.[13]

Omnichannel and digital platforms: Insurtech's omnichannel and digital platforms create consistent and seamless customer experiences across multiple channels. Whether through websites, mobile apps, social media or call centres, insurers can engage with customers in a unified manner. This approach extends reach, offers convenience and choice, and elevates customer satisfaction and engagement. Customers gain access to their policies, account management, claims submission and support at their convenience.

Content marketing and social media: Content marketing and social media play pivotal roles in building trust, credibility and awareness among customers and prospects. Insurtech empowers insurers to educate their audience, providing valuable information and showcasing their values and social impact. These platforms facilitate ongoing engagement, feedback collection and the generation of referrals and reviews.[14]

In summary, insurtech transforms the insurance industry by tailoring communication and engagement to individual customer preferences. By employing AI, data analytics, omnichannel platforms and digital marketing, insurers can offer more relevant, efficient and empathetic interactions with their customers. This not only enhances customer satisfaction but also positions insurers to adapt to the evolving landscape of the insurance industry.

Conclusion

In conclusion, insurtech stands at the forefront of revolutionizing the insurance industry, ushering in transformative changes that significantly impact the customer experience. This evolution is characterized by the seamless streamlining of processes and communication, resulting in the expeditious and efficient handling of insurance claims. Additionally, insurtech offers an array of digital tools that simplify policy management and fosters convenient interactions between customers and insurance providers, thereby elevating the standards of customer service to encompass responsive support throughout the entire policy life cycle.

Furthermore, insurtech's influence extends to personalization and transparency, enabling insurers to tailor policies to individual customer needs and render insurance policies and pricing more transparent. The paramount consideration of data privacy ensures a secure and reliable customer experience. The provision of educational tools empowers customers to make well-informed decisions about their coverage options.

Data analytics emerges as a key component in insurers' efforts to better comprehend and cater to their customers, ultimately leading to heightened customer retention and loyalty. Insurtech's inherent adaptability ensures that insurance offerings evolve in tandem with shifting customer expectations.

By offering digital tools and enhancing accessibility, insurtech simplifies the process of comparing and purchasing insurance policies while simultaneously automating routine tasks and reducing paperwork. This streamlined approach contributes to an elevated customer service experience, ensuring that customers receive timely support and assistance as needed.

Moreover, insurtech empowers customers to play an active role in managing their risk and insurance needs, making insurance more accessible and engaging. The advent of insurance aggregator platforms and digital marketplaces provides customers with a convenient one-stop-shop for finding the best coverage.

Lastly, insurtech empowers insurance companies to tailor their communication and engagement strategies to individual customer preferences through the strategic implementation of AI, data analytics, omnichannel platforms and digital marketing. This results in interactions that are not only more relevant and efficient but also characterized by a higher degree of empathy, ultimately culminating in an enhanced overall customer experience.

As we transition to Chapter 5, we will delve into the realm of insurtech and risk management, exploring how technology and innovation are redefining insurers' abilities to assess, mitigate and respond to risks effectively. From data analytics and predictive modelling to proactive risk prevention, insurtech continues to reshape the landscape of risk management in ways that are both transformational and adaptable. Join us in the exploration of these pioneering developments in the intersection of insurtech and risk management.

Notes

1   '5+ Insurtech Marketing Techniques | Disruptive Technologies for …', colorwhistle, 17 Jul. 2023. colorwhistle.com/insurtech-marketing-techniques/ (archived at https://perma.cc/QQ4R-SJ5N).

2   '5+ Insurtech Marketing Techniques | Disruptive Technologies for …', colorwhistle, 17 Jul. 2023. colorwhistle.com/insurtech-marketing-techniques/ (archived at https://perma.cc/VR6D-PCSH).

3   '5+ Insurtech Marketing Techniques | Disruptive Technologies for …', colorwhistle, 17 Jul. 2023. colorwhistle.com/insurtech-marketing-techniques/ (archived at https://perma.cc/WCA5-KPTV).

4   'Lemonade Sets World Record with 2-second AI Insurance Claim', AI, 14 Jun. 2023. aimagazine.com/articles/lemonade-sets-world-record-with-2-second-ai-insurance-claim (archived at https://perma.cc/G9V9-XATY).

5   'Virtual Assistants vs Chatbots: What's the Difference?' Freshworks, 5 Nov. 2020. www.freshworks.com/freshdesk/customer-engagement/virtual-assistant-chatbot-blog/ (archived at https://perma.cc/9KXG-72WU).

6   'Cyber Insurance', RSA Insurance, December 19, 2023.

7   'The Lemonade Foundation Turns to Blockchain to Protect Subsistence Farmers from Climate Change', Lemonade, 22 Mar. 2022. investor.lemonade.com/news-and-events/news/news-details/2022/The-Lemonade-Foundation-Turns-to-Blockchain-to-Protect-Subsistence-Farmers-from-Climate-Change/default.aspx (archived at https://perma.cc/SCC7-W8ZN).

8   'Lemonade: This $5 Billion Insurance Company Likes to Talk Up its AI. Now It's in a Mess Over It', CNN, 27 May 2021. www.cnn.com/2021/05/27/tech/lemonade-ai-insurance/index.html (archived at https://perma.cc/Y6FT-XFHJ).

9   'Policygenius Review: Compare Quotes for Car Insurance, Homeowners Insurance, and More', Business Insider, 12 Apr. 2021. www.businessinsider.com/personal-finance/policygenius-review (archived at https://perma.cc/9FVX-KLRT).

10   'Policygenius Review 2023 – Insurance', Money Under 30. www.moneyunder30.com/insurance/reviews/policygenius/ (archived at https://perma.cc/SC8L-AQU4).

11   'The Insurtech for Embedded Protection', Cover Genius. covergenius.com/ (archived at https://perma.cc/8QTQ-7845).

12   'Insurers Need New Communication Strategies – or Risk Burnout', Insurtech, 25 Jun. 2023. insurtechdigital.com/articles/insurers-need-new-communication-strategies-or-risk-burnout (archived at https://perma.cc/9SRG-LESF).

13   '5+ Insurtech Marketing Techniques | Disruptive Technologies for ...', colorwhistle, 17 Jul. 2023. colorwhistle.com/insurtech-marketing-techniques/ (archived at https://perma.cc/66LM-X26F).

14   '5+ Insurtech Marketing Techniques | Disruptive Technologies for ...', colorwhistle, 17 Jul. 2023. colorwhistle.com/insurtech-marketing-techniques/ (archived at https://perma.cc/3AMF-8ZDD).

5

Insurtech and risk management

Introduction

Risk assessment plays a pivotal role across a multitude of industries, encompassing insurance, finance, healthcare and beyond. Its core mission involves scrutinizing potential threats and uncertainties that have the capacity to impact individuals, businesses or organizations. Traditionally reliant on manual methodologies and historical data, risk assessment has, however, undergone a profound metamorphosis with the advent of technology.

Today, it embraces predictive modelling and forecasts that project the future, incorporating data sources such as weather forecasts and beyond. In this article, we embark on an exploration of the profound impact that data analytics, artificial intelligence (AI) and machine learning (ML) have had on the landscape of risk assessment. Our focal point will be on the ways in which insurtech companies are adeptly leveraging data to construct increasingly precise risk profiles.

A variety of technologies, spanning the Internet of Things (IoT), robotic process automation (RPA), biometrics and digital identity, undeniably contribute to the landscape of risk assessment. However, my unwavering assertion is that AI and machine learning constitute the bedrock upon which these transformative advancements are built. In essence, AI and machine learning serve as the keystone technologies orchestrating the seamless integration of these other innovations.

Consequently, it is my unwavering belief that AI and machine learning hold the pre-eminent position as the most pivotal technologies within the domain of risk assessment.

In this chapter, we delve into the multifaceted realm of insurtech and risk management, focusing our lens on the underwriting and claims functions.

The evolution of risk assessment

For many years, risk assessment primarily relied on historical data and manual analysis. This approach had limitations, including the inability to adapt to rapidly changing environments. Additionally, it often failed to capture complex patterns and trends in data.

The rise of data-driven risk assessment: Data is the lifeblood of modern risk assessment. With the growth of data analytics, organizations can now collect and process vast volumes of structured and unstructured data from various sources. This includes data on customer behaviour, social media activity, weather patterns, geolocation data and more. By harnessing this data, risk assessment has become more granular and comprehensive.

AI-powered risk assessment: AI plays a pivotal role in modern risk assessment. AI algorithms can process and analyse data at speeds and scales that were previously unimaginable. This technology enables organizations to automate and optimize tasks such as underwriting, claims handling, customer service and fraud detection. For example, AI-powered systems can quickly identify fraudulent claims by analysing patterns in historical data. These systems continuously learn from new data, improving their accuracy over time. This reduces human errors, biases and operational costs.

Machine learning and risk modelling: Machine learning, a subset of AI, is instrumental in risk modelling. Machine learning algorithms can detect hidden patterns and correlations in data that human analysts might miss. This leads to more accurate risk assessment models.

Machine learning models can adapt and evolve as new data becomes available. This adaptability is crucial in assessing risks associated with dynamic and evolving scenarios. For instance, machine learning can provide early warnings and predictions by analysing historical patterns and trends.

Insurtech's data-driven revolution

The insurance technology (insurtech) sector is at the forefront of leveraging data for risk assessment. These companies are redefining how insurance operates by harnessing cutting-edge technologies. Insurtech firms are particularly skilled at developing precise risk profiles for individuals and businesses.

Developing precise risk profiles: Insurtech companies utilize data to create highly accurate risk profiles for individuals and businesses. For example, they can assess an individual's health, driving habits or property characteristics to determine insurance premiums accurately. By tailoring coverage based on real-time data, insurtech firms provide more personalized and cost-effective insurance options.

Business risk assessment: Beyond individual risk assessment, data analytics, AI and machine learning are transforming how businesses evaluate risks. For industries such as supply chain management and manufacturing, these technologies offer insights into potential disruptions and vulnerabilities. This proactive approach allows businesses to mitigate risks effectively.

Challenges and ethical considerations: While data-driven risk assessment offers numerous advantages, it also comes with challenges. Data privacy and security are paramount concerns. Organizations must handle sensitive data responsibly and comply with regulatory and ethical standards.

Ethical considerations also come into play when using data for risk assessment. Fairness, transparency and bias mitigation are critical aspects that organizations must address to ensure ethical risk assessment practices.

Future trends in risk assessment

Looking ahead, the future of risk assessment holds exciting possibilities. Emerging technologies, such as quantum computing and advanced predictive analytics, will further enhance our ability to understand and manage risks. Additionally, the integration of risk assessment with blockchain technology promises more secure and transparent transactions. Chapter 8 will delve deeper into the future of insurtech trends.

The vision of perfect information

Envision a world where information flows seamlessly, and every risk is priced with pinpoint accuracy. In this ideal realm, risk assessment takes on a whole new dimension. For example, when securing a building, the insurance cost seamlessly integrates into the building's overall price. This happens because information is so precise and effortlessly accessible.

To elaborate further, let's consider life insurance. At present, life insurance factors in the inefficiencies and uncertainties of life events. However, in a world of perfect pricing and information, the need for traditional life insurance as we know it might diminish. With precise knowledge of when major life events will occur, individuals could meticulously plan and save for them, for example, for funerals.

Now, contemplate insuring high-risk properties, like those in flood-prone or hurricane-prone areas. If real estate professionals have access to perfect information regarding these risks, property prices would inherently include the equivalent of insurance. In this scenario, traditional insurance might not be as necessary.

Furthermore, in a world where risks are so precisely known, even events like pandemics or rare accidents become predictable. This would likely lead to a decline in insurance premiums as the element of unpredictability vanishes. Essentially, in this idealized world of perfect information and pricing, traditional insurance products could become less relevant, and insurance premiums would decrease as risks become more predictable, ultimately reshaping the entire insurance landscape.

However, it's essential to acknowledge that, while advancements in data and technology provide us with a clearer understanding of many risks, complete predictability remains elusive. While some data, such as weather forecasts, financial market trends and actuarial calculations, is available and aids in risk assessment, we are not yet capable of foreseeing every future event with absolute certainty.

In this context, insurance continues to serve a vital role in hedging against the remaining uncertainties. Insurance products fundamentally offer financial protection and compensation to individuals or businesses in the event of unforeseen risks or uncertainties. This fundamental purpose requires a delicate balance when pricing them for an unpredictable and continually evolving future.

Moreover, the widespread global operations of insurtech companies, providing products that span multiple jurisdictions, introduce additional layers of intricacy to the regulation of this industry. Effectively navigating the regulatory landscape within both the insurance and insurtech sectors can indeed be a daunting undertaking. Regulations are often finely tailored to specific geographical areas, with each country within these regions maintaining its unique regulatory framework. For enterprises engaged in operations that transcend multiple jurisdictions, this situation presents both a challenge and a substantial hurdle. Acquiring the necessary licences, adeptly managing risks and crafting comprehensive risk management strategies that not only align with various regional regulations but also encompass the entirety of their global activities become formidable tasks.

Navigating risk in the world of insurtech

In this exploration of the insurtech landscape, we delve into some of the critical risks faced by insurtech firms and the strategies deployed to manage them effectively.

Regulatory compliance: One of the foremost challenges for insurtech firms is ensuring regulatory compliance within the diverse jurisdictions they operate in. This entails adherence to a spectrum of laws and regulations, including risk-based capital assessments, stress testing and own risk and solvency evaluations. In addition, insurtech companies must maintain product and service standards defined by principles of fairness, transparency and ethics. Effectively managing this risk involves proactive engagement with regulators, securing requisite licences and approvals, conducting periodic audits and reviews and embracing industry best practices.

Data security and privacy: At the core of insurtech operations lies extensive data collection, processing and storage, drawn from various sources encompassing customers, partners, sensors and social media. This wealth of data is invaluable, yet its sensitivity poses significant risks, such as cyberattacks, breaches or misuse. To mitigate these threats, insurtech firms must institute robust data governance protocols, fortified by encryption, authentication and comprehensive backup and recovery systems.

Customer trust and satisfaction: In the fiercely competitive insurtech landscape, nurturing and preserving customer trust and satisfaction is a perpetual endeavour. Customers demand not only the highest quality but also expect services that are swift, convenient and personalized. Furthermore, they seek assurance in the form of reliability, accuracy, fairness and transparency. To effectively manage this risk, insurtech companies must deliver value-added services, engage with customers proactively, furnish clear and timely information, fulfil their commitments diligently and actively solicit feedback to fuel continuous improvement.

Technology innovation and disruption: The insurtech domain operates within the whirlwind pace of technological evolution, featuring innovations like AI, machine learning, blockchain, cloud computing and IoT. While these technologies hold the promise of enhancing products and services, they simultaneously pose challenges and competitive threats. Managing the risk associated with technological evolution requires investments in research and development, the adoption of adaptable methodologies, fostering collaboration with partners and stakeholders and the vigilant monitoring of dynamic market trends.

As we navigate the multifaceted landscape of insurtech, it's evident that managing risks is not merely a necessity but a strategic imperative. The success and resilience of insurtech firms hinge on their ability to confront these challenges head-on, implementing agile strategies that safeguard regulatory compliance, data integrity, customer satisfaction and technological innovation. In this dynamic arena, the mastery of risk is a defining characteristic of insurtech leaders poised to shape the future of the insurance industry.

Revolutionizing risk assessment with data analytics, AI and machine learning

Data analytics, AI and machine learning are spearheading a transformation in risk assessment processes. These cutting-edge technologies are ushering in faster, more precise and dynamically adaptable methods for analysing and managing diverse types of risks. Here's how these technologies are reshaping risk assessment:

Enhanced data analytics: Data analytics plays a pivotal role in gathering and processing vast quantities of both structured and unstructured data from various sources, including customer behaviour, social media, weather patterns and geolocation data. This empowers the creation of more intricate and comprehensive risk profiles and segments. As a result, the quality and reliability of risk data and information improve and it becomes easier to identify novel or emerging risks, potentially necessitating the development of new products or services.

Automation and optimization with AI and machine learning: AI and machine learning introduce automation and optimization into crucial tasks like underwriting, claims handling, customer service and fraud detection. Advanced algorithms and models, capable of learning from data and refining their performance over time, are deployed. This reduces human errors, minimizes biases and trims costs associated with risk assessment. Furthermore, it accelerates and streamlines the decision-making process related to risk.[1,2]

Proactive risk management: AI and machine learning generate forward-looking scenarios and predictions by leveraging historical patterns and trends. Techniques like natural language processing (NLP), user and event behaviour analytics or smart contracts are harnessed for this purpose. The outcome is a more proactive and preventive approach to risk management, featuring alerts, guidance or incentives designed to curtail the frequency and severity of losses or claims.

Secure risk transfer mechanisms: AI and machine learning also contribute to the creation of secure and transparent risk transfer mechanisms, such as blockchain and distributed infrastructure. These mechanisms facilitate more efficient transactions and data sharing among various stakeholders within the risk ecosystem. Consequently, the potential for fraud or disputes along the risk value chain diminishes. Additionally, compliance with regulatory and ethical standards governing the collection, storage and utilization of personal data within the risk sector is bolstered.

These are some of the ways in which data analytics, AI and machine learning are revolutionizing risk assessment processes. Their impact extends beyond mere process optimization, creating added value for both customers and insurers through improvements in the quality, speed and cost-effectiveness of risk management.

Predictive analytics transforms underwriting in insurtech

Predictive analytics in underwriting represents a technological leap forward, a game-changer in the world of insurance. At its core, it involves the strategic use of data, algorithms and machine learning techniques to assess risk profiles and determine tailored premiums for insurance policies. In this section, we delve deep into the profound impact of predictive analytics, particularly within the context of insurtech. We will explore how this innovation empowers insurers to enhance risk prediction, streamline underwriting processes, offer proactive risk management solutions and establish more secure risk transfer mechanisms.

Predictive analytics revolutionizes the accuracy and granularity of risk assessment. Drawing from an array of data sources such as customer behaviour, social media, weather patterns, geolocation data or industry-specific insights, it crafts remarkably comprehensive and nuanced risk profiles and segments. This newfound depth empowers insurers to craft highly customized and competitive pricing and coverage options. Furthermore, it positions them to swiftly identify new or emerging risks, proactively adapting with new products or services as the landscape evolves.[3,4]

Predictive analytics isn't just about precision; it's about efficiency too. The technology streamlines underwriting processes by automating and optimizing key tasks. Utilizing advanced algorithms and machine learning models that continually learn from data, predictive analytics slashes human errors and biases, leading to cost reductions. In addition, it supercharges the speed of underwriting decisions, ensuring policyholders aren't left waiting.

Predictive analytics doesn't stop at assessment; it extends into proactive risk management. By generating forward-looking scenarios and predictions using techniques like NLP, user and event behaviour analytics and smart contracts, it empowers insurers to provide timely alerts, valuable advice or enticing incentives. These offerings work in tandem to reduce the frequency and severity of losses or claims, a boon for both policyholders and insurers.[5]

Another dimension of predictive analytics in underwriting is the creation of transparent and secure risk transfer mechanisms. Here, technologies like blockchain and distributed infrastructure come into play. They facilitate more efficient transactions and seamless data sharing among diverse stakeholders within the risk ecosystem. The result? A notable reduction in the potential for fraud or disputes throughout the risk value chain. Furthermore, this approach ensures adherence to the rigorous regulatory and ethical standards governing the collection, storage and utilization of personal data in the risk industry.[6]

In summary, predictive analytics, especially in the context of insurtech, has ushered in a new era for underwriting. It empowers insurers to achieve unprecedented precision, efficiency and security in risk assessment and management. Policyholders benefit from more tailored coverage and pricing, while insurers benefit from streamlined processes and proactive risk mitigation. Predictive analytics, alongside other insurtech innovations, ensures the insurance industry is better equipped than ever to navigate the complexities of today's risk landscape.

Examples of insurtech innovations in predictive underwriting

TrueMotion: TrueMotion is at the forefront of insurtech, harnessing smartphone sensor technology to evaluate and score drivers based on their behaviour, with a particular focus on distracted driving. The insights generated by TrueMotion assist underwriters in attracting and retaining the safest and most profitable drivers. This innovative approach not only enhances road safety but also contributes to more accurate and selective underwriting, ultimately reducing risk for insurers.[7,8]

Goji: Goji revolutionizes insurance purchasing by leveraging personal history to connect buyers with the most suitable and cost-effective insurers. The platform collates and shares this valuable information with leading underwriters. By including an individual's driving history as part of the application process, insurers can swiftly provide tailored quotes based on specific risk profiles. This not only streamlines the underwriting process but also enables precise and prudent pricing, mitigating risk for insurers.[9,10]

Habit Analytics: Habit Analytics is an insurtech trailblazer that utilizes data collected from smartphones and connected home devices to construct comprehensive behavioural patterns. These patterns empower insurers to make informed decisions regarding services, product offerings and risk modelling. The integration of real-time data into underwriting models enhances their accuracy and enables insurers to optimize pricing decisions. This data-driven approach not only bolsters underwriting but also contributes to the development of more finely tuned risk assessment models.[11]

Intelliarts: Intelliarts is an industry leader offering machine learning solutions tailored for insurance underwriting. Among its offerings is automated submission triaging, which employs cutting-edge machine learning algorithms to filter incoming applications and assign them to underwriters in the most efficient manner. This not only expedites the underwriting process but also ensures that applications are routed to the most suitable experts, improving overall efficiency and accuracy in risk assessment.[12]

These examples underscore how insurtech is driving innovation in the insurance industry by incorporating predictive modelling and data-driven approaches to enhance underwriting efficiency, reduce risk and provide more tailored solutions to customers.

Telematics and IoT in risk mitigation

In recent years, the integration of telematics and the IoT has ushered in a new era of risk management, particularly in the realms of motor and property insurance. These technologies have revolutionized how insurers assess and mitigate risks, offering more precise and data-driven strategies to enhance safety and reduce potential liabilities.

Monitoring driving behaviour

Telematics, often associated with motor insurance, involves the utilization of connected devices and sensors integrated into vehicles to closely monitor driving behaviour. These devices capture a wealth of data, including speed, acceleration, braking patterns and even when and how frequently a vehicle is used. This reservoir of data provides insurers with profound insights into an individual's driving tendencies. This shift from traditional reliance on historical and demographic data for risk assessment to real-time behavioural analysis has brought about a transformative change in the landscape of motor insurance pricing.

This transformation is marked by a shift away from the conventional one-size-fits-all insurance premiums towards a highly personalized pricing model tailored intricately to individual driving habits. For instance, a cautious driver who consistently adheres to speed limits and practices safe braking is duly rewarded with reduced premiums, while a high-risk driver may face heightened insurance costs. Telematics, therefore, not only allows insurers to finely calibrate their pricing but actively encourages safer driving practices. This, in turn, can lead to a tangible reduction in accidents and insurance claims.

An exemplary illustration of this approach is Progressive's Snapshot program. This initiative employs a telematics device that conveniently plugs into a vehicle's diagnostic port. This unobtrusive device continually records and transmits driving data, providing insurers with the means to offer precisely calibrated premiums that accurately mirror a driver's safety practices. Beyond pricing, telematics goes a step further by fostering safer driving behaviours through real-time feedback and incentives. Consequently, it plays a pivotal role in significantly reducing both accident frequency and insurance claims. Telematics devices have indeed reshaped the landscape of motor insurance by capturing a wealth of data related to driving behaviour. These sophisticated devices meticulously measure aspects like speed, acceleration, braking, cornering, mileage, time of day and location. By harnessing this treasure trove of information, insurers can comprehensively evaluate the risk profile of drivers. The outcome is a paradigm shift from one-size-fits-all premiums to highly personalized insurance rates based on individual driving habits.[13]

Enhancing home security

IoT devices have also made significant inroads in the property insurance sector, particularly in enhancing home security. Smart home technologies, such as connected security cameras, motion detectors and smart locks, are seamlessly integrated into homeowners' daily lives. These devices continuously monitor and transmit data related to home security to both homeowners and insurers.

Consider, for instance, a smart security system's capability to instantaneously notify homeowners and insurers of a break-in, fire or water leak in the home. With components including smoke detectors, water leak sensors, motion detectors, smart locks, cameras and thermostats, these systems enable immediate responses that can potentially avert substantial property damage and curtail insurance claims. In light of these risk-reducing benefits and resulting cost savings for insurers, property insurance providers often extend incentives or discounts to homeowners who embrace these IoT-based security systems.

A prime example of this technological evolution is Nest, a company at the vanguard of this movement. Nest offers an array of smart home devices engineered to detect and pre-empt incidents such as fires, thefts or water damage. By seamlessly integrating these devices into their homes, homeowners actively contribute to risk mitigation while relishing a safer and more secure living environment.

Promoting health and well-being

The influence of the IoT reaches beyond motor and property insurance, extending its reach into the realms of health and life insurance. In these domains, IoT devices play a pivotal role by continuously monitoring a wide array of health and wellness factors. These include heart rate, blood pressure, physical activity, sleep quality and medication adherence. Insurers leverage this extensive pool of health-related data to perform comprehensive assessments of customer health status and evaluate associated risk factors.

Take, for example, Fitbit, a prominent company renowned for its wearable devices capable of measuring diverse health metrics and tracking physical activity levels. These IoT devices empower insurers to design tailored products and services that cater to individual health needs. Furthermore, IoT devices actively engage customers in managing their health and well-being. They provide real-time feedback and incentives that encourage healthier choices, ultimately contributing to the reduction of health-related risks. This innovative integration of IoT monitoring is revolutionizing the landscape of health and life insurance, fostering a future of more personalized and proactive coverage.[14]

Environmental monitoring

Beyond motor and property insurance, IoT-enabled environmental monitoring plays a pivotal role in risk mitigation. Weather-related events, such as floods, hurricanes and wildfires, pose substantial risks to both insurers and policyholders. IoT devices, including weather sensors and remote environmental monitoring stations, enable insurers to track these events in real-time.

By monitoring environmental conditions, insurers can proactively notify policyholders of impending risks and provide guidance on how to minimize potential damage. This not only serves to protect policyholders but also allows insurers to mitigate their own exposure to high-value claims by helping customers prepare and take preventative actions.

For instance, Digi International specializes in delivering IoT-driven environmental monitoring solutions designed for a wide spectrum of applications, encompassing air quality, water quality, soil conditions, weather patterns and wildlife habitats. Their innovative solutions leverage an array of sensors and interconnected devices to adeptly gather and transmit environmental data. This data is then subjected to meticulous processing and analysis, seamlessly integrating the power of edge computing and cloud services. The outcome is a suite of solutions that not only detects and forestalls pollution but also optimizes resource management, fostering an environment that champions sustainability.[15]

In summary, the integration of telematics and IoT technologies marks a revolutionary era in risk mitigation for the insurance industry. These innovations empower insurers to transcend traditional data sources by incorporating real-time, behaviour-driven data into their risk assessment processes. Whether it's analysing driving behaviour, reinforcing home security, promoting health and well-being or vigilantly monitoring environmental conditions, these technologies provide insurers with the means to offer finely tailored coverage and incentives. The outcome is a reduction in risks, an enhancement of safety and the delivery of enhanced value to both policyholders and the broader insurance sector.

By harnessing the potential of telematics and IoT, the insurance industry undergoes a profound transformation in its approach to risk management. Whether it's revolutionizing motor insurance through the analysis of driving habits, enhancing property insurance via smart home solutions, or promoting healthier living in health and life insurance, these technologies enable insurers to provide pricing that is increasingly precise, services that are highly proactive, transactions that are exceptionally secure and customer experiences that are deeply personalized. The adoption of telematics and IoT by the insurance industry propels it toward a future defined by heightened safety, increased efficiency and an unwavering commitment to customer satisfaction.

In the ever-evolving landscape of insurance, the integration of technology has brought about remarkable transformations, particularly in the realms of claims processing and fraud detection. The advent of insurtech, a portmanteau of insurance and technology, has ushered in an era where the traditional, often cumbersome, methods of handling claims have given way to streamlined and efficient processes. Moreover, AI has emerged as a powerful tool in the arsenal of insurers, enhancing their ability to detect fraudulent claims with unprecedented accuracy. In this article, we delve into how insurtech is revolutionizing claims processing through automation and data analysis while shining a light on the pivotal role AI plays in detecting fraudulent claims, ultimately resulting in significant cost savings for insurers.

The role of AI in fraud detection

One of the perennial challenges for insurers has been the detection of fraudulent claims. Fraudulent claims not only result in substantial financial losses but also erode the trust between insurers and policyholders. AI has emerged as a formidable ally in this battle against fraud.[16,17,18]

AI-powered systems are adept at sifting through vast datasets and identifying anomalies or patterns indicative of fraud. These systems can analyse a multitude of variables, including claimant behaviour, historical claims data, medical records and external data sources, to flag claims that warrant closer scrutiny. For example, if a claimant has a history of filing claims for similar injuries in a short span of time, it may raise a red flag.

NLP is another facet of AI that comes into play during fraud detection. It can be used to parse unstructured data, such as medical notes or claim descriptions, to identify inconsistencies or suspicious language.

Moreover, AI systems can continuously learn and adapt to evolving fraud tactics. As fraudsters become more sophisticated, AI algorithms evolve alongside, becoming increasingly adept at identifying new and intricate forms of fraud.

Incorporating AI into fraud detection doesn't just benefit insurers. It also acts as a deterrent, as potential fraudsters are aware of the advanced systems in place to detect illegitimate claims. This, in turn, discourages fraudulent activities.

Example use cases

Behaviour analysis: AI examines a claimant's historical behaviour, identifying patterns of repeated claims for similar injuries in a short period, prompting further investigation.

NLP: NLP analysis unstructured data within medical records or claim descriptions, flagging claims with inconsistent or suspicious language.

Adaptive algorithms: AI algorithms evolve to detect new and sophisticated fraud tactics employed by fraudsters, ensuring ongoing effectiveness in fraud detection.

Deterrence effect: The mere presence of advanced AI-based fraud detection systems discourages potential fraudsters from engaging in fraudulent activities, promoting ethical behaviour in insurance claims.

AI's role in fraud detection is instrumental in safeguarding insurers and policyholders from fraudulent activities while fostering a climate of trust and integrity within the insurance industry

Here are examples of how AXA, a prominent French life insurance company, and CNA Financial, a major insurer, harness AI-based fraud detection software:

AXA and Darktrace

AXA partnered with the UK-based start-up Darktrace to implement an AI fraud detection solution aimed at detecting and handling threats posed by advanced cyber criminals. This partnership was particularly crucial for AXA as it sought to monitor its extensive network and proactively contain emerging threats before they could escalate into more significant problems.[19]

Darktrace's Enterprise Immune System software, a central component of the solution, is designed to learn and adapt to the behaviour of computer and network users throughout the workday. By recognizing patterns in user behaviour, the software can correlate data to establish relationships between different users' roles and activities.

Once these patterns are established, the software leverages its autonomous response component, known as Antigena, to take action against detected threats. Antigena is capable of suspending users within AXA's network whose behaviour aligns with pre-defined indicators of data security threats, claims fraud or preparations for fraudulent activities.

This partnership with Darktrace demonstrates how AXA harnesses AI-based solutions not only for fraud detection but also for safeguarding its digital infrastructure against cyber threats. The software's ability to detect anomalies and emerging threats helps

AXA proactively address security concerns while maintaining the integrity of its operations.

AXA's adoption of AI-based fraud detection and threat prevention technology exemplifies the insurance industry's commitment to using advanced technology to enhance security and protect both the company and its policyholders from potential risks and fraudulent activities.

CNA FINANCIAL AND SHIFT TECHNOLOGY

CNA Financial sought to streamline and automate its claims fraud detection process while gaining a better understanding of the context surrounding detected fraud. To achieve these objectives, they partnered with Shift Technology, a company specializing in AI-driven fraud detection solutions. CNA Financial became the first company to implement Shift Technology's FORCE software solution.[20]

The key goal for CNA Financial was to optimize its special investigations efforts by focusing on the most suspicious claims with predetermined analytical paths. This approach ensured that all known fraud methods were thoroughly investigated within their claims.

Shift Technology's FORCE software not only automated the fraud detection process but also provided critical context related to observed fraud situations. This context guidance helped in determining the most appropriate resolution for each case.

By using AI-based predictive analytics and fraud detection technology, CNA Financial significantly enhanced its ability to identify potential fraud while ensuring that every suspicious claim received the appropriate level of scrutiny. This not only improved the efficiency of their claims processing but also contributed to better fraud prevention and management.

CNA Financial's collaboration with Shift Technology exemplifies how insurers are leveraging AI solutions to optimize fraud detection, enhance claims management and ultimately protect their business interests and policyholders from fraudulent activities. This innovative approach reflects the insurance industry's commitment to embracing technology to improve operational efficiency and security.

The takeaway

The fusion of insurtech and AI in the realms of claims processing and fraud detection represents a dynamic shift within the insurance industry. It not only simplifies the claims journey for policyholders but also arms insurers with potent tools to effectively combat fraudulent activities. As insurtech continues to evolve and AI advances in sophistication, the insurance landscape stands on the brink of further enhancements in efficiency, precision and overall customer satisfaction. In this harmonious blend of technology and insurance, the future holds great promise.

Insurtech's role in claims transformation

Insurtech plays a pivotal role in reshaping the claims process by harnessing a synergy of automation and data analysis, leveraging a range of cutting-edge technologies. These encompass AI, machine learning, RPA, NLP and blockchain. Here's how insurtech revolutionizes claims processing:

Automation and efficiency: Insurtech deploys advanced algorithms and models capable of learning from data and continuously improving their performance. This automation optimizes various tasks, including underwriting, claims handling, customer service and fraud detection. By doing so, it mitigates human errors and biases while concurrently reducing operational costs. Moreover, it significantly enhances the speed and efficiency of claims decision-making.

Data extraction and analysis: Insurtech excels in the extraction, analysis and validation of both structured and unstructured claims data, encompassing documents, images and videos. This meticulous scrutiny elevates the accuracy and reliability of claims assessments. Additionally, insurtech enables remote management and automation of various claims functions, such as inspections, appraisals and settlements.

Proactive claims management: Employing techniques like NLP, user and event behaviour analytics and smart contracts, insurtech generates forward-looking scenarios and predictions based on historical patterns and trends. This proactive approach empowers the delivery of preventive claims management solutions. These encompass alerts, guidance or incentives designed to reduce the frequency or severity of losses and claims.

Transparent and secure transactions: Insurtech seamlessly integrates advanced technologies like blockchain and distributed infrastructure to establish transparent and secure claims transfer mechanisms. These mechanisms streamline transactions and facilitate data sharing among various stakeholders within the claims ecosystem. Consequently, they minimize the potential for fraud or disputes along the claims value chain. Furthermore, they ensure compliance with rigorous regulatory and ethical standards governing the collection, storage and utilization of personal data in the claims industry.

AI-enhanced fraud detection: AI emerges as a formidable asset in identifying fraudulent claims. By sifting through extensive datasets from diverse sources, including customer behaviour, social media, weather patterns, geolocation data and industry-specific information, AI discerns fraud patterns and anomalies indicative of illicit activities. It also provides contextual guidance to investigators, facilitating the verification and resolution of suspicious claims. Beyond fraud detection, AI can uncover other issues affecting the claims process, such as improper payments, waste or abuse. This multifaceted application of AI in claims processing results in substantial savings for insurers, encompassing billions of dollars in reimbursements and expense reductions.

In summary, insurtech, bolstered by the analytical capabilities of AI, stands as a transformative force in the claims processing landscape, enhancing efficiency, precision and security while minimizing risks and losses for insurers.

Safeguarding sensitive data

In the ever-evolving landscape of insurtech, cybersecurity emerges as an indispensable pillar. These innovative companies stand as custodians of a vast trove of sensitive customer data, ranging from personal particulars and financial records to health histories and claims archives. The magnitude of this responsibility cannot be overstated, for in the digital age, the ramifications of a cyber breach are far-reaching.

Cyberattacks have the potential to shatter the confidentiality, integrity and accessibility of this data. The consequences are dire, encompassing reputational damage, punitive regulatory fines, legal entanglements and irate customers. To navigate these perilous waters, insurtech firms must fortify their defences with robust cybersecurity measures, not only to safeguard their data assets but also to align with stringent regulatory mandates.[21]

Insurtech companies are rising to this challenge through a multifaceted approach that emphasizes adaptability, defence-in-depth, technological innovation, user education and collaborative networking:

A risk-based approach: Insurtech firms are embracing a risk-based approach to cybersecurity. This method involves identifying the data assets that hold the highest value and exhibit the greatest vulnerabilities. These critical assets are then subjected to rigorous assessments that weigh potential threats and their associated impacts. Subsequently, the firms prioritize the application of suitable controls and mitigation strategies, ensuring that finite resources are directed effectively to protect the most sensitive data.[22]

Layered defences: A layered defence strategy is another cornerstone of insurtech cybersecurity. By employing a diverse range of security solutions across different layers of their systems, such as encryption, firewalls, antivirus software, multi-factor authentication and vigilant monitoring, insurtech companies establish a formidable security perimeter. This multi-tiered approach significantly bolsters their resilience against an array of cyber threats.

Leveraging cloud-based services: Cloud-based platforms and services play a pivotal role in insurtech cybersecurity. These solutions offer scalability, flexibility and cost-effectiveness, while simultaneously providing advanced security features such as automated data backup, disaster recovery and stringent access controls. By entrusting sensitive data to cloud environments, insurtech firms enhance their data protection capabilities and reduce the risk of data loss or system downtime.[23]

User education: Recognizing that the strength of cybersecurity lies not just in technology but in user behaviour, insurtech companies are actively educating and training both their employees and customers. This includes imparting knowledge on creating and managing strong passwords, identifying and evading phishing attempts, the importance of software updates and the criticality of promptly reporting security incidents. By fostering a cybersecurity-conscious culture, insurtech firms further bolster their defences.[24]

Collaborative networking: Insurtech firms understand the collective nature of cybersecurity challenges. Consequently, they actively collaborate with various stakeholders within the insurance industry, spanning regulators, peer companies, technology vendors and strategic partners. These collaborative efforts entail the sharing of vital information, insights and best practices on cybersecurity matters, ultimately fortifying the entire industry against cyber threats.

One example of an insurtech start-up that offers solutions for cybersecurity is Coalition. Coalition, an insurtech start-up based in San Francisco, offers comprehensive cybersecurity solutions for businesses. They provide a holistic approach that includes cybersecurity assessments and recommendations to identify and rectify vulnerabilities, real-time threat monitoring and alerts to prevent cyberattacks, incident response and recovery services in case of a breach and cyber liability coverage to protect against financial losses and legal liabilities resulting from cyber incidents.[25,26]

Blockchain revolution in insurance

Blockchain's capacity to create an immutable history of insurance policies and claims also aids in fraud detection and prevention. By analysing historical data on the blockchain, insurers can identify patterns and anomalies that may indicate fraudulent activities. This proactive approach enables insurers to take action before fraudulent claims are paid out, saving significant financial resources.

In addition to fraud prevention, blockchain enhances data security and privacy. Personal and sensitive information can be stored in a decentralized manner, reducing the risk of data breaches. Policyholders have greater control over their data, granting access only to authorized parties through cryptographic keys.

Blockchain technology has emerged as a game-changer in the insurance industry, promising to elevate transparency and trust through secure and verifiable transactions involving multiple stakeholders. Its applications, particularly in the realm of smart contracts, have the potential to significantly reduce fraud, disputes and friction in the customer experience. Let's delve into some illustrative use cases demonstrating how blockchain can transform these areas:

Smart contracts for automated processes: Smart contracts, nestled within the blockchain, are self-executing agreements that activate based on predefined conditions. They offer automation capabilities across various insurance processes, from policy issuance to premium collection and claims management. For example, consider a smart contract that automatically triggers a payout for a delayed or cancelled flight in a travel insurance policy, bypassing cumbersome manual interventions and paperwork. Additionally, smart contracts can facilitate parametric insurance, where payouts are triggered by specific, predefined parameters such as rainfall, temperature or earthquake magnitude. This streamlined approach simplifies the insurance process, lowers associated costs and benefits individuals in remote or underinsured regions.

Fraud prevention and dispute resolution: Blockchain's inherent nature as a distributed ledger creates an immutable and shared record of transactions and events. This transparency serves as a potent tool in reducing fraud and disputes within the insurance sector. By storing policy details and ownership on a blockchain, the technology can thwart issues like double-booking or double-claiming of insurance policies. Furthermore, blockchain can act as a fraud deterrent by utilizing data from trusted sources like IoT devices, sensors or third-party providers to validate the occurrence and severity of incidents. When disputes do arise, blockchain provides a transparent, auditable trail of evidence, simplifying arbitration or litigation processes.

Enhancing the customer experience: Blockchain is set to revolutionize the customer experience within the insurance landscape. It does so by boosting the speed, efficiency and convenience of insurance services. For instance, the technology can facilitate peer-to-peer (P2P) insurance, where customers collectively pool their premiums and share risks without intermediaries. This model empowers communities to self-insure and trust the blockchain for transparent and fair payouts. Microinsurance, another application, offers low-cost, short-term coverage for specific events or activities, making insurance more accessible and tailored to individual needs. Lastly, blockchain enables cross-border insurance, allowing customers to access insurance products and services from different geographical regions with ease.

In conclusion, blockchain's transformative potential in the insurance industry is indisputable. Through smart contracts, fraud reduction and improved customer experiences, this technology is poised to reshape the way insurance is conducted, making it more efficient, secure and customer-centric. As its adoption continues to expand, the insurance sector is on the cusp of a new era defined by transparency, trust and enhanced service delivery.

In conclusion, blockchain technology is poised to revolutionize the insurance industry by enhancing transparency, trust and efficiency. Through the implementation of blockchain-based smart contracts, fraud detection and prevention and secure data management, insurers can provide a more reliable and customer-centric insurance experience while reducing costs and risks associated with fraud and disputes. As blockchain adoption continues to grow, the insurance industry is on the brink of a transformative shift towards a more transparent and secure future.

Examples of insurtech start-ups leveraging blockchain technology

Dynamis: Dynamis harnesses Ethereum, a blockchain-based smart contract platform, to provide a unique peer-to-peer unemployment insurance solution. Customers have the flexibility to craft personalized policies and collaborate with others who share similar employment-related risks. The start-up goes the extra mile by using social media data to verify the employment status of its customers, reinforcing trust and credibility.[27]

InsurETH: This start-up capitalizes on Ethereum's blockchain to offer blockchain-based travel delay insurance. Customers can acquire policies that automatically trigger payouts in the event of flight delays or cancellations. To ensure the validity of claims, the platform relies on data from reliable sources like flight trackers, elevating transparency and instilling trust.[28]

Teambrella: Teambrella embraces blockchain to create a P2P insurance platform that encompasses a broad spectrum of risks, ranging from car accidents to pet illnesses and bike thefts. Customers have the opportunity to form teams with others who share similar insurance needs and preferences. What sets Teambrella apart is its unique approach, where customers collectively determine the outcome of each claim and the corresponding payout, democratizing the insurance process.

These insurtech start-ups serve as prime examples of how blockchain technology is revolutionizing the insurance landscape. By facilitating peer-to-peer models, enhancing transparency and employing smart contracts, they offer pioneering solutions that cater to the evolving demands and expectations of insurance customers. The expanding role of blockchain in insurtech promises a future marked by heightened efficiency, equity and customer empowerment.

In summation, the pivotal role of cybersecurity in insurtech cannot be overstated. As these companies continue to digitize and innovate, they must steadfastly uphold their commitment to safeguarding sensitive customer data. By adopting a comprehensive and proactive approach to cybersecurity, insurtech firms not only protect their data assets but also bolster trust, ensuring a secure and thriving future for the industry in the digital era.

Insurtech regulatory considerations and challenges

Insurtech, which embodies the fusion of cutting-edge technology with traditional insurance services, is revolutionizing the insurance industry by enhancing efficiency, accessibility and affordability. However, this innovative sector also encounters a spectrum of regulatory challenges and considerations, stemming from the highly regulated nature of the insurance industry and the novel methodologies it introduces.

One of the primary concerns for insurtech companies is compliance with existing insurance laws and regulations. These laws are not uniform and vary extensively across different regions and countries. They include various aspects like licensing requirements, solvency norms, consumer protection measures and specific regulations tailored to different insurance products. For insurtech firms, especially those operating on an international scale, understanding and adhering to this complex regulatory landscape is crucial.

Data privacy and security are also paramount. Insurtech companies often process vast amounts of personal data due to their reliance on data analytics, AI and IoT devices. Consequently, they must strictly adhere to data protection laws such as Europe's GDPR, ensuring the security and privacy of this data to maintain consumer trust and meet regulatory standards.

The integration of blockchain technology and smart contracts in insurtech brings unique regulatory challenges, including the legal recognition of smart contracts and the management of data within blockchain networks. Regulators are working to adapt legal frameworks to these emerging technologies, addressing their cross-border nature and implications.

Moreover, solvency and risk management are vital regulatory areas for insurtech firms involved in underwriting and bearing risks.

These companies must maintain adequate capital reserves for potential claims and exhibit effective risk management practices for regulatory compliance.

Consumer protection and transparency are fundamental from a regulatory viewpoint. Insurtech companies are expected to ensure clear and understandable policy terms, pricing structures and claims processes. They also have the responsibility to ensure that their algorithms and AI-driven decisions are fair and non-discriminatory.

Regulatory sandbox environments provide a unique opportunity for insurtech companies to experiment with innovative products and services in a more relaxed regulatory setting. However, transitioning from these environments to full-scale operations involves navigating a complex set of regulations.

For insurtech companies offering cross-border services, compliance with the insurance and financial regulations of each country they operate in adds another layer of complexity, challenging given the diversity of international regulatory landscapes.

Cybersecurity is another critical area. Due to the digital nature of insurtech services, these companies must adhere to stringent cybersecurity regulations to protect against data breaches and other cyber threats.

Partnerships with traditional insurance firms, a common practice in the insurtech industry, can create unique regulatory challenges. These often involve navigating the division of responsibilities and liabilities between the technology-focused insurtech entities and the traditional insurers.

In conclusion, while insurtech companies bring significant innovation and efficiency to the insurance sector, they also face a broad range of regulatory challenges. Successfully navigating these challenges is crucial for the sustainable operation of insurtech companies, balancing the drive for innovation with the necessity for compliance. Regulators must adapt to this changing environment and develop frameworks that balance innovation and consumer protection, ensuring that the evolving regulations are applicable and fair for the diverse and fast-evolving insurtech sector.

Transforming risk management in insurance

Insurtech, the innovative blend of technology in the insurance sector, is significantly transforming risk management practices. As risks evolve due to technological progress, climate change and changing consumer behaviours, insurtech is at the forefront, offering solutions that enable insurers to adapt and manage these risks more effectively.

Utilization of advanced data analytics and predictive modelling: Insurtech harnesses the power of big data analytics and predictive modelling, allowing insurers to evaluate risks with greater accuracy. By analysing extensive data from diverse sources, such as social media, IoT devices and traditional data points, insurance companies can obtain a more profound understanding of risk factors. This leads to more precise underwriting and optimized pricing of insurance policies.

Enhanced fraud detection mechanisms: Insurtech incorporates AI and machine learning, significantly bolstering the capacity of insurance companies to detect and prevent fraud. These technologies are adept at identifying patterns and inconsistencies in claims data, potentially flagging fraudulent activities and thus curbing financial losses.

Promotion of usage-based insurance (UBI) models: Particularly prevalent in motor insurance, insurtech has been instrumental in advancing UBI models. Through telematics, which monitors driving behaviour, insurers can more accurately assess individual risks, paving the way for personalized premium plans and promoting safer driving habits.

Risk prevention with IoT integration: IoT plays a crucial role in real-time monitoring and mitigation of risks. Smart home sensors, for example, can promptly alert homeowners and insurers to potential hazards like leaks or fires, enabling rapid responses and mitigating severe damages.

Blockchain application in risk management: Blockchain technology introduces a secure and transparent method to handle contracts and claims. Smart contracts automate and streamline claims processing, reduce fraud potential and ensure adherence to contract terms, enhancing overall risk management.

Addressing emerging risks: Insurtech is pivotal in developing insurance products for new and emerging risks, such as cyber insurance for data breaches and coverage for autonomous vehicles, ensuring that insurance solutions remain relevant and effective.

Improving customer engagement and education: Insurtech enhances customer engagement through mobile apps and online platforms. Educating customers about risk mitigation and preventive strategies reduces claim likelihood and bolsters overall risk management.

Climate risk assessment capabilities: In response to climate change, insurtech employs advanced modelling techniques to predict and manage risks associated with extreme weather events, aiding in the strategic planning and pricing of insurance products.

Fostering collaborative ecosystems: Insurtech encourages collaboration among insurers, technology companies and other stakeholders. This collective approach facilitates data and insight sharing, leading to improved risk assessment and management.

Ensuring regulatory compliance: Insurtech also plays a crucial role in maintaining compliance with the dynamic regulatory landscape, a key aspect of risk management. Automated compliance checks are instrumental in avoiding legal and financial repercussions.

In conclusion, insurtech is revolutionizing risk management in the insurance industry. By leveraging AI, IoT, blockchain and other technologies, it enables more accurate risk assessment, effective fraud detection and efficient claims processing. Insurtech not only helps insurers keep pace with emerging risks and regulatory shifts but also fundamentally changes the way risk is managed in the insurance sector.

Cyber risk assessment and insurance solutions

Insurtech companies are playing an increasingly important role in assessing cyber risks and providing cyber insurance solutions. As cyber threats evolve and become more sophisticated, these companies leverage cutting-edge technology and innovative approaches to offer effective cyber insurance products. Here are some key ways in which insurtech companies assess cyber risks and develop their insurance solutions, along with illustrative use cases:

Advanced data analytics and AI: Insurtech firms use big data analytics and AI to analyse patterns and trends in cyber incidents. This helps in identifying potential vulnerabilities and common attack vectors. For instance, an insurtech company might use AI to analyse data breaches across various industries, understanding the most targeted data types and entry points used by hackers.

Risk assessment tools and algorithms: Many insurtech companies develop sophisticated tools and algorithms to assess an organization's cyber risk profile. These tools often consider factors like the company's IT infrastructure, data storage practices, employee cybersecurity awareness and past incident history. For example, a tool might score a company's risk level based on its use of firewalls, encryption and intrusion detection systems.

Real-time monitoring and threat intelligence: Insurtech firms often offer real-time monitoring services as part of their cyber insurance packages. They utilize threat intelligence feeds to stay updated on the latest cyber threats and vulnerabilities, helping clients to proactively address potential security issues. A use case here could be an insurtech firm that provides a dashboard to clients, showing real-time data on potential threats and suggested actions.

Customized insurance policies: By using the data and insights gained from their analyses, insurtech companies can offer customized cyber insurance policies that cater to the specific needs and risk profiles of different businesses. For instance, a small e-commerce store and a large financial institution would have vastly different cyber risk profiles and insurance needs.

Collaboration with cybersecurity firms: To enhance their risk assessment capabilities, insurtech companies often collaborate with cybersecurity firms. This partnership allows them to incorporate specialized knowledge about cyber threats into their insurance products. A case in point could be an insurtech partnering with a cybersecurity firm to assess the risk level of companies in the financial sector, considering the latest trends in financial cybercrimes.

Claims handling and post-breach response: Insurtech companies not only focus on risk assessment but also on efficient claims handling and post-breach response. They often provide services such as legal assistance, public relations support and forensic analysis in the event of a cyber incident. For example, an insurtech company might have a rapid response team that assists a client in mitigating damage and navigating legal requirements following a data breach.

In summary, insurtech companies are at the forefront of tackling cyber risks by employing advanced technologies and methodologies for risk assessment and developing customized insurance solutions. Their approach includes a combination of real-time monitoring, data analytics, collaboration with cybersecurity experts and tailored insurance products, making them essential players in managing and insuring against cyber risks in various industries.

Conclusion

In concluding Chapter 5 on 'Insurtech and Risk Management', we have seen how insurtech is revolutionizing the way risks are identified, analysed and managed in the insurance industry. This evolution, driven by advanced technologies like AI, predictive analytics, IoT and other emerging technologies, marks a significant shift from traditional risk management practices.

The chapter highlighted the transformative impact of data-driven approaches in understanding and mitigating risks. The use of telematics for monitoring and IoT for proactive risk assessment illustrates how technology is making risk management more precise and responsive.

As we transition to Chapter 6, 'Insurtech and Claims', the focus shifts from assessing and managing risks to how these risks materialize in the form of claims. This next chapter will explore how the same technological innovations influencing risk management are also reshaping claims processing.

We will delve into the ways insurtech is simplifying and streamlining the claims process, making it faster, more efficient and more user-friendly. The advancements in automated claims handling, AI for fraud detection and real-time processing demonstrate how technology is enhancing the overall experience of filing and settling claims.

Chapter 6 will bridge the gap between risk management and claims processing, showing how advancements in one area complement and enhance the other, ultimately leading to a more integrated and efficient insurance life cycle. As we move forward, we'll see how insurtech is not just about managing risks but also about effectively resolving claims, closing the loop in the insurance journey.

Notes

1   'Can AI Be Used for Risk Assessments?' ISACA, 28 Apr. 2023. www.isaca.org/resources/news-and-trends/industry-news/2023/can-ai-be-used-for-risk-assessments (archived at https://perma.cc/NSD4-FPH2).

2   'Machine Learning and AI for Risk Management', SpringerLink, 7 Dec. 2018. link.springer.com/chapter/10.1007/978-3-030-02330-0_3 (archived at https://perma.cc/5X84-2Y8E).

3   'How Data and Analytics Are Redefining Excellence in P&C Underwriting', McKInsey, 24 Sep. 2021. www.mckinsey.com/industries/financial-services/our-insights/how-data-and-analytics-are-redefining-excellence-in-p-and-c-underwriting (archived at https://perma.cc/SX56-DXG3).

4   'Underwriting Applications of Predictive Analytics', CAS, 1 Mar. 2017. www.casact.org/newsletter-article/underwriting-applications-predictive-analytics (archived at https://perma.cc/UTF7-R3DT).

5   'Predictive Analytics in Insurance: Pricing and Underwriting Dynamics', Polestar, 9 Jun. 2023. www.polestarllp.com/blog/predictive-analytics-insurance-pricing-underwriting-dynamics (archived at https://perma.cc/6MQ7-XFFM).

6   'Predictive Analytics in Life Underwriting – Friend, not Foe', PartnerRe, 21 Feb. 2022. www.partnerre.com/opinions_research/predictive-analytics-in-life-underwriting-friend-not-foe/ (archived at https://perma.cc/C6RL-Y8LQ).

7   'How Data and Analytics Are Redefining Excellence in P&C Underwriting',
    24 Sep. 2021. www.mckinsey.com/industries/financial-services/our-insights/
    how-data-and-analytics-are-redefining-excellence-in-p-and-c-underwriting
    (archived at https://perma.cc/6YAB-RB3T).

8   'How Insurtechs Are Transforming Insurance Underwriting – 7 Examples',
    30 Aug. 2018. insuranceblog.accenture.com/how-insurtechs-are-transforming-
    insurance-underwriting-7-examples (archived at https://perma.cc/XE5V-8SNF).

9   'How Insurtechs Are Transforming Insurance Underwrit-ing – 7 Examples',
    30 Aug. 2018. insuranceblog.accenture.com/how-insurtechs-are-transforming-
    insurance-underwriting-7-examples (archived at https://perma.cc/39M7-
    RE2E).

10 'How Insurtechs Are Transforming Insurance Underwrit-ing – 7 Examples',
    Accenture, 30 Aug. 2018. insuranceblog.accenture.com/how-insurtechs-are-
    transforming-insurance-underwriting-7-examples (archived at https://perma.
    cc/VZJ5-G5YX).

11 'How Insurtechs Are Transforming Insurance Underwriting – 7 Examples',
    Accenture, 30 Aug. 2018. insuranceblog.accenture.com/how-insurtechs-are-
    transforming-insurance-underwriting-7-examples (archived at https://perma.
    cc/U528-5DNG).

12 'Using Machine Learning to Increase Underwriting Efficiency', 18 May 2022.
    www.ai.intelliarts.com/post/using-machine-learning-to-increase-underwriting-
    efficiency (archived at https://perma.cc/LX9P-L8XH).

13 'Telematics and the Future of Risk Management', AgentSync, 26 May 2022.
    agentsync.io/blog/technology/why-telematics-is-future-of-risk-management
    (archived at https://perma.cc/4KX6-CM2D).

14 'Telematics in Insurance Industry', IRJET, 1 Apr. 2021. www.irjet.net/archives/
    V8/i3/IRJET-V8I3546.pdf (archived at https://perma.cc/95WG-BLBG).

15 'IoT-Based Environmental Monitoring: Types and Use Cases', 15 Apr. 2022.
    www.digi.com/blog/post/iot-based-environmental-monitoring (archived at
    https://perma.cc/98RZ-3QWP).

16 'Using AI to Prevent Insurance Fraud', ITL, 4 Oct. 2023.
    www.insurancethoughtleadership.com/ai-machine-learning/using-ai-prevent-
    insurance-fraud (archived at https://perma.cc/CWP9-E8R3).

17 'The Future of Insurance Fraud Detection is Predictive Analytics', 23 Jun.
    2022. whatfix.com/blog/insurance-fraud-detection/ (archived at https://perma.
    cc/5SZJ-6DYW).

18 'Artificial Intelligence-Based Fraud Detection in Insurance', Emerj, 13 Dec.
    2019. emerj.com/ai-sector-overviews/artificial-intelligence-fraud-detection-
    insurance/ (archived at https://perma.cc/522R-3YDF).

19 'Artificial Intelligence-Based Fraud Detection in Insurance', Emerj, 13 Dec. 2019. emerj.com/ai-sector-overviews/artificial-intelligence-fraud-detection-insurance/ (archived at https://perma.cc/T5FX-3JNZ).

20 'Artificial Intelligence-Based Fraud Detection in Insurance', Emerj, 13 Dec. 2019. emerj.com/ai-sector-overviews/artificial-intelligence-fraud-detection-insurance/ (archived at https://perma.cc/78TL-XP5Z).

21 'Insurtech Cybersecurity: An Evolving Space', InsurTech, 21 Jun. 2021. insurtechdigital.com/insurtech/insurtech-cybersecurity-evolving-space (archived at https://perma.cc/K2MA-P3EW).

22 'Cyber Trends 2021: IT Security in Insurtech', InsurTech, 17 May 2021. insurtechdigital.com/technology-and-ai/cyber-trends-2021-it-security-insurtech (archived at https://perma.cc/DBT8-HKCM).

23 '5 Cybersecurity Threats Hitting Insurance Companies in 2022', InsurTech, 20 Mar. 2022. insurtechdigital.com/insurtech/5-cybersecurity-threats-hitting-insurance-companies-in-2022 (archived at https://perma.cc/48J9-AVVN).

24 'Three Major Insurtech Cybersecurity Risks in 2022', InsurTech, 18 Nov. 2021. insurtechdigital.com/insurtech/three-major-insurtech-cybersecurity-risks-2022. (archived at https://perma.cc/H54E-V9K3).

25 'Top 10 Cyber Insurance Startups and Insurtechs', 10 Feb. 2023. insurtechdigital.com/articles/top-10-cyber-insurance-startups-and-insurtechs (archived at https://perma.cc/9AKG-G55V).

26 'Discover 5 Top Cyber Insurance Startups', StartUs Insights. www.startus-insights.com/innovators-guide/cyber-insurance-startups/ (archived at https://perma.cc/EN9V-ZKSR).

27 'The 4 Insurtech Blockchain Disruptors to Know', Foresight Factory, 15 Jun. 2017. www.foresightfactory.co/4-insurtech-blockchain-disruptors-know/ (archived at https://perma.cc/8BFF-D99C).

28 'The 4 Insurtech Blockchain Disruptors to Know', Foresight Factory, 15 Jun. 2017. www.foresightfactory.co/4-insurtech-blockchain-disruptors-know/ (archived at https://perma.cc/9MWA-LCHG).

6

Insurtech and claims

Introduction

As we transition from Chapter 5, which delved into the innovative ways insurtech is reshaping risk management, we now turn our focus to another critical facet of the insurance industry: claims processing. In this chapter, we will explore how insurtech is revolutionizing the claims landscape, transforming traditional practices into a more streamlined, efficient and customer-centric process.

Claims processing has always been at the heart of the insurance industry. It is the moment when the insurer fulfils its promise to the policyholder, a critical touchpoint that significantly influences customer satisfaction and trust. Traditionally, this process has been manual, paper-intensive and time-consuming, often leading to delays, increased costs and customer frustration. However, the advent of insurtech has begun to dramatically alter this landscape.

Leveraging advanced technologies such as artificial intelligence (AI), machine learning (ML), blockchain and the Internet of Things (IoT), insurtech companies are not only speeding up the claims process but also making it more transparent and accurate. These technological interventions are minimizing human errors, detecting fraud more effectively and enhancing the overall customer experience.

This chapter will provide an in-depth look at the various ways in which insurtech is influencing claims processing. From automated claims handling and real-time data analytics to mobile-first customer interfaces and proactive fraud detection, the scope of transformation is vast and varied. We will also examine case studies and real-world examples to understand the practical application of these technologies in the insurance claims process.

Moreover, we will discuss the challenges and opportunities that come with implementing these technological solutions, including the integration of new systems with traditional insurance processes, regulatory hurdles and the need for balance between automation and human oversight.

By the end of this chapter, readers will gain a comprehensive understanding of how insurtech is not just altering the mechanics of claims processing, but also redefining the relationship between insurers and their customers. As we move forward into an increasingly digital and connected world, the role of insurtech in claims processing is set to become more pivotal, marking a significant shift in how the insurance industry operates and delivers value to its clients.

Traditional methods of claims processing in the insurance industry

Traditional methods of claims processing in the insurance industry are characterized by a series of manual steps and extensive paperwork, which can often result in a lengthy and cumbersome process. Here are the key components of this traditional approach:

Claim initiation: Traditionally, the process begins with the policyholder filing a claim, usually after an incident has occurred. This is typically done over the phone, through mail or in person at an insurance office. The policyholder is required to fill out claim forms and provide necessary documentation to support their claim.

Data collection and documentation: This step involves collecting all relevant data and documentation related to the claim. It includes gathering police reports, medical records, witness statements, photographs of the incident and other pertinent information. The policyholder often bears the responsibility for providing these documents, which can be time-consuming.

Claims adjustment and investigation: Once the claim is filed, a claims adjuster is assigned to the case. The adjuster's role is to investigate the claim, assess the damage and determine the insurance company's liability. This process often involves on-site inspections, interviews with the claimant and witnesses and consultations with experts.

Manual review and processing: The adjuster manually reviews all the information and documentation related to the claim. Based on this review, they make a decision on claim approval or denial. This process can be lengthy, as it involves various levels of verification and adherence to policy terms.

Settlement and payout: If a claim is approved, the insurance company then calculates the settlement amount based on the policy's coverage and the assessed damage. The payout process itself can be time-consuming, as it often involves several administrative steps and final approvals.

Communication with the policyholder: Throughout the claims process, communication with the policyholder is typically done via phone calls, emails or letters. This communication is essential for requesting additional information, providing updates on the claim's status and explaining the reasons for claim decisions.

Record keeping and reporting: Insurers maintain records of all claims and their outcomes. These records are often kept in paper files or traditional databases, which can make retrieval and analysis of past claims data cumbersome.

Fraud detection and prevention: In the traditional model, fraud detection primarily relies on the adjuster's expertise and experience. Suspicious claims may undergo additional scrutiny, but the process largely depends on manual effort and judgement.

The traditional claims processing method, while thorough, is often criticized for being slow, prone to human error and customer-unfriendly due to its lack of transparency and speed. This has led to a growing interest in modernizing the process through insurtech innovations.

Evolution of insurtech in addressing traditional claims processing challenges

Insurtech has evolved remarkably to address the numerous challenges inherent in traditional claims processing methods. By integrating advanced technologies and innovative approaches, insurtech solutions have transformed the once cumbersome and time-consuming process into one that is more efficient, accurate and customer-friendly.

Digital and automated claims processing: One of the most significant evolutions in insurtech has been the shift from manual to digital claims processing. Automated systems powered by AI and machine learning algorithms can handle routine tasks such as data entry, document scanning and initial claim assessments. This automation not only speeds up the process but also reduces human error, leading to more accurate claims handling.

Enhanced customer experience through technology: Traditional claims processes often suffered from a lack of transparency and slow communication. Insurtech has addressed these issues by implementing customer-friendly technologies like mobile apps and online portals. These platforms allow policyholders to file claims, upload necessary documents and track the status of their claims in real-time, greatly enhancing the customer experience.

Advanced data analytics for accurate assessment: Insurtech utilizes big data analytics to process vast amounts of information quickly and accurately. This capability enables a more thorough and nuanced understanding of each claim, leading to fairer and more precise assessments. Predictive analytics also play a role in identifying potential issues before they escalate, aiding in proactive claims management.

Integration of IoT for real-time data: The use of IoT devices in insurtech has brought a new dimension to claims processing. For instance, in motor insurance, telematics devices can provide real-time data on vehicle usage and driver behaviour, aiding in swift and accurate accident assessments. In home insurance, smart home technologies can detect and report incidents like leaks or fires immediately, enabling faster response.

Blockchain for transparency and fraud detection: Blockchain technology is being leveraged to create immutable records of claims and policies, enhancing transparency and trust between the insurer and the insured. This technology also plays a crucial role in fraud detection, as the blockchain ledger makes it difficult to alter or forge documents and claim histories.

Personalized claims processing: AI and machine learning enable insurtech companies to offer personalized claims experiences. By analysing a customer's history, preferences and behaviour, insurtech platforms can tailor the claims process to individual needs, making it more user-friendly and efficient.

Regulatory compliance and flexibility: As regulatory environments evolve, insurtech platforms are designed to be flexible and adaptable to new laws and standards. This adaptability ensures that the claims process remains compliant with current regulations, avoiding legal complications and maintaining high standards of operation.

In summary, the evolution of insurtech has been pivotal in addressing the inefficiencies and limitations of traditional claims processing. Through technology and innovation, insurtech has made claims processing faster, more accurate, transparent and customer-centric, while also enhancing the overall efficiency and reliability of the insurance industry.

Technology-driven claims processing

Insurtech has incorporated a range of advanced technologies to revolutionize claims processing in the insurance industry. These technologies are designed to enhance efficiency, accuracy and customer satisfaction. The predominant technologies used in insurtech for claims processing include:

AI and machine learning: AI and machine learning algorithms are at the forefront of insurtech claims processing. They are used for automating tasks such as reviewing claim forms, assessing damage through images and videos and making initial determinations on claims. Machine learning models improve over time, learning from past claims data to make more accurate assessments and decisions.

Blockchain technology: Blockchain offers a secure and transparent way to record transactions, which is crucial in the claims process. It provides immutable records of claims and policies, enhancing trust and transparency. Blockchain technology is also instrumental in fraud detection, as it makes it harder to alter or forge documents and claim histories.

IoT: IoT devices, especially in motor and home insurance, play a vital role in claims processing. In motor insurance, telematics devices collect data about vehicle usage and driver behaviour, which is crucial after accidents. For home insurance, sensors can detect and report incidents like water leaks or fires, facilitating faster claims processing.

Natural language processing (NLP): NLP is used to analyse customer communication and extract relevant information from claim documents automatically. It helps in understanding and processing the large volumes of unstructured data typically involved in claims, such as adjuster notes, repair estimates and medical reports.

Robotic process automation (RPA): RPA is used for automating repetitive and rule-based tasks that are common in the claims process. This includes data entry, form processing and updating customer records. RPA helps in reducing the processing time and minimizing human errors.

Predictive analytics: This technology uses historical data to predict future outcomes. In claims processing, predictive analytics can forecast the likelihood of a claim being fraudulent or the potential cost of a claim based on similar past incidents. This helps insurers in proactive decision-making and resource allocation.

Mobile applications: Mobile apps are increasingly being used to improve the customer experience in claims processing. They allow customers to file claims, upload documents and photos and communicate with their insurer directly from their smartphones. Some apps also include features like chatbots for instant assistance and GPS for location-based services.

Cloud computing: Cloud technology provides the necessary infrastructure for storing and processing the large amounts of data involved in claims. It offers scalability, flexibility and accessibility, enabling insurers to manage claims more efficiently and securely.

These technologies, individually and in combination, are enabling insurtech companies to transform the traditional claims process into a more streamlined, accurate and customer-friendly experience. They reflect the ongoing evolution of the insurance sector towards greater digitalization and innovation.

Streamlining the claims process

The integration of advanced technologies in insurtech has significantly streamlined the claims process, offering stark improvements over traditional methods. Here's how these technologies make a difference:

Enhanced speed and efficiency with automation: Technologies like AI, machine learning and RPA automate various aspects of the claims process that were previously done manually. Tasks like data entry, initial claims assessment and document processing are now handled quickly and efficiently, reducing the time from claim filing to resolution.

Improved accuracy and reduced human error: AI and machine learning algorithms analyse claims with a level of precision that minimizes errors. This accuracy is particularly evident in assessing damages and estimating repair costs, where AI algorithms can evaluate photos and videos to provide accurate damage assessments, reducing the likelihood of human error.

Real-time data processing with IoT: IoT devices, particularly in motor and home insurance, provide real-time data that is crucial for prompt claims processing. For instance, telematics in vehicles can immediately supply data post-accident, enabling quicker claims filing and processing, while home sensors can detect and report incidents like leaks or fires instantly.

Enhanced fraud detection: The use of blockchain technology and advanced data analytics has bolstered the ability to detect fraudulent claims. Blockchain creates an immutable record of transactions, making it difficult to falsify claim histories, while predictive analytics can identify patterns indicative of fraud.

Personalized customer experience: Technologies like mobile apps and NLP offer a more personalized and user-friendly claims process. Policyholders can easily file claims, upload necessary documentation and communicate with their insurer through mobile apps, while NLP enhances customer service by processing and responding to customer enquiries more effectively.

Streamlined communication and documentation: Cloud computing and NLP facilitate better management and accessibility of claim-related documents and data. Cloud platforms offer scalable and secure storage, making it easier to access and share information, while NLP tools can swiftly process and categorize large volumes of unstructured data, such as adjuster notes and medical reports.

Predictive analytics for proactive claims handling: Predictive analytics enable insurers to anticipate potential issues and streamline claims processing. By analysing historical data, insurers can identify trends and patterns, helping them to allocate resources more effectively and manage claims more proactively.

Reduced costs and improved resource allocation: The efficiency and accuracy brought by these technologies lead to cost savings for insurance companies. Automated processes reduce the need for extensive manual labour, while improved accuracy and fraud detection minimize financial losses from erroneous or fraudulent claims.

In summary, insurtech technologies have brought about a transformative shift in the claims process. Compared to traditional methods, they offer increased speed, accuracy and efficiency, along with enhanced customer experience and fraud detection capabilities. This technological integration signifies a major advancement in the way insurance companies handle claims, leading to better outcomes for both insurers and policyholders.

Automation in claims management

Automated claims management systems in insurtech are characterized by several key features that significantly enhance the efficiency and effectiveness of the insurance claims process. These features represent a shift from traditional, manual claims handling to a more streamlined, technology-driven approach. Here are the essential features of these systems:

Automated data entry and processing: These systems utilize advanced technologies to automatically input and process data. This includes the extraction and analysis of information from claims forms, emails and other documents, significantly reducing the time and effort required for manual data entry.

AI-powered damage assessment: Utilizing AI, particularly machine learning and image recognition algorithms, these systems can accurately assess the extent of damage from photos or videos submitted by claimants. This capability is particularly prevalent in motor and property insurance claims.

Real-time claims tracking and updates: Automated systems provide real-time updates on the status of a claim, both to the insurer and the policyholder. This feature ensures transparency and keeps all parties informed throughout the claims process.

Fraud detection algorithms: By analysing patterns and anomalies in claims data, AI-driven fraud detection tools can identify potentially fraudulent claims. These systems compare new claims against historical data to flag suspicious cases, thereby reducing the incidence of fraud.

Integrated communication tools: These systems often include integrated communication platforms, allowing for seamless interaction between claimants, adjusters and other stakeholders. This feature facilitates quicker resolution of queries and more efficient claims processing.

Predictive analytics for risk assessment: Automated claims systems use predictive analytics to assess the risk associated with a claim. By analysing historical claims data, these systems can predict the likelihood of future claims and their potential impact, aiding in more informed decision-making.

Customizable workflow automation: Insurtech claims systems offer customizable workflows that can be tailored to the specific needs and policies of an insurance company. This flexibility allows insurers to optimize the claims process according to their operational models and customer needs.

Document management and storage: These systems provide efficient document management solutions, securely storing and organizing all claim-related documents. Cloud-based storage ensures that data is accessible from anywhere, enhancing the efficiency of the claims processing.

Mobile accessibility: With the ubiquity of smartphones, many automated claims systems are designed for mobile access. This allows policyholders to file claims, upload documents and track their claim status conveniently from their mobile devices.

Regulatory compliance: Automated claims management systems are built to comply with industry regulations and standards. They ensure that all claims are processed in accordance with legal requirements, helping insurance companies avoid regulatory issues.

In summary, automated claims management systems in insurtech are equipped with a range of features that streamline the claims process. From AI-driven assessments to fraud detection and mobile accessibility, these systems are transforming the traditional claims landscape into a more efficient, transparent and customer-centric model.

Real-world examples of improved efficiency in claims handling through automation

Automation in insurance claims handling has led to significant improvements in efficiency, accuracy and customer satisfaction. Here are a few real-world examples that highlight the impact of automation in the claims process:

Lemonade: A technology-driven insurance company, uses an AI-powered system named AI Jim to handle and process claims. In a notable instance, AI Jim settled a theft claim in just three seconds, a process that traditionally could take days or even weeks. This was achieved by the AI system running 18 anti-fraud algorithms and approving the claim almost instantly after the customer submitted the claim via the mobile app.

EvolutionIQ: This start-up harnesses the power of AI to revolutionize claims processing for insurers and reinsurers. It intelligently utilizes data from a multitude of sources, including policy documents, medical records and third-party reports, to automate and optimize claims procedures. By doing so, it ensures precise and consistent claims outcomes. Furthermore, EvolutionIQ provides valuable analytics and insights that empower insurers to enhance their claims performance and bolster customer satisfaction.[1]

Tractable: Tractable stands out by employing computer vision technology to assess vehicle and property damage based on photographs. It not only evaluates the extent of damage but also predicts repair costs and guides claimants through the necessary steps. This innovation accelerates the claims settlement process, combats fraud and elevates the overall customer experience for insurers.[2]

Snapsheet: Snapsheet offers a versatile cloud-based platform designed to facilitate end-to-end digital claims management for insurers. It empowers customers to effortlessly submit claims through various channels, including a mobile app, web portal or chatbot. The platform employs AI to validate claims, estimate damages and process payments swiftly. Additionally, Snapsheet provides insurers with valuable analytics and reporting tools to optimize claims operations and reduce costs effectively.[3]

Alan: Alan is a trailblazing digital health insurance provider that simplifies the claims process for its customers. It grants access to a network of healthcare professionals and doctors online, enabling users to book appointments and receive instant reimbursements. Alan goes beyond traditional health insurance by offering preventive care services, including telemedicine, wellness programmes and mental health support, further enhancing the overall healthcare experience for its policyholders.[4]

These examples demonstrate how automation and technological innovation in the insurance sector are streamlining the claims process, making it faster, more efficient and more responsive to customer needs. The adoption of AI, mobile technology, drones and other digital tools is setting new standards for claims handling in the insurance industry.

Fraud detection and prevention

Techniques and technologies employed by insurtech to detect and prevent insurance fraud

Insurtech companies leverage a variety of advanced techniques and technologies to combat insurance fraud, a persistent and costly issue in the insurance industry. These innovative approaches have greatly enhanced the ability to detect and prevent fraudulent activities. Here are some of the key techniques and technologies used:

AI and machine learning: AI and machine learning algorithms analyse large datasets to identify patterns and anomalies indicative of fraudulent activities. These systems can learn from historical fraud data and continually improve their detection capabilities.

Predictive analytics: Predictive analytics tools use historical data to predict the likelihood of fraud. By analysing past claims and known fraud cases, these tools can flag claims that exhibit similar characteristics for further investigation.

NLP: NLP is used to analyse unstructured data, such as claimant interviews or adjuster notes. It can detect inconsistencies or suspicious language patterns that may suggest fraudulent behaviour.

Telematics and IoT data analysis: In motor insurance, telematics devices track vehicle usage and driver behaviour, providing data that can be analysed for signs of fraud, such as staged accidents. In home insurance, IoT sensors can detect and report conditions that contradict claims, like water sensors disputing a flood claim.

Blockchain technology: Blockchain creates immutable and transparent records of transactions and policies, making it harder for individuals to fabricate or alter past insurance claims or policy information.

Social media analysis: Insurtech companies use social media monitoring tools to cross-verify claimant's statements and activities. Inconsistencies between a claim and public social media posts can be red flags for fraud.

Image and video analysis: Advanced image recognition software analyses photos and videos submitted in claims to detect signs of tampering or inconsistencies that could indicate fraud.

Anomaly detection systems: These systems are designed to identify outliers or abnormal patterns in claims data. Anomalies that deviate significantly from typical patterns can trigger further investigation.

Fraud detection databases: Insurers often contribute to and utilize shared fraud detection databases that contain information about known fraudsters and fraudulent activities, which can be cross-referenced against new claims.

Biometric verification: Biometric technologies like facial recognition or voice analysis can be used to verify the identity of claimants, reducing the risk of identity fraud in claims processing.

By integrating these technologies and techniques, insurtech companies are not only enhancing their ability to detect and prevent insurance fraud but are also contributing to a more secure and trustworthy insurance ecosystem. This technological approach to fraud detection underscores the insurtech industry's commitment to protecting both insurers and policyholders from the financial and reputational damages caused by fraudulent activities.

Impact of insurtech's fraud detection methods on the insurance industry

The implementation of advanced fraud detection methods by insurtech companies has significantly impacted the insurance industry in several key areas. These techniques and technologies have not only enhanced the ability to combat fraud but also brought about broader changes in the sector. Here's how:

Reduction in financial losses: The primary impact of effective fraud detection is the considerable reduction in financial losses due to fraudulent claims. Insurtech tools can identify and prevent fraudulent activities before claims are paid, saving insurance companies millions of dollars annually.

Increased efficiency and speed of claims processing: With automated fraud detection systems, legitimate claims can be processed faster. Insurers can allocate fewer resources to fraud investigation for each claim, speeding up the overall claims process and improving efficiency.

Improved customer trust and satisfaction: By reducing fraudulent claims, insurers can offer more competitive premiums to their customers. Additionally, the quicker processing and settlement of legitimate claims enhance customer trust and satisfaction.

Enhanced data analytics capabilities: The use of AI, machine learning and predictive analytics for fraud detection has also improved the industry's data analytics capabilities. Insurers can leverage these insights for better risk assessment and product development.

Strengthened regulatory compliance: Advanced fraud detection methods help insurers comply with regulatory requirements regarding fraud prevention. This compliance is crucial for maintaining a company's reputation and avoiding legal repercussions.

Creation of more accurate risk models: By identifying patterns and anomalies in claims data, insurtech tools aid in creating more accurate risk models. These models can be used for pricing insurance products more effectively and tailoring them to specific customer segments.

Fostering industry collaboration: The fight against insurance fraud often involves sharing data and insights across companies and platforms. This collaboration fosters a more united front against fraud in the industry.

Encouraging technological advancement: The success of insurtech in fraud detection encourages further investment and innovation in technology within the insurance industry. This drive towards innovation keeps the industry at the forefront of technological advancements.

Redefining the role of insurance professionals: With AI and automation taking over routine tasks, insurance professionals are free to focus on more complex, analytical and customer-focused roles, thereby redefining their functions within the industry.

Public perception and market stability: Effective fraud prevention contributes to a positive public perception of the insurance industry. This perception is crucial for maintaining market stability and attracting new customers.

In summary, the implementation of sophisticated fraud detection methods by insurtech companies has a wide-ranging impact on the insurance industry. It has led to financial savings, improved operational efficiencies, enhanced customer experiences and spurred a wave of technological and collaborative innovation, all of which contribute to a stronger, more resilient insurance sector.

Enhancing customer experience in claims

In the previous chapter, we shed light on how insurtech has revolutionized the insurance claims process. The traditional claims journey, once intricate and time-consuming, has undergone a remarkable transformation due to insurtech's adoption of automation, data analysis and digitalization, resulting in a considerable enhancement of customer satisfaction.

This section explores the diverse ways in which insurtech, a disruptive influence in the insurance sector, significantly contributes to enriching the customer experience throughout the claims process. Insurtech has reshaped the interaction between insurers and policyholders, rendering the entire process more efficient, transparent and user-centric. Here are the key areas of exploration:

Efficiency and simplicity in claims submission

Streamlined claims filing: Insurtech innovations have simplified the claims submission process. Policyholders can now swiftly and effortlessly submit claims via user-friendly mobile apps and web interfaces, making the experience less daunting and more user-friendly.

AI-driven claims analysis: Post-claim submission, AI technologies play a pivotal role in efficiently analysing claims against policy terms and historical data. This includes considering factors such as coverage limits, deductibles and specific circumstances, ensuring accurate and comprehensive claim assessments.

Automated settlements: Insurtech platforms have introduced automated payout systems for qualifying claims, significantly reducing the waiting time for settlements and elevating customer satisfaction.

Advancements in damage assessment

Innovative assessment tools: The utilization of drones equipped with high-resolution cameras for on-site damage evaluation represents a significant advancement. Combined with machine learning algorithms, this technology enables more precise and rapid estimations of repair costs, minimizing human error and expediting the claims resolution process.

Enhancing customer experience through insurtech

Simplified filing and enhanced transparency: Digital platforms simplify the claims filing experience, reducing frustration. Real-time updates and faster processing times, facilitated by automation and AI, contribute to increased transparency and customer satisfaction.

Continuous support and accessibility: The provision of round-the-clock support through digital channels, including chatbots and AI assistants, ensures ongoing assistance and convenience for customers.

Digital document handling: The capability to upload documents digitally streamlines the evidence submission process.

Robust fraud detection: Advanced fraud detection mechanisms strengthen customer trust by ensuring fairness and integrity in the claims process.

Self-service features: Insurtech platforms often offer self-service options, granting customers greater control over managing their claims and accessing information.

Integration with auxiliary services: Seamless integration with additional services, such as car rentals or home repairs, provides comprehensive support to customers in need.

Predictive analytics usage: Predictive analytics tools play a critical role in anticipating customer needs during the claims process, enabling insurers to provide proactive support and guidance.

In summary, the integration of insurtech into claims processing signifies a significant shift away from traditional, manual approaches toward a more streamlined, transparent and customer-centric paradigm. The incorporation of AI, digital platforms, predictive analytics and other advanced technologies has not only bolstered the operational efficiency of claims processing but has also profoundly enriched the overall customer experience within the insurance industry.

Use of data analytics in claims

Data analytics is a powerful tool used to enhance the assessment and processing of insurance claims. Here's how it contributes to making the process smoother and more efficient:

Claims prioritization and fraud detection: Data analytics quickly identifies and prioritizes claims based on their urgency and potential for fraud. This ensures that genuine claims receive prompt attention while fraudulent ones are detected early.

Resource allocation and efficiency: By automating routine tasks, data analytics frees up insurance professionals to focus on complex cases and customer interactions, leading to a more efficient claims process.

Improved customer experience: Real-time updates provided by data analytics keep policyholders informed about the status of their claims. This transparency enhances the overall customer experience during the claims journey.

Accurate damage assessment: Advanced tools like drones equipped with high-resolution cameras and machine learning algorithms allow for precise and rapid estimation of repair costs in property damage claims.

Claims reserving: Data analytics helps insurers calculate the appropriate amount of funds to set aside for future claim payments, ensuring financial stability and compliance with regulatory requirements.

Customer insights: By analysing data, insurers gain valuable insights into customer needs and behaviours. This information enables them to tailor insurance solutions to individual customers, increasing satisfaction and retention.

Regulatory compliance: Data analytics ensures that insurance companies adhere to regulatory guidelines, reducing the risk of legal issues and penalties.

In summary, data analytics plays a vital role in modernizing and optimizing the insurance claims process. It facilitates faster decision-making, improves customer interactions and helps insurers manage resources more effectively.

Harnessing the power of data analytic

By harnessing the power of data analytics, insurers can make informed decisions that enhance efficiency, customer satisfaction and fraud prevention. Here are examples of how data-driven approaches have influenced decision-making in claims management:

Fraud detection and prevention: Data analytics is used to identify patterns and anomalies in claims data that may indicate fraudulent activity. Insurers can proactively investigate suspicious claims, saving costs and maintaining the integrity of their operations.

Predictive analytics for claim severity: By analysing historical claims data, predictive models can estimate the potential severity of a claim. Insurers can allocate resources more effectively, prioritizing high-severity claims for faster resolution.

Claims prioritization: Data-driven algorithms assess the urgency and complexity of claims. High-priority claims, such as those involving injuries or significant property damage, are processed with greater attention and speed.

Automation of routine tasks: Data-driven automation streamlines routine claims processing tasks, reducing manual intervention. For example, when a claim meets specific criteria, automated systems can approve and process payments quickly.

Damage assessment with drones: Drones equipped with high-resolution cameras collect real-time data on property damage. Machine learning algorithms process this data to estimate repair costs accurately and expedite the claims resolution process.

Customer experience enhancement: Data analytics tracks customer interactions and feedback during claims processing. This information helps insurers identify areas for improvement in customer service, leading to higher satisfaction rates.

Claims reserving: Predictive analytics models use historical data to estimate future claim payments accurately. Insurers can allocate appropriate financial reserves to ensure they have sufficient funds to meet future claim obligations.

Personalized customer interactions: Data-driven insights into customer preferences and behaviours enable insurers to provide personalized communication, advice and services, enhancing the overall customer experience.

Performance metrics: Insurers use data analytics to measure the performance of claims teams. Metrics like claims processing times and customer satisfaction scores inform decision-making to improve efficiency.

Regulatory compliance: Data-driven tools help insurers ensure compliance with regulations. By monitoring and analysing claims data, insurers can identify and address potential compliance issues proactively.

These examples illustrate how data-driven approaches have become essential in shaping decisions related to claims management, leading to more efficient processes, improved customer experiences and enhanced fraud prevention measures.

The role of mobile applications in claims

Mobile applications have transformed various aspects of our lives, and the insurance industry is no exception. The use of mobile apps in filing and managing insurance claims has brought convenience and efficiency to policyholders and insurers alike. In this discussion, we'll explore the significant roles that mobile applications play in the process of filing and managing insurance claims.

Effortless claims filing: Mobile apps enable policyholders to file insurance claims with ease. Instead of navigating complex websites or making phone calls, users can simply open the app and follow intuitive prompts to submit their claims. This convenience reduces barriers to filing claims, ensuring that legitimate claims are reported promptly.

Immediate documentation: When an incident occurs, mobile apps allow policyholders to capture and attach photos, videos or other relevant documents directly to their claim. This documentation provides insurers with valuable evidence for assessing the claim's validity and estimating damages.

Real-time updates: Mobile apps keep policyholders informed about the status of their claims in real time. Users can track the progress of their claims, view estimated timelines for resolution and receive notifications when key milestones are reached. This transparency reduces uncertainty and anxiety associated with the claims process.

Digital communication: Mobile apps facilitate direct and instant communication between policyholders and claims adjusters. Users can exchange messages, share additional information or seek clarifications within the app. This streamlined communication accelerates the claims resolution process.

Claims tracking and history: Mobile applications allow policyholders to access their claims history and track previous and ongoing claims. This historical data can be valuable for policyholders when making decisions about coverage or for insurers when assessing risk.

Digital signatures: Mobile apps often include the capability for policyholders to provide digital signatures for required documents. This eliminates the need for physical paperwork and speeds up the claims processing timeline.

Convenient payments: In cases where a claim is approved, mobile apps facilitate secure electronic payments directly to policyholders' bank accounts. This convenience ensures that policyholders receive their settlements quickly and hassle-free.

Emergency assistance: Some insurance mobile apps offer emergency assistance features, such as roadside assistance for motor insurance. Policyholders can request immediate help in emergencies, further enhancing the value of their insurance coverage.

Policy information access: Beyond claims management, mobile apps provide access to policy information, including coverage details, premiums and policy documents. This information is readily available to users whenever they need it.

Customer feedback and improvement: Insurance companies can collect feedback from users through their mobile apps, allowing them to identify areas for improvement in their claims processes and overall customer experience.

In conclusion, mobile applications have revolutionized the way insurance claims are filed and managed. They offer policyholders convenience, transparency and real-time communication, while insurers benefit from improved efficiency and data collection. As technology continues to advance, the role of mobile apps in insurance claims is likely to expand further, enhancing the overall customer experience in the insurance industry.

Here are some examples of how mobile apps have successfully transformed the claims process in the insurance industry:

USE CASE: TRŌV'S DOCUMENT SUBMISSION VIA MOBILE APP

Trōv, a San Francisco-based digital insurance leader, has leveraged AI technology to simplify the claims process. With their mobile app, policyholders can easily submit required documents. Instead of spending money on printouts and photocopies, users can simply snap pictures of their documents using their smartphones.[5] This intuitive feature streamlines the claims documentation process and eliminates the need for physical paperwork.

USE CASE: ROOT INSURANCE'S BEHAVIOUR-BASED MOTOR INSURANCE APP

Root Insurance has made waves in the United States by revolutionizing motor insurance through its smartphone app.[6] The app tracks driving behaviours and collects data directly from users' smartphones. By analysing driving habits such as speed, braking and handling, Root Insurance determines personalized insurance rates. This data-driven approach allows policyholders to get motor insurance tailored to their driving performance, potentially leading to lower premiums for safe drivers. Root Insurance's app has transformed the way motor insurance is priced and offered, making it more individualized and fairer.

These examples demonstrate how mobile apps have enabled insurers to embrace data-driven approaches, enhance customer experiences and simplify the claims process for policyholders.

Integration with traditional systems

The integration of insurtech with traditional insurance systems has brought about a significant transformation in the way insurance claims are processed and managed. Insurtech solutions seamlessly merge with existing systems to streamline and enhance the claims process, offering benefits to both insurers and policyholders. In this discussion, we will explore how insurtech integrates with traditional insurance systems and the advantages it brings to the claims management process.

Streamlined data exchange: Insurtech platforms are designed to integrate smoothly with the existing data infrastructure of traditional insurers. This allows for seamless data exchange between the two systems. When a claim is filed, insurtech systems can access relevant policyholder information, coverage details and historical data from the traditional system. This integration minimizes data entry errors, reduces duplication of efforts and accelerates the claims assessment process.

Enhanced automation: One of the key advantages of insurtech integration is enhanced automation. Insurtech solutions utilize AI-driven algorithms and data analytics to assess claims rapidly and accurately. These technologies can validate claims against policy terms, coverage limits and historical data, all while cross-referencing with external data sources when necessary. The automation of these tasks significantly reduces manual interventions and speeds up claims processing.

Improved customer experience: Insurtech integration aims to enhance the overall customer experience during the claims process. Policyholders can file claims through user-friendly mobile apps or web interfaces, making the process more accessible and convenient. Real-time updates on claim status and automated communication keep policyholders informed and engaged. This customer-centric approach not only increases satisfaction but also fosters loyalty.

Data-driven decision-making: Insurtech systems provide valuable insights through data analytics. By integrating with traditional systems, they can access a wealth of historical claims data. This data-driven approach enables insurers to make informed decisions regarding claims settlements, fraud detection and risk assessment. Predictive analytics also play a role in proactively identifying potential issues and mitigating risks.

Efficient document management: Insurtech integration often includes digital document management. Policyholders can upload documents, photos and videos through mobile apps, eliminating the need for physical paperwork. This digital evidence submission expedites the verification process and reduces administrative burdens for both insurers and claimants.

The integration of insurtech with traditional insurance systems has revolutionized the claims process. By seamlessly merging these technologies, insurers can leverage automation, data analytics and customer-centric features to enhance efficiency, accuracy and customer satisfaction. This integration represents a fundamental shift towards a more agile and responsive insurance industry that benefits both insurers and policyholders.

Challenges in integrating new technologies with traditional systems

The integration of new technologies with traditional systems, often referred to as digital transformation, is a crucial aspect of modernizing various industries, including insurance. While this integration brings numerous benefits, it also presents challenges, particularly in the context of the insurance sector. In this discussion, we will explore the main challenges in integrating new technologies with traditional insurance systems and how these challenges are being addressed.

LEGACY SYSTEM COMPATIBILITY

Challenge: Traditional insurers often rely on legacy systems that have been in place for many years. These legacy systems may not be inherently compatible with modern technology solutions, making integration complex.

Solution: To address this challenge, insurers can opt for modular solutions that can work alongside legacy systems. APIs (Application Programming Interfaces) and middleware can bridge the gap between old and new systems, allowing data to flow seamlessly. Additionally, some insurers choose to gradually replace legacy systems with more modern alternatives over time.

DATA SECURITY AND PRIVACY

Challenge: The insurance industry handles vast amounts of sensitive customer data. Integrating new technologies can pose data security and privacy risks if not handled carefully.

Solution: To mitigate these risks, insurers must implement robust cybersecurity measures and compliance protocols. Encryption, multi-factor authentication and regular security audits are essential. Furthermore, insurers must adhere to data privacy regulations, such as GDPR in Europe, to ensure customer data is handled responsibly and transparently.

CHANGE MANAGEMENT

Challenge: Employees accustomed to traditional processes may resist or struggle with the adoption of new technologies. Change management can be a significant challenge.

Solution: Insurers should invest in comprehensive training programmes for their employees to ensure they are comfortable with the new technologies. Clear communication about the benefits of digital transformation is essential to gain buy-in from staff. In some cases, involving employees in the decision-making process can alleviate resistance.

COSTS AND ROI

Challenge: Implementing new technologies can be costly and insurers may be concerned about the return on investment (ROI) of these initiatives.

Solution: Insurers should conduct thorough cost-benefit analyses to assess the potential ROI of technology integration. They can also explore cloud-based solutions, which often have lower upfront costs and scalable pricing models. Demonstrating the long-term advantages, such as increased efficiency and customer satisfaction, can justify the initial expenses.

REGULATORY COMPLIANCE

Challenge: The insurance industry is subject to various regulatory frameworks, which can be complex and differ by region. Ensuring compliance with these regulations while integrating new technologies is challenging.

Solution: Insurers must work closely with legal and compliance teams to navigate regulatory requirements. Collaborating with technology vendors who have experience in the insurance sector and compliance expertise can simplify the process. Staying informed about evolving regulations is also crucial.

While integrating new technologies with traditional insurance systems presents challenges, these obstacles can be overcome with careful planning, strategic investments and a commitment to modernization. The insurance industry stands to gain significantly from digital transformation, including improved efficiency, enhanced customer experiences and increased competitiveness in the evolving marketplace. Addressing these challenges is essential to realize these benefits.

Future trends in insurtech and claims

The insurtech industry is poised for exciting future developments that will revolutionize claims processing. These innovations aim to enhance customer experiences, streamline operations and adapt to changing insurance preferences. Let's explore some of the predicted future developments in insurtech related to claims processing.

AI FOR SMARTER CLAIMS

Prediction: AI will play a central role in improving claims processing by expediting routing, assessment and settlements, while also enhancing the customer experience.

Explanation: AI-powered algorithms will enable quicker and more accurate claims routing by analysing claim details and directing them to the appropriate experts. Additionally, AI will facilitate personalized pricing, detect fraudulent claims and offer risk prevention recommendations. For instance, AI can automatically process and verify claims documents, significantly reducing processing times.

DIGITAL PLATFORMS AND ECOSYSTEMS

Prediction: Digital platforms will connect insurers, customers and service providers, creating seamless and integrated claims experiences.

Explanation: These platforms will offer end-to-end solutions, from quick response via mobile drones for damage assessment to access to in-network repair shops. Smart contracts on digital ecosystems will automate claims settlements based on predefined conditions, reducing disputes and expediting payouts. Such platforms will enhance transparency and reduce the need for intermediaries.

INNOVATIVE INSURANCE MODELS AND PRODUCTS

Prediction: Insurtech will introduce new insurance models and products that align with evolving customer needs, allowing for greater flexibility and customization.

Explanation: Customers will have access to innovative policies such as pay-as-you-go, pay-as-you-live and freedom-to-move insurance. These policies will enable customers to adjust their coverage and premiums based on their usage, behaviour and lifestyle changes. For example, motor insurance premiums can be based on actual driving habits monitored through telematics.

ADVANCED TECHNOLOGIES INTEGRATION

Prediction: Insurtech will integrate advanced technologies like optical character recognition (OCR), image analysis, blockchain and telematics to streamline claims processing and reduce manual interventions.

Explanation: OCR technology will extract information from documents, reducing the need for manual data entry. Image analysis, combined with mobile apps, will allow policyholders to submit claim evidence quickly through photos and videos. Blockchain will enhance security and transparency in claims records, while telematics data will provide insights for motor claims assessments, such as accident reconstruction and driver behaviour analysis.

The future of insurtech in claims processing promises a more efficient, customer-centric and technologically advanced landscape. These predicted developments will not only benefit insurers by reducing costs and improving risk management but also enhance the overall experience for policyholders, making the claims process smoother and more tailored to their evolving needs and preferences.

Emerging technologies are set to play a pivotal role in enhancing efficiency, accuracy and overall customer satisfaction. In this discussion, we will explore how these innovations are poised to transform the insurance claims landscape in the future.

- AI and machine learning:
  - Enhanced claims assessment: AI-driven algorithms will analyse claims data more comprehensively, leading to faster and more accurate claim assessments.
  - Automated claims handling: AI-powered chatbots and virtual assistants will expedite claims processing, reducing the need for manual interventions.
  - Fraud detection: AI will be crucial in identifying fraudulent claims through pattern recognition and anomaly detection.

- Telematics and IoT:
  - o Usage-based insurance: Telematics devices will continue to monitor driving behaviour, allowing insurers to offer personalized, pay-as-you-drive policies.
  - o Preventive measures: IoT devices in homes and vehicles will provide real-time data, enabling insurers to offer proactive risk mitigation services.
  - o Accurate assessment: Data from IoT devices will facilitate more precise claims assessments, reducing disputes and expediting settlements.
- Blockchain technology:
  - o Transparent transactions: Blockchain will ensure transparent and tamper-proof claims records, reducing disputes and fraud.
  - o Smart contracts: Claims processing will be automated through self-executing smart contracts, enabling faster settlements.
  - o Data security: Blockchain will enhance data security, safeguarding sensitive customer information.
- Digital platforms and ecosystems:
  - o Integrated services: Digital platforms will connect insurers, policyholders and service providers in a seamless ecosystem, offering end-to-end claims solutions.
  - o Mobile apps: User-friendly mobile apps will simplify claims reporting and provide real-time updates, improving customer experience.
  - o Efficient dommunication: Digital platforms will enhance communication between insurers and customers, fostering trust and transparency.
- Predictive analytics:
  - o Anticipatory claims handling: Predictive analytics will enable insurers to anticipate claims and proactively offer assistance or guidance to policyholders.

o Dynamic pricing: Premiums and coverage will be dynamically adjusted based on real-time data, optimizing pricing for policyholders.

o Risk prevention: Predictive insights will assist in identifying and mitigating risks before they result in claims.

As we venture into the future, these emerging technologies will not only streamline the claims process but also redefine the insurance industry's approach to customer service and risk management. The synergy between data-driven decision-making and automation will lead to a more efficient, transparent and customer-centric claims landscape, ultimately benefiting both insurers and policyholders.

Conclusion

This chapter has shed light on the transformative influence of insurtech on the insurance claims process. We've witnessed how automation, data analytics and mobile applications have revolutionized claims management, making it more efficient, transparent and customer-centric. Fraud detection has become increasingly sophisticated and the integration of insurtech with traditional systems has paved the way for a more streamlined approach.

Looking ahead, the prospects for insurtech in claims processing are promising. Emerging technologies like AI, digital platforms and predictive analytics are poised to further enhance the efficiency and personalization of claims services.

Now, as we transition to Chapter 7, we will explore how the insurance industry is actively investing in insurtech to shape the future of insurance. This investment is driving innovation, improving customer experiences and reshaping the insurance landscape in profound ways.

Notes

1 'EvolutionIQ Secures $21M to Streamline Insurance Claims Processing with AI', Insurtech Insights, 12 Apr. 2022. www.insurtechinsights.com/evolutioniq-secures-21m-to-streamline-insurance-claims-processing-with-ai/ (archived at https://perma.cc/75DW-PTMS).

2 'Four Insurtech Startups Shaking Up the Insurance Industry', Forbes, 9 Jul. 2019. www.forbes.com/sites/alisoncoleman/2019/07/09/four-insurtech-startups-shaking-up-the-insurance-industry/ (archived at https://perma.cc/RTY2-EE8W).

3 'Snapsheet Secures Strategic Investment from State Farm Ventures, Fueling Digital Innovation in Claims', PR Newswire, 18 Jul. 2023. www.prnewswire.com/news-releases/snapsheet-secures-strategic-investment-from-state-farm-ventures-fueling-digital-innovation-in-claims-301878914.html (archived at https://perma.cc/SUP6-HRHR).

4 'Alan Raises $220 Million for its Health Insurance and Healthcare Superapp', Alan, 19 Apr. 2021. techcrunch.com/2021/04/19/alan-raises-220-million-for-its-health-insurance-and-healthcare-super-app/ (archived at https://perma.cc/YA25-5QTR).

5 '5+ Insurtech Marketing Techniques | Disruptive Technologies for ...', colorwhistle, 17 Jul. 2023. colorwhistle.com/insurtech-marketing-techniques/ (archived at https://perma.cc/GW5E-PMFL).

6 '5+ Insurtech Marketing Techniques | Disruptive Technologies for ...', colorwhistle, 17 Jul. 2023. colorwhistle.com/insurtech-marketing-techniques/ (archived at https://perma.cc/9AF7-2ZLV).

7

Investing in insurtech

Introduction

As a founder navigating the ever-evolving landscape of insurtech, my journey to secure vital investment capital for Tapoly proved to be both enlightening and arduous. In this chapter I share my experiences and the strategies I deployed, which not only facilitated the acquisition of the necessary funding for Tapoly but also shaped the course of our company.

One of the first challenges I encountered was the high level of competition in the insurtech industry. There are currently 3,475 insurtech companies operating worldwide, with over 1,500 new ones entering the market in the last five years, according to the Porch 2021 Report. This means there are a lot of innovative start-ups all trying to get the attention of potential investors, which also leads to more investment in the industry. As a 2021 McKinsey report pointed out, global investment in insurtech exceeded $11 billion in 2021.[1]

Standing out in this crowded field requires more than just a great idea. You need to create a compelling story about your business. In my experience, showing our idea actually worked and was gaining traction was a big challenge, especially since we were one of the first in this new area. This made it more difficult to prove that our product was what customers wanted.

One of the invaluable lessons I learned early in this journey was the significance of recognition and credibility. In the fiercely competitive landscape, capturing investor attention hinged on establishing Tapoly as an award-winning enterprise. We relentlessly worked towards creating a product and service that garnered accolades, effectively setting us apart as a preferred choice for potential investors and bolstering our reputation.

Financial considerations for insurtech

When launching an insurtech start-up, financial planning is crucial. Your funding needs can differ greatly based on your role in the value chain. For ventures concentrating on technology development, substantial capital is often essential. Creating tech solutions usually demands significant time, potentially ranging from several years to even decades, to effectively introduce your product to the market. Additionally, the process of developing a tech platform tends to involve considerable expenses. This is primarily due to the significant time and financial investments required for hiring tech talent and assembling your team. Moreover, if your venture delves into deep tech such as AI or quantum computing, the lead time to market and realize commercialization timeline may stretch over a couple of decades before you begin generating revenue.[2]

On the other hand, if your emphasis is on distribution, you may have the opportunity to demonstrate traction and generate sales more quickly. However, it's important to note that if you operate as a digital managing general agent (MGA), you might need to allocate additional time for product development and gain approval from insurers. This process, along with the time required for regulatory licensing by financial authorities, adds to the overall financial considerations when founding your Insurtech business.

If your business combines both technology and distribution, you'll need extra capital to effectively manage these dual operations. These two components have completely different revenue models, expenses and timeframes for market entry and are subject to distinct regulations. Moreover, the diverse tax rules and benefits can add complexity to your business story when seeking investments and fundraising opportunities.

Cultural disparities in investment

Drawing from my personal experience in securing international investments, it's clear that the investment culture in the UK diverges significantly from that in other regions. In the United States, investors tend to be less risk averse, readily allocating capital at an early stage with the expectation of substantial returns. In contrast, the UK and Europe lean towards a more cautious approach, where investors often seek incentives like government sponsorship programmes and tax relief schemes such as SEIS/EIS in the UK to encourage participation in early-stage ventures.

SEIS and EIS exemplify two prominent UK government initiatives aimed at fostering investment in small and medium-sized businesses. The Seed Enterprise Investment Scheme (SEIS) and Enterprise Investment Scheme (EIS) offer tax relief incentives to individual investors who acquire new shares in eligible companies. Similar programmes can be found in numerous other countries, all geared towards stimulating investment in start-ups and nurturing entrepreneurial growth.

Moreover, the United States boasts a more mature and vibrant start-up ecosystem that supports companies from their inception to post-exit stages. This comprehensive support structure has contributed to the United States becoming home to a significant number of insurtech unicorns, setting an example for other regions seeking to foster similar success stories. Subsequently, other prominent locations include the United Kingdom with 313 companies, Germany with 130 and Canada with 122.[3]

The statistics reveal a strong correlation between the prevailing culture, the robustness of the start-up ecosystem, government tax incentives and support, as well as insurance expertise with the number of insurtech start-ups that can successfully enter the international market and achieve unicorn status. It's important to emphasize that the investment ecosystem in the United States is not only more mature but also larger, providing substantial support for international expansion and business growth. These factors collectively contribute to the higher presence of unicorns in the region.

The global tapestry of insurtech investments:
Unravelling regional nuances

As we venture further into the realm of insurtech investments, it is clear that these financial endeavours take on distinct regional flavours, each characterized by its unique set of challenges and opportunities. In this section, we explore the global landscape of insurtech investments and decipher the unique characteristics that define these investments in various regions. Additionally, we will delve into the world of unicorn insurtech companies and examine case studies of start-ups that have successfully navigated through different funding stages, achieving remarkable growth.

North America: The epicentre of innovation

North America, particularly the United States, stands as a true epicentre of innovation in the insurtech realm. With a staggering 1,370 insurtech companies, the United States boasts an impressive 44 per cent share of the global insurtech market. This dominance is driven by a fiercely competitive market environment and a robust entrepreneurial spirit that characterizes the region.

What sets the United States apart is not only its attractive market but also its insatiable demand. Here, a potent blend of venture capital, entrepreneurial zeal and unwavering commitment to technological progress fuels a continuous stream of investments.

The United States has maintained a thriving ecosystem marked by robust investment inflows, with Silicon Valley serving as a renowned hub for insurtech innovation and significant venture capital. Regulatory frameworks and consumer behaviours in North America influence distinctive investment dynamics, aligning with the optimistic outlook for insurtech outcomes.

In this landscape, health insurance-related insurtechs take centre stage, drawn by the vast market opportunity and the resistance to disruption by health sector incumbents. The global health insurance market's substantial growth, particularly in the American market, makes it an attractive space for insurtechs. However, the deeply entrenched and resistant nature of the US health sector demands substantial financial backing to compete with established players.

Three notable case studies illustrate the success and impact of American health sector insurtechs:

Case study – Oscar Health: Founded in New York in 2012, Oscar Health has redefined American healthcare with its member-centric approach. The company's dedication to simplifying health insurance through innovative digital tools, mobile apps and telemedicine services has led to substantial investments totalling $1.6 billion. Oscar Health achieved a remarkable valuation of $9.5 billion during its IPO in March 2021 and now serves 250,000 customers across nine states.

Case study – Bright Health: Established in 2015, Bright Health has emerged as a transformative force in American healthcare, focusing on seamless and transparent healthcare experiences. Their strategic partnerships with healthcare providers have attracted over $1.5 billion in investments. Bright Health's successful IPO in June 2021 valued the company at approximately $12 billion, positioning it as a key player in the industry.

Case study – Clover Health: Clover Health, founded in 2014, addresses the complexities of the American healthcare system with data-driven, personalized health insurance experiences. With investments totalling $925 million, Clover Health's commitment to leveraging data-driven approaches culminated in a SPAC merger in January 2021, valuing the company at approximately $3.7 billion. This milestone underscores Clover Health's dedication to enhancing healthcare accessibility and quality through technology-driven solutions.

North America, led by the United States, remains at the forefront of insurtech innovation and investment. The region's vibrant ecosystem, characterized by relentless innovation and substantial funding, continues to reshape the insurance landscape, with a particular focus on health insurance-related insurtechs. These companies are not only making significant strides in enhancing healthcare experiences but also attracting considerable investments, reaffirming their potential to drive positive change in the industry.

Europe: A diverse spectrum of investments

Europe's insurtech landscape contains diverse insurance markets, regulatory landscapes and consumer behaviours. The continent offers a range of investment opportunities, from established insurance markets in Western Europe to emerging insurtech hubs in the East. Europe's insurtech ecosystem benefits from a wealth of knowledge influenced by the Lloyd's of London market.

Three notable case studies highlight Europe's insurtech innovation:

Case study – ManyPets (formerly Bought by Many): Based in the UK, ManyPets revolutionized pet insurance with online, form-free claims and streamlined payment processes. They secured significant investments, raising nearly $500 million and achieving a valuation exceeding $2 billion by June 2021.

Case study – Alan: A digital health insurance pioneer in France, Alan aimed to address healthcare inefficiencies. They raised over $550 million and reached a valuation of €2.7 billion ($2.69 billion) in May 2022, emphasizing their commitment to transforming healthcare.

Case study – Wefox: Operating from Berlin, Wefox aimed to disrupt the insurance industry. They secured substantial funding, with a Series D round of $400 million and reached a milestone of 2 million customers.

These case studies exemplify Europe's dynamic and diverse insurtech landscape, offering a glimpse into the multitude of investment opportunities it holds. Europe continues to foster insurtech innovation and disruption, making it an exciting frontier for investors and entrepreneurs poised to shape the future of the insurance industry across the continent and beyond, drawing from the rich history and expertise influenced by the historic Lloyd's of London market.

Asia-Pacific: A dynamic investment arena

The Asia-Pacific region offers a dynamic and diverse landscape for insurtech investments, with varying levels of technology adoption and complex regulatory frameworks. Some countries in the region embrace insurtech enthusiastically, while others proceed cautiously in integrating technology into their insurance markets. The region is particularly notable for its significant markets, such as China's expansive offerings in health, life and property insurance, and India's rapidly growing sector.

Three notable case studies highlight the diversity and growth in the Asia-Pacific insurtech landscape: specific to life, motor and health care.

Case study – Digit Insurance (India): Founded in 2017, Digit Insurance has rapidly grown to a valuation of $3.5 billion in just five years. It caters to previously uninsured Indian customers, offering motor, travel and health insurance coverage. With substantial fundraising and plans for an IPO, Digit Insurance exemplifies the insurtech boom in India.

Case study – bolttech (Singapore): Established in 2020, bolttech operates an AI-based ecosystem connecting insurance providers and distributors globally. With a valuation of $1 billion, it serves 7.7 million customers and transacts over $5 billion worth of premiums, reshaping insurance distribution on a global scale.

Case study – ZhongAn (China): Founded in 2013, ZhongAn is China's largest online insurance company with a diverse range of ecosystem-oriented insurance products. With a valuation of $5.169 billion, it serves over 524 million clients and underwrites billions of policies, showcasing its significant presence and impact in China's insurtech sector.

In summary, insurtech investments vary across regions, reflecting the unique characteristics, regulatory environments and consumer behaviours in each area. Understanding these regional nuances is essential to unlocking the full potential of insurtech investments in the insurance sector's transformation.

Key factors influencing investment decisions

Investors in the insurtech realm prioritize one fundamental aspect: a solid return on investment (ROI). They are inclined to invest in insurtech companies that demonstrate the potential for substantial ROI. To secure their desired returns, investors seek insurtech solutions that effectively address critical issues faced by target customers. As outlined in Chapter 1, insurtech emerges to tackle fundamental challenges and gaps in the insurance industry, including evolving customer expectations, enhancing operational efficiency, driving product innovation and improving risk management.

Investors exhibit a distinct preference for certain types of insurtech companies due to the inherent advantages and growth prospects these categories offer. Here's why these specific value insurtech prepositions often rank high in investor preference:

Deep technology: Investors show keen interest in insurtech companies that harness cutting-edge technologies like artificial intelligence, machine learning, data analytics and blockchain. These technologies empower companies to optimize their operational efficiency, reduce costs and elevate customer experiences. Such enhancements often translate into higher profitability and increased competitiveness in the market, making these companies particularly enticing for investors.

Digital distribution platforms: Insurtech companies that provide digital distribution platforms are favoured by investors because they simplify the insurance purchasing process for customers. These platforms enhance customer acquisition and retention rates, a factor highly appreciated by investors. The transparency and convenience they offer can lead to increased policy sales, presenting a compelling proposition for investors.

Data analytics and predictive modelling: Investors are drawn to insurtech firms specializing in data analytics and predictive modelling. These companies possess the capability to analyse extensive datasets for precise risk assessment and competitive policy pricing. Investors value this predictive capability, recognizing its potential to significantly enhance profitability and risk management within the insurance industry.

Claims automation: Insurtech start-ups that focus on automating claims processing through technologies like artificial intelligence and computer vision are highly attractive to investors. Streamlining claims settlements not only leads to improved customer satisfaction but also reduces operational costs for insurance companies. Investors recognize the potential for significant cost savings and improved efficiency, making these start-ups an attractive investment opportunity.

Customer engagement solutions: Companies offering solutions to boost customer engagement and communication in the insurance sector are well regarded by investors. Enhanced customer engagement often translates into higher policy retention rates and increased opportunities for cross-selling additional products. Investors acknowledge the value of these improved customer relationships.

Specialized insurance segments: Investors are intrigued by insurtechs targeting specialized insurance segments, such as cyber insurance, pet insurance or parametric insurance. These niche markets present opportunities for rapid growth and reduced competition, factors that appeal to investors seeking high potential returns.

Global expansion potential: Insurtech companies with global expansion potential and scalability are particularly appealing to investors. Investors seeking substantial growth opportunities beyond initial markets are attracted to insurtechs capable of expanding their reach and adapting to different regions.

Track record and growth: Investors favour insurtech firms with a proven track record of growth, customer acquisition and revenue generation. Demonstrated scalability and profitability are key indicators of a company's attractiveness to investors.

Investors gravitate towards specific insurtech categories because they recognize the inherent advantages and growth opportunities these companies offer. The alignment of these insurtechs with technological trends, market demand and profitability potential makes them attractive investment prospects for savvy investors.

Successful insurtech use cases and key investors

Insurtech, a dynamic sector that employs technology to revolutionize the insurance industry, garners substantial investments from various sources. Below is a list of ten successful insurtech use cases, along with key investors involved:

Root: Root, a US-based insurtech, offers personalized motor insurance based on driving behaviour. Utilizing telematics, AI and mobile technology, it rewards safe drivers with lower rates. In its IPO in October 2020, Root raised $724 million, with investors including Drive Capital, Ribbit Capital and Tiger Global Management.

Hippo: US-based Hippo offers home insurance integrated with smart home devices and proactive protection. Utilizing IoT, AI and big data, it monitors and mitigates risks, reducing claims costs and enhancing customer satisfaction. In a SPAC merger with Reinvent Technology Partners Z in July 2021, Hippo secured $350 million, with investors like Dragoneer Investment Group, Lennar Corporation and Mitsui Sumitomo Insurance.

Next Insurance: Next Insurance, also based in the US, specializes in tailored and affordable insurance for small businesses. It simplifies and streamlines the insurance process for small business owners using online platforms, AI and automation. Next Insurance raised $250 million in its Series D round in September 2020, with investors including CapitalG, Munich Re Ventures and FinTLV Ventures.

Wefox: Wefox, headquartered in Germany, operates a digital platform for insurance distribution and management. It connects customers, brokers and insurers through an integrated marketplace offering personalized and transparent products and services. In June 2021, Wefox secured $650 million in its Series C round, with investors such as Target Global, OMERS Ventures and Salesforce Ventures.

Zego: Zego, based in the UK, provides flexible, usage-based insurance for gig workers and fleets. Leveraging telematics, IoT and mobile technology, it offers customized, pay-per-mile coverage for drivers and riders. Zego raised $150 million in its Series C round in March 2021, with investors including DST Global, General Catalyst and TransferWise.

Alan: Alan, a France-based insurtech, offers health insurance and healthcare services for individuals and businesses. Utilizing digital platforms, AI and data science, it provides straightforward pricing, claims processing and benefits. In April 2021, Alan secured €185 million in its Series D round, with investors like Coatue Management, Dragoneer Investment Group and Index Ventures.

Waterdrop: Waterdrop, headquartered in China, operates an online platform for mutual aid, crowdfunding and insurance. It employs social media, blockchain and big data to provide affordable healthcare financing solutions for millions of Chinese people. In May 2021, Waterdrop raised $360 million in its IPO, with investors including Tencent Holdings, Boyu Capital and Swiss Re.

PolicyBazaar: PolicyBazaar, an India-based insurtech, runs an online marketplace for insurance comparison and purchase. Utilizing web aggregators, chatbots and analytics, it offers unbiased and transparent information on various insurance products from different insurers. In November 2021, PolicyBazaar raised $870 million in its IPO, with investors like SoftBank Vision Fund II, Temasek Holdings, Info Edge (India) Ltd and numerous others.

Diversity, equity and inclusion (DEI) consideration

DEI is not just a matter of social responsibility; it's a strategic choice for investors. Companies that prioritize DEI tend to outperform peers in various aspects, including profitability, innovation and talent retention. A diverse and inclusive workplace is also better equipped to navigate changing market conditions.

DEI plays a pivotal role in the ongoing transformation of the insurance industry. Diverse perspectives are essential to driving innovation in this sector, leading to more customer-centric solutions. In the insurtech sector, DEI helps mitigate risks associated with narrow perspectives in risk assessment. Biases in underwriting, claims processing and pricing can be reduced through DEI, minimizing the risk of financial losses. It also ensures that insurtech companies effectively cater to diverse customer bases. Tailoring products and services to under-represented communities can lead to market expansion and increased market share. In addition, DEI-driven companies tend to be more resilient and are viewed favourably by socially conscious investors. It aligns with ethical investment values and enhances a company's reputation and sustainability.

DEI is a strategic imperative. Its adoption not only improves business performance but also fosters innovation, expands market reach and contributes to positive social impact. For investors, integrating DEI into their investment strategies aligns with long-term sustainability and ethical considerations while presenting significant opportunities for growth.

Include DEI KPIs in insurtech

Incorporating DEI key performance indicators (KPIs) within insurtech operations is a forward-looking approach that not only aligns with ethical values but can also drive long-term sustainability and profitability in the industry. Here's a step-by-step guide tailored to the insurtech perspective:

Recognize the relevance of DEI in insurtech: Start by understanding why DEI is essential in the insurtech sector. DEI can enhance customer understanding, reduce biases in decision-making, attract top talent and protect your company's reputation.

Select DEI-focused business strategies: Embrace business strategies that prioritize diversity, equity and inclusion. This may involve fostering a diverse workforce, fostering an inclusive company culture or developing products and services tailored to underserved markets.

Review and enhance DEI policies and initiatives: Evaluate your company's existing DEI policies and initiatives. Consider factors such as the diversity of your team, pay equity practices, anti-discrimination measures and community engagement efforts. Ensure they align with your DEI goals.

Integrate DEI metrics into operational practices: As part of your day-to-day operations, incorporate DEI metrics and measurements. Gather data on employee demographics, turnover rates, the effectiveness of diversity training programmes and the impact of inclusion efforts.

Set measurable DEI objectives: Collaborate with your leadership team to establish clear and quantifiable DEI performance objectives. These goals may include increasing diversity in leadership positions, reducing pay disparities or launching initiatives to engage with under-represented communities.

Monitor and report on DEI progress: Continuously track your insurtech company's progress toward achieving its DEI objectives. Regularly report on DEI KPIs to maintain transparency and accountability within your organization.

Promote DEI industry-wide: Engage with the broader insurtech community to advocate for DEI principles. Participate in industry discussions, conferences and collaborations that focus on diversity and inclusion. Partner with other insurtech leaders and industry associations to drive change.

Adopt a long-term perspective: Recognize that the full impact of DEI initiatives may take time to materialize. Stay committed to the long-term success of your DEI-focused insurtech operations.

Evaluate financial and DEI performance concurrently: Continuously assess your financial performance alongside your progress in achieving DEI goals. Ensure that DEI initiatives are not only viewed as ethical responsibilities but also as drivers of business growth.

By integrating DEI KPIs into your insurtech operations, you can contribute to a more inclusive industry while potentially improving your company's financial performance and resilience over the long run. Remember that each insurtech operation may require a tailored approach, and active engagement with your workforce and stakeholders is critical for success.

ESG (environmental, social and governance) consideration

ESG considerations are increasingly important for insurtech companies seeking investment for several key reasons:[4]

Attracting ethical and impactful investors: Many investors, including institutional funds and venture capital firms, are prioritizing ESG-aligned investments. Insurtech companies that can demonstrate a commitment to sustainable and ethical business practices are more likely to attract capital from these investors. ESG-focused investors are often interested in supporting businesses that align with their values and contribute positively to society and the environment.

Mitigating investment risks: ESG factors can directly impact an insurtech company's risk profile. For example, failing to address environmental risks related to climate change or social risks related to fair labour practices can lead to operational, legal and reputational risks that may negatively affect the company's financial performance and its attractiveness to investors. By proactively addressing ESG risks, insurtech firms can enhance their investment appeal.

Meeting regulatory and market expectations: Regulatory bodies and market stakeholders are increasingly emphasizing ESG disclosure and reporting. Insurtech companies that align with these expectations are better positioned to navigate regulatory requirements and respond to market demands. Compliance with ESG-related regulations and standards is crucial for maintaining investor confidence and avoiding legal issues.

Enhancing reputation and differentiation: An insurtech company with a strong ESG focus can stand out in a competitive market. It can use its commitment to sustainability, ethical practices and societal impact as a differentiator, attracting customers, partners and investors who value ESG-aligned businesses. A positive reputation can lead to increased brand loyalty and investor interest.

Long-term sustainability: ESG considerations are closely linked to the long-term sustainability and resilience of insurtech businesses. Addressing environmental and social issues, such as climate change or customer data privacy, can help insurtech firms adapt to evolving market conditions, customer preferences and regulatory changes, ensuring their continued success.

Access to impact investment funds: Some insurtech companies may seek funding from impact investment funds, which specifically target businesses that generate positive social and environmental impacts alongside financial returns. Aligning with ESG principles can open doors to these impact-focused funding sources, expanding the pool of potential investors.

Risk mitigation for investors: ESG-focused companies are often seen as better equipped to manage risks associated with environmental and social factors. Investors may view ESG-aligned insurtech firms as more resilient and capable of addressing emerging risks, which can reduce their own investment risks.

Talent attraction: Companies that prioritize ESG values tend to attract employees who are passionate about environmental and social causes. Having a strong ESG orientation can help insurtech companies attract and retain top talent, fostering innovation and growth.

ESG considerations are important for insurtech companies seeking investment because they can help attract ethical and impactful investors, mitigate investment risks, meet regulatory and market expectations, enhance reputation and differentiation, ensure long-term sustainability, access impact investment funds, reduce risk for investors and attract top talent. Insurtech firms that embrace ESG principles are better positioned to secure investment and thrive in a socially conscious and competitive investment landscape.

Incorporate ESG into insurtech operation

Incorporating ESG principles into insurtech operations involves several key steps:

Assessment: Begin by assessing your current operations to identify areas where ESG considerations can be integrated. This includes evaluating environmental impact, social responsibility and governance practices.

Define ESG objectives: Clearly define your ESG objectives and goals. Determine what environmental initiatives you can undertake, how you can contribute to social causes and how you can improve governance within your organization. ESG principles are increasingly utilized by investors and stakeholders to evaluate a company's sustainability and ethical impact. These ESG values align with the United Nations Sustainable Development Goals (SDGs), which comprise 17 objectives aimed at creating a more sustainable and improved global future by 2030.

Integration into products and services: Incorporate ESG criteria into your insurtech products and services. Consider offering insurance products that address environmental risks (e.g. climate-related coverage), support social causes (e.g. inclusive policies) and adhere to strong governance principles (e.g. transparency in underwriting).

Risk assessment: Assess the impact of ESG factors on your risk profile. Understand how environmental events (e.g. natural disasters), social trends (e.g. changing demographics) and governance practices (e.g. compliance with regulations) affect your business.

Data and technology: Leverage data and technology to support ESG integration. Use data analytics to assess and mitigate environmental and social risks. Implement technologies that improve governance, transparency and reporting.

Stakeholder engagement: Engage with stakeholders, including customers, investors, employees and regulators, to understand their ESG expectations and concerns. Consider their feedback in shaping your ESG strategy.

Reporting and transparency: Establish robust reporting mechanisms to disclose your ESG efforts and performance. Transparency is essential in demonstrating your commitment to ESG to investors and customers.

Training and culture: Foster an ESG-focused culture within your organization. Provide training and awareness programmes for employees to ensure everyone understands and supports ESG goals.

Partnerships: Collaborate with organizations, NGOs or other insurtechs that share similar ESG values. Partnerships can amplify your impact and expand your reach.

Compliance: Stay updated on ESG regulations and standards in your region and industry. Ensure compliance with reporting requirements and adapt your operations as needed.

Continuous improvement: ESG integration is an ongoing process. Regularly review and refine your ESG strategy based on performance, changing market dynamics and stakeholder feedback.

Incorporating ESG into insurtech operations not only aligns your business with sustainability and ethical principles but can also enhance your attractiveness to investors, customers and partners who prioritize ESG considerations.

Funding insurtech

In the insurtech start-up landscape, various investment types are linked to different stages of funding. Here's a breakdown of the primary investment categories and their associated stages:

SEED INVESTMENT

Angel investors: Typically individual investors offering funds from $10,000 to $500,000 in exchange for equity. They often bring industry knowledge and can provide vital advice. To connect with them, explore local angel investor groups, participate in pitch events or use online platforms such as AngelList.

Start-up incubators and accelerators: These programmes offer funding, mentorship and resources. They are great for networking with potential investors. Prominent examples include Y Combinator, Techstars and 500 Startups. It's important to choose a programme that aligns with your industry focus and development stage.

EARLY-STAGE INVESTMENT

Venture capital (VC) firms: These firms usually invest between $1 million and $10 million. They are professional outfits managing funds from various sources and specialize in supporting start-ups and early-stage companies. Research VC firms that have a focus on your industry and development stage.

Corporate venture arms and strategic partners: These entities, often part of larger corporations, typically provide funding in the range of $500,000 to $5 million.

Online investment platforms: Platforms like Kickstarter, Indiegogo (for crowdfunding) or Crowdcube and Seedrs (for equity crowdfunding) can be effective for raising funds from a broad base of individual investors.

LATE-STAGE INVESTMENT

Growth equity funds: These funds often invest in the range of $10 million to $50 million.

Private equity firms and sovereign wealth funds: These firms usually deal with larger investments, typically ranging from $50 million to $100 million. Sovereign wealth funds, owned by governments, also fall into this category with similar investment ranges.

IPO (INITIAL PUBLIC OFFERING) STAGE

Public investors: In an IPO, general public investors purchase shares, usually involving investments of $100 million or more.

The amounts mentioned are indicative ranges and can vary depending on specific conditions, the start-up's developmental stage and the company valuation. Selecting the right investment category and securing suitable funding is vital for the growth and success of insurtech start-ups.

Securing investor meetings

Identifying where to find investors is a critical step for entrepreneurs. Here are some effective strategies to consider when seeking potential investors:

Networking events: Participate in industry-specific conferences, seminars and networking gatherings. These are excellent venues to connect with potential investors, establish relationships and present your business idea.

Join industry associations: Become a member of relevant industry associations or chambers of commerce. They often have direct links to investors and offer valuable networking opportunities.

Engage with local start-up communities: Immerse yourself in your local entrepreneurial scene. Attend start-up meet-ups, engage with co-working spaces and participate in local start-up events to find investor connections.

Leverage online networking platforms: Utilize platforms like LinkedIn to connect with potential investors. Engaging in group discussions and networking online can broaden your reach.

Start-up competitions and pitch events: Enter competitions and pitch events designed for start-ups. These events can draw the attention of investors, whether you win or simply participate.

Seek mentors and advisors: Connect with experienced mentors and advisors who have investor networks. Their guidance and introductions can be invaluable.

Friends and family: Consider initial funding from friends and family who support your vision. Ensure transparency about risks and formalize any agreements.

Corporate partnerships: Look for partnership opportunities with larger corporations in your industry. Many have venture arms or innovation programmes investing in start-ups.

Government funding: Explore government grants, subsidies and programmes designed to support start-ups, offering non-dilutive funding options.

Pitch competitions and demo days: Participate in these events hosted by various institutions like universities or accelerators. These platforms can significantly raise your visibility among investors.

Online research platforms: Use resources like Crunchbase, PitchBook or CB Insights to research potential investors and their investment patterns.

Consult professional advisors: Engage with legal, financial and business advisors familiar with the start-up ecosystem. They can offer introductions or advice on connecting with investors.

When seeking investors, remember that the right fit is crucial. Aim for investors who share your vision and understand your industry and growth stage. A strong relationship and a persuasive pitch are key to attracting the ideal investors for your start-up's success.

Evaluating insurtech: Key advice for founders

As a founder in the insurtech sector seeking investment, it's critical to understand investor expectations and present your start-up effectively. Here's an expanded guide to assist you in this endeavour:

Comprehensive market analysis: Develop a deep understanding of your specific insurtech market segment. Research its dynamics, key challenges and emerging opportunities. Demonstrating this knowledge will show investors your ability to navigate and capitalize on market conditions.

Navigating the regulatory environment: Stay informed about the regulatory landscape in all your operational regions. Understanding compliance requirements and demonstrating adaptability to regulatory changes can significantly increase investor confidence.

Robust technology infrastructure: Your technology should not only be innovative but also scalable and secure. Emphasize robust data privacy and security measures in place, as these are critical concerns in the insurance sector.

Customer acquisition and sustainability: Evaluate and present your customer acquisition strategies and costs. It's important to align these with your funding requirements and long-term business plans, demonstrating a sustainable growth trajectory.

Detailed competitive landscape analysis: Clearly identify your key competitors and articulate what differentiates your start-up – be it a unique value proposition, technological edge or innovative service model.

Team composition and expertise: Highlight the strengths of your team, emphasizing their industry experience and diverse skill sets. Show how this collective expertise contributes to innovative solutions and problem-solving.

Business model clarity: If your business model is complex or dual in nature, explain it coherently. Investors need to understand how each aspect contributes to your overall strategy and success.

Strategic alliances and partnerships: Showcase any strategic partnerships or alliances that expand your market reach, enhance your resource pool or provide competitive advantages.

Clear exit strategy: Outline potential exit strategies, whether it's acquisition, an IPO or another route. This should align with your long-term business objectives and provide a clear trajectory for potential investors.

Risk management and mitigation: Acknowledge specific risks associated with the insurtech domain, from regulatory challenges to evolving market dynamics. Demonstrating a proactive approach to risk management will be key.

Preparation for due diligence: Have comprehensive due diligence materials ready, including detailed financials, legal documentation, customer testimonials and third-party evaluations. This preparation demonstrates your seriousness and professionalism.

Innovation and adaptability: Emphasize your start-up's innovative aspects and its adaptability to changing market and technological landscapes. Investors are often attracted to companies that show potential for growth and flexibility in dynamic environments.

Growth metrics and projections: Present clear and realistic growth metrics and projections. This should include user acquisition rates, revenue forecasts and scalability plans, providing a clear picture of your start-up's potential for success.

By addressing these key areas effectively, insurtech founders can significantly enhance their appeal to potential investors, positioning their start-ups for success in a highly competitive and evolving industry.

Investment tips for founders

Securing investment is a vital aspect of driving growth for insurtech start-ups. To navigate this challenging landscape successfully, here are comprehensive tips to enhance your fundraising efforts:

Align with investor profiles: Tailor your pitch to align with the specific preferences of potential investors. Whether they have a penchant for B2B models, early-stage start-ups or particular insurtech niches, understanding their investment focus is crucial.

Identifying the right investors: Look for investors who not only provide financial backing but also bring valuable industry expertise and a collaborative mindset to the table. Their experience in the insurtech sector can be a game-changer for your start-up.

Leveraging networking opportunities: Actively engage in industry events, seminars and networking gatherings. These are prime venues to meet potential investors, establish connections and showcase your business idea.

Developing a compelling pitch: Construct a clear, engaging pitch that effectively highlights your start-up's unique value proposition. Focus on articulating the market opportunity, scalability potential and how your solution addresses specific pain points in the insurtech domain.

Evidence of traction: Present solid proof of your start-up's progress. This can include metrics on customer acquisition, revenue growth, successful pilot projects or strategic partnerships that demonstrate market validation and potential for future growth.

Financial expertise: Be adept with your finances. This includes being able to project future revenues and expenses, showcasing a path to profitability and understanding your burn rate.

Showcasing a robust team: Emphasize the strengths of your team, highlighting their industry experience, technical expertise and dedication. Investors often bet on teams, so showing a well-rounded and capable team is key.

Ready for due diligence: Organize all necessary documentation and data for the due diligence process. Be prepared to substantiate your business model, market potential and operational capabilities.

Understanding valuation realities: Approach valuation discussions with a well-informed perspective, understanding current market trends and being prepared for realistic and sometimes tough negotiations.

Diversifying funding sources: Consider various funding avenues – from angel investors to venture capital, crowdfunding and strategic partnerships. This approach can help reduce reliance on a single source and potentially bring in a broader range of expertise and networks.

Regulatory compliance and legal framework: Ensure that your start-up adheres to all relevant legal and regulatory requirements. In the insurtech sector, compliance is particularly crucial given the stringent regulatory environment.

Warm introductions and networking: Utilize your personal and professional networks for introductions to potential investors. A referral or introduction from a trusted source can significantly enhance the credibility of your pitch.

Consistent follow-up: Keep the lines of communication open with potential investors after initial meetings. Prompt follow-ups indicate professionalism and a serious commitment to your venture.

Staying resilient in fundraising: Maintain persistence in your fundraising journey. Rejection is common; what matters is your ability to refine your approach continuously and explore new avenues.

Understanding diverse investor timelines: Recognize that each investor operates on different timelines for decision-making. Patience and flexibility are key during this process.

Mentorship and advisory: Seek insights and advice from experienced mentors or advisors in the start-up ecosystem. Their guidance can be invaluable in refining your pitch and strategy.

Pitch perfection through practice: Repeatedly rehearse your pitch to ensure a confident and polished presentation. Being prepared for any question or challenge during the pitch is crucial.

Value-added investors: Look beyond the capital. Investors who can offer mentorship, industry connections and strategic insights can provide immense value.

Commitment beyond immediate investment: Stay committed to the long-term vision of your start-up. Securing investment is just one step in the journey; sustaining and growing your business is the ongoing challenge.

Barrier to entry in the insurtech industry

The barrier to entry in the insurtech industry can be considered relatively high compared to some other industries. Several factors contribute to this higher barrier. The insurance industry is heavily regulated in most countries to protect consumers and ensure financial stability. Navigating these regulations, obtaining the necessary licences and meeting capital requirements can be time-consuming and expensive.

Starting an insurtech company often requires a significant amount of capital to cover potential claims and maintain financial stability. This capital requirement can be substantial compared to many other tech-based start-ups.

Insurtech companies need a deep understanding of the insurance industry, including underwriting, risk management and pricing. Building this expertise takes time and often requires partnerships with experienced professionals.

Insurtech relies heavily on advanced technologies like artificial intelligence and data analytics. Developing and implementing these technologies effectively can be challenging and may require substantial investment.

Trust is crucial in the insurance industry, and new insurtech start-ups must work to gain the trust of potential policyholders, which can be a time-consuming process.

The insurtech sector has become increasingly competitive, with numerous start-ups and established insurers entering the space. Standing out and gaining market share can be challenging.

However, it's important to note that the barrier to entry can vary within the insurtech sector itself. Some insurtech start-ups focus on niche markets or specific insurance products, which may have lower barriers compared to those aiming for broader market penetration.

Overall, while the barrier to entry in insurtech is relatively high due to regulatory, capital and expertise requirements, it's not necessarily higher than other heavily regulated industries like banking or healthcare. Success in the insurtech industry often depends on innovation, strategic partnerships and the ability to address specific pain points within the insurance ecosystem.

Valuation metrics and multiples for insurtech companies

Valuation multiples for insurtech companies can vary widely based on several factors, including the company's growth prospects, financial performance, competitive positioning and the overall market conditions. Here are some common valuation metrics and multiples used in the insurtech industry:

Revenue multiple: This multiple is calculated by dividing the company's total revenue by its valuation. The revenue multiple can vary significantly, with early-stage start-ups often commanding lower multiples than more established companies. Typical revenue multiples for insurtechs can range from 2× to 5× or higher, depending on growth and profitability.

Earnings before interest, taxes, depreciation and amortization (EBITDA) multiple: EBITDA is a measure of a company's operating profitability. The EBITDA multiple is calculated by dividing a company's EBITDA by its valuation. Insurtech companies with strong profitability and growth potential may command higher EBITDA multiples, often ranging from 5× to 10× or more.

Price-to-sales (P/S) ratio: The P/S ratio compares a company's market capitalization (or valuation) to its total revenue. This ratio is commonly used for high-growth technology companies, including insurtechs. A P/S ratio of 5× to 10× or higher is not uncommon for fast-growing insurtech start-ups.

Price-to-earnings (P/E) ratio: The P/E ratio compares a company's stock price to its earnings per share (EPS). While insurtech start-ups may not always have positive earnings, more mature companies in the sector may use this metric. P/E ratios can vary widely, but technology-focused insurtechs may have higher P/E ratios than traditional insurers.

Book value multiple: The book value multiple compares a company's market capitalization to its book value, which is the net asset value of the company's equity. Insurtechs with substantial tangible assets may use this metric. The book value multiple can vary based on the composition of assets and liabilities.

Growth metrics: Investors often consider growth metrics like the compound annual growth rate (CAGR) of revenue or user base when valuing insurtech companies. Higher growth rates can justify higher valuation multiples.

Comparable company analysis (Comps): Investors may compare the valuation multiples of an insurtech company to those of similar publicly traded or privately held peers to assess relative valuation.

It's important to note that valuation in the insurtech sector can be highly subjective and influenced by factors such as market sentiment, investor appetite for technology-driven solutions and industry trends. Early-stage start-ups may focus more on potential and growth, while established insurtechs with proven business models may emphasize profitability and cash flow.

Ultimately, the valuation of an insurtech company is determined through negotiations between the company and potential investors or buyers, and it should reflect the unique characteristics and circumstances of the business.

Changing landscape of insurtech investment

Investment in insurtech is undergoing a significant transformation, reflecting the dynamic nature of the industry and the growing recognition of its potential. Here are some key ways in which investment in insurtech is changing:

Growing investment volume: Perhaps the most noticeable change is the sheer volume of investment pouring into insurtech. In the early days, it was a relatively niche area, but now it's attracting billions of dollars in funding annually. This influx of capital is a clear sign that investors see real opportunities in the space.

Diverse investor base: Initially, insurtech attracted attention primarily from venture capital firms. However, the investor base has diversified considerably. Now, you have traditional insurance companies, private equity firms, corporate venture arms and even tech giants like Google and Amazon getting involved. This diversification brings different perspectives, expertise and resources to the table.

Global reach: While insurtech started in regions like the USA and UK, it's no longer confined to a few geographic hotspots. Investment in insurtech is becoming more global, with start-ups emerging from various parts of the world. Investors are also looking beyond their borders to tap into promising opportunities worldwide.

Focus on different sub-segments: Initially, insurtech investments were broad and exploratory. Now, investors are becoming more targeted. They're looking at specific sub-segments within insurtech, such as health insurance, property and casualty, or digital distribution platforms. This focus allows for more specialized innovation and solutions.

Later-stage funding: As the insurtech landscape matures, we're seeing more later-stage funding rounds. Companies that have proven their concepts and gained traction are now seeking growth-stage investments to scale their operations and expand into new markets.

Exit strategies: Investors are increasingly thinking about exit strategies. Whether it's through mergers and acquisitions or initial public offerings (IPOs), they're looking for opportunities to cash in on their investments. This creates a sense of urgency and accountability for insurtech start-ups to deliver results.

Focus on sustainability: With the growing emphasis on ESG factors, some investors are specifically seeking out insurtech companies that align with sustainable practices and responsible business models.

Integration with traditional insurers: Insurtech is no longer seen as a disruptor that will replace traditional insurance companies. Instead, there's a trend towards collaboration and integration. Many traditional insurers are investing in or partnering with insurtech start-ups to leverage their technology and enhance their own operations.

In summary, investment in insurtech is evolving from a niche interest to a major force in the insurance industry. This evolution includes a larger pool of investors, a focus on specific sub-segments, a global perspective and a growing emphasis on sustainability and collaboration with traditional insurers. As the insurtech landscape continues to mature, we can expect even more changes and innovations in the future.

Conclusion

In this chapter, we have explained the intricate landscape of insurtech investment, shedding light on the founder's journey, financial considerations, cultural disparities and the regional nuances that shape the global tapestry of insurtech investments. From the innovation epicentre of North America to the diverse spectrum of investments in Europe and the dynamic arena of Asia-Pacific, we explored the key factors influencing investment decisions in the insurtech space.

We delved into successful insurtech use cases and the key investors driving their growth, providing insights into the evolving trends in insurtech investment. Additionally, we emphasized the growing importance of DEI considerations in insurtech investments and discussed how investment inclusivity and the incorporation of DEI KPIs can reshape the insurtech landscape.

Furthermore, we explored the significance of ESG criteria in insurtech operations, highlighting the steps to incorporate ESG principles and the impact of ESG on investment decisions. Funding insurtech ventures and evaluating investment opportunities were also integral aspects of our journey.

As we conclude this chapter, it is evident that the insurtech industry is evolving at a remarkable pace, driven by innovation, technology and a commitment to sustainability and inclusivity. Insurtech founders seeking investment can leverage the insights shared here to navigate the complex investment landscape, while investors can harness these insights to make informed decisions and contribute to the growth and transformation of the insurtech ecosystem.

In the ever-evolving world of insurtech, one thing remains constant: the pursuit of innovation and the desire to create a more resilient, inclusive and sustainable insurance industry for the benefit of all. As we continue to witness ground-breaking developments in insurtech, it is clear that the journey has only just begun, and the future promises even greater opportunities and advancements in this dynamic industry.

Notes

1 'Global Perspectives on Insurtechs', McKinsey, 30 Sep. 2021. www.mckinsey.com/industries/financial-services/our-insights/global-perspectives-on-insurtechs (archived at https://perma.cc/WT8J-BBB2).

2 'What Does It Take to Scale a Deeptech Company?', Cambridge Future Tech, 17 Feb. 2021. camfuturetech.com/tech-nation-what-does-it-take-to-scale-a-deeptech-company/ (archived at https://perma.cc/Q76J-UR92).

3 'Report: What Is the State of InsurTech in 2021?', Porch, 8 Mar. 2021. https://porch.com/advice/report-state-insurtech-2021 (archived at https://perma.cc/SK3V-2LA5).

4 'ESG: A Growing Sense of Urgency', PwC. pwc.com/us/en/industries/financial-services/library/next-in-insurance-top-issues/esg-insurance-industry.html (archived at https://perma.cc/6XTP-TXN2).

8

The future of insurtech

Introduction

Our journey so far has covered the history, the present and the trans-formative changes within the insurtech landscape.

Now our focus shifts towards uncharted territory – the future of insurtech. This subject piques my interest as a founder in this field. It's crucial to understand that the future of insurtech isn't solely a consequence of time passing; rather, it's a realm we actively shape through our current efforts. The strategies and insights we've gathered serve as the foundation for envisioning the insurtech landscape of tomorrow.

Speaking of the future, there are several trends in insurtech that are poised to leave a profound impact on the insurance industry in the coming years.

Artificial intelligence (AI) and natural language processing (NLP) are both likely to shape the future. Insurtech is increasingly leveraging these technologies to automate critical tasks such as underwriting, claims processing, customer service and fraud detection. A prime example is Zurich, which is actively exploring the integration of ChatGPT AI technology in areas like claims processing and modelling.[1]

The adoption of blockchain technology and distributed infrastructure is also revolutionizing the way transactions and data sharing occur within the insurance ecosystem. For instance, the consortium of insurers known as B3i is diligently working on a blockchain-based platform designed for reinsurance contracts.

Insurtech is driving the development of innovative connectivity solutions and devices that can gather and transmit real-time data from customers and assets. Real-time data collection through connectivity solutions enables more dynamic and personalized risk assessment and pricing. Trōv, an on-demand gadget insurer that empowers customers with a smartphone app to toggle their coverage as needed[2] shows the potential of these types of solutions.

The insurtech landscape is advancing through automation technologies like robotics, drones and self-driving cars. These technologies promise to reduce human errors, enhance safety and lower claims costs. Lemonade, an insurtech trailblazer, employs a chatbot named Maya to manage policy sales and claims payouts.[3,4]

The emergence of trust architecture and digital identity solutions is enhancing the security and privacy of customer data and transactions. Civic, for instance, offers a decentralized identity verification platform that insurers can utilize to verify customers' identities without storing their personal information.[5,6]

Exploring the unseen

We explore the emerging technologies, regional nuances and evolving trends that will play a significant role in shaping the future of insurtech. Our focus will be on understanding how innovations such as AI, environmental, social and governance (ESG) considerations and changing customer preferences are poised to impact our industry. This exploration holds personal significance for me, as I have had the privilege of witnessing the entrepreneurial spirit and innovation that are integral to the insurtech ecosystem. As founders and industry insiders, we are not mere observers; we actively participate in driving this transformation. Our start-ups, our visionary ideas and our unwavering commitment contribute to moulding the insurtech landscape.

Throughout this chapter, we will draw connections between the insights we've gathered in the book, creating a holistic understanding of the insurtech landscape. This comprehensive perspective serves as both a navigational tool and a compass, guiding us toward opportunities and challenges on the horizon.

As we embark on this final phase of our journey I encourage you to embrace it with the mindset of a founder and an innovator. Let's envision the possibilities, anticipate the disruptions and collaboratively chart a course for the future of insurtech.

The subsequent concluding chapter will provide us with the opportunity to consolidate our insights, contemplate their broader implications and visualize how insurtech will continue to redefine the insurance industry.

So, let's venture into the uncharted territory of insurtech's future as founders and visionaries, ready to shape the exciting prospects that lie ahead.

Setting the stage for the future

The landscape of the insurance industry teeters on the brink of a profound transformation, shaped by the relentless march of technology, evolving customer expectations and emerging global trends. It's imperative to set the stage and grasp the intricate dynamics at play.

The insurance industry boasts a rich history steeped in stability and tradition, a hallmark of its resilience through time. Nevertheless, the onset of the 21st century ushered in a new era where innovation, digitalization and customer-centricity seized the spotlight, simultaneously injecting an element of instability into the equation. This transformative shift is primarily attributed to the rise of insurtech.

It's important to acknowledge the multifaceted nature of the insurance industry, which offers diverse protection and risk management services to individuals and businesses alike. The perception of whether this industry leans more towards stability or instability is subject to a complex interplay of factors, including the economic environment, regulatory frameworks, competitive landscapes, technological innovations and the challenges posed by societal and environmental changes.

Indeed, there exist differing perspectives on this matter.

On one hand, proponents argue that the insurance industry has long been synonymous with stability. They point to its extensive history of innovation and adaptability, highlighting its pivotal role in fortifying the financial system and supporting the broader economy. For instance, European Central Bank asserts, 'The insurance sector has traditionally been regarded as a relatively stable segment of the financial system. This is mainly because most insurers' balance sheets, unlike those of banks', are composed of relatively illiquid liabilities that protect insurers against the risk of rapid liquidity shortages that can and do confront banks.'[7]

On the other hand, critics contend that the insurance industry grapples with increasing challenges and uncertainties. These challenges emanate from the ever-evolving macroeconomic landscape, heightened customer expectations, intensified competition from newcomers and the emergent risks stemming from climate change and cyber threats. As PwC (PricewaterhouseCoopers) articulates, 'The stability that insurers have long relied on for predictable risk pricing and consistent growth is disappearing. There's been a succession of short-term crises so far this century. In the past three years alone, the world has experienced a pandemic, sometimes violent political unrest, severe supply chain disruptions, global conflict, high inflation and multiple historically extreme weather events.'[8]

In light of these varying viewpoints, it's evident that the insurance industry's path towards stability or instability remains subject to a dynamic interplay of forces, rendering its future a matter of ongoing exploration and adaptation.

Insurtech trends

The insurance industry is on the brink of a profound transformation, influenced by a convergence of factors that span evolving customer preferences, technological advancements, surging cyber threats and heightened regulatory scrutiny. In the future, we envision that the landscape will be defined by these pivotal trends.

ON-DEMAND AND PERSONALIZED INSURANCE PRODUCTS

Insurance providers are actively pivoting towards on-demand and highly personalized insurance offerings, driven by cutting-edge technologies like the Internet of Things (IoT), telematics and AI. These innovations empower insurers to gain real-time insights into policyholders' behaviours, leading to remarkably tailored coverage options.

For instance, motor insurers now offer usage-based insurance, leveraging AI algorithms to calculate premiums based on actual driving patterns. The future extends this trend to other sectors, such as health insurance. Wearable devices and health data could become integral in crafting individualized policies and pricing, with AI-driven data analysis orchestrating this personalization.

Use case: Envision a world where your health insurance adjusts its premium based on real-time data from your smartwatch, tracking daily exercise routines, heart rate and overall health. Simultaneously, your motor insurance adapts to your driving behaviour, incentivizing both healthier living and safe driving practices.

ADVANCEMENT AND ADOPTION OF TECHNOLOGY

The insurance sector embraces emerging technologies at an accelerating pace. AI and machine learning (ML) revolutionize underwriting, claims processing and fraud detection. Blockchain brings transparency and security to policy underwriting and administration, while IoT revolutionizes risk assessment through real-time data on insured assets.

List of emerging tech: Quantum computing, 5G connectivity, augmented reality (AR), virtual reality (VR) and advanced data analytics loom large as disruptive forces reshaping the insurance landscape.

ECOSYSTEM EXPANSION FOR ADDED VALUE

In the evolving landscape, insurance providers are broadening their horizons beyond traditional coverage. They are venturing into a broader ecosystem, offering complimentary services to enhance customer stickiness and bolster profitability. This ecosystem approach provides policyholders with added value, further solidifying their loyalty.

Use case: Insurance companies may offer services such as home security systems, wellness programmes or risk assessment consultancy, creating a holistic customer experience that extends beyond insurance coverage.

RISK MANAGEMENT IN THE AGE OF CYBER THREATS

The surge in cybercrime compels insurance companies to introduce specialized cyber insurance products. These policies encompass a spectrum of digital threats, from data breaches to ransomware attacks. Emerging technologies like AI and big data analytics play pivotal roles in proactively identifying and mitigating cyber risks, even before they materialize.

Use case: AI-powered cybersecurity tools continually monitor network traffic, swiftly detecting and neutralizing potential threats, ensuring the security of sensitive data.

INCREASED REGULATION AND DATA PROTECTION

With the expanding collection of customer data and reliance on advanced technologies, robust data protection and privacy regulations become imperative. Governments and regulatory bodies impose stringent rules on data handling and customer consent. To safeguard customer information, insurers invest in fortified cybersecurity measures and compliance frameworks.

Use case: Blockchain technology secures customer consent and data access permissions, ensuring compliance with stringent data protection regulations.

The future of insurance will see a landscape characterized by personalization, technology-driven solutions and cyber resilience. Insurers must adapt nimbly to these changes, harnessing emerging technologies to meet evolving customer expectations, proficiently manage risks and navigate a progressively regulated environment.

Anticipating the challenges and opportunities

While the future holds immense promise for the insurance industry, it also presents challenges that must be navigated. Insurers will need to strike a delicate balance between innovation and regulation, all while meeting the evolving needs of customers.

MEETING THE NEEDS OF EMERGING MARKETS

As we explore the future of insurtech, it's crucial to turn our attention to the promising opportunities and distinct challenges presented by emerging markets. In the evolving landscape of insurtech, it is the dynamic expanse of emerging markets that also demands our focus.

Emerging markets refer to geographic regions characterized by swift economic growth, industrialization and technological advancement. These regions include areas in Asia, Africa, Latin America and certain parts of Eastern Europe.

Chief among these distinctive traits is the notable rise of middle-class populations. Fuelled by increasing incomes and improved living standards, a substantial and diverse middle class is emerging. This demographic shift carries profound implications for the insurance sector, as an ever-growing number of individuals and families seek financial security and protection through insurance products and solutions.

Simultaneously, the rapid urbanization prevalent in these markets plays a pivotal role in this transformation. Currently, over half of the world's population in countries like China, India, Indonesia and Vietnam resides in urban areas. This urban resurgence is accompanied by significant increases in per capita income, with expectations of a remarkable rise by 30 per cent to 50 per cent. Consequently, the middle class in these regions increasingly gravitates toward enhanced quality, greater diversity and augmented convenience in their consumption patterns.

In addressing the unique needs of emerging markets, microinsurance takes centre stage as a critical component. Microinsurance, a specialized branch of insurance tailored to cater to the financial protection needs of low-income individuals and small businesses, becomes instrumental in bridging the insurance gap and extending financial security to underserved populations. Within this narrative, insurtech innovations play a pivotal role in rendering microinsurance accessible and cost-effective, thereby fostering greater financial inclusion.

Emerging markets present a unique set of challenges and needs that are significantly different from developed economies, particularly in the context of insurance. These needs stem from a combination of economic, social and environmental factors that define the lives of individuals and businesses in these regions.

Protection against unique risks: People in emerging markets often face risks specific to their geographical and socio-economic environment. This includes agricultural risks due to climate variability, health risks due to inadequate healthcare facilities and risks associated with informal or small-scale business operations.

Affordability and accessibility: The majority of the population in emerging markets may not have disposable income to allocate towards traditional insurance premiums. Hence, affordability is a critical need. Additionally, insurance services need to be accessible in remote or less developed areas where conventional banking and insurance infrastructures may be sparse.

Financial literacy and trust: There's often a lack of awareness and understanding of insurance as a concept. Moreover, there can be a general mistrust towards financial institutions, making it essential to offer transparent, simple and trustworthy insurance solutions.

Catering to informal economies: Many individuals in emerging markets are part of the informal economy or run small-scale businesses that aren't typically covered by traditional insurance policies.

Adaptability to local conditions: Products need to be adaptable to local conditions, customs and languages to ensure they are relevant and comprehensible to the intended users.

Microinsurance addresses these specific needs through several key characteristics:

Low-cost premiums: Microinsurance products are designed with low premiums, making them affordable for low-income individuals and families.

Tailored coverage: Policies are specifically designed to cover risks prevalent in these areas, such as micro health insurance covering common local diseases, or micro crop insurance tailored to specific agricultural conditions.

Simplified terms and conditions: Microinsurance products are simplified in terms of language and policy conditions, making them easier to understand for people with limited financial literacy.

Local distribution networks: Microinsurance often leverages local distribution networks, such as microfinance institutions, non-governmental organizations (NGOs) or mobile network operators, to reach customers in remote areas.

Flexible payment options: Payment schemes are often flexible, catering to the irregular income patterns typical in these markets. This could include mobile money platforms, which are widely used in many emerging markets.

Building trust through community engagement: Microinsurance providers often work closely with local communities to build trust and educate potential customers about the benefits of insurance.

Innovation through technology: Leveraging technology, particularly mobile and digital platforms, microinsurance can reach a wider audience more efficiently. This tech-driven approach also aids in gathering data to design better-suited products and services.

Risk pooling and sharing: Microinsurance models often involve community-based risk pooling, which is culturally aligned with many societies in emerging markets where community support systems are strong.

In essence, microinsurance is not just an insurance product scaled down in terms of cost and coverage; it is a fundamentally different approach to insurance, designed to be deeply aligned with the unique needs, conditions and preferences of individuals and businesses in emerging markets. Through microinsurance, the goal of broader financial inclusion becomes more achievable, offering protection and stability to those who need it most.

THE INFLUENCE OF ADVANCED TECHNOLOGY

It's important to note that these technological changes are not just incremental improvements; they represent significant advancements that simplify the process of obtaining insurance. Thanks to the widespread use of smartphones, digital payment systems and internet access, insurance services are now more accessible to a broader audience than ever before. Insurtech start-ups are leading the way in utilizing these technologies to create innovative and scalable insurance solutions, narrowing the accessibility gap and aligning insurance services with the evolving needs of our customers.

THE IMPORTANCE OF ESG

ESG is a critical metric for assessing a company's performance in areas such as environmental sustainability, social responsibility and effective governance practices. Its importance within the insurance industry is likely to grow in the future because it influences both the demand for insurance products and the methods of creating and delivering these products.

Insurtech firms can contribute by:

- Utilizing data and analytics to measure and communicate ESG-related risks and impacts. This helps them offer more accurate insurance pricing.

- Developing innovative insurance solutions that align with the preferences of customers concerned about ESG issues. This includes offerings like green insurance, microinsurance and social impact insurance.

- Collaborating with traditional insurers, regulators and other stakeholders to provide additional services that promote ESG objectives, such as addressing climate change and enhancing financial inclusion.

- Ensuring their own business practices align with ESG principles, including waste reduction, diversity promotion and transparent and ethical operations.

By taking these measures, insurtech companies can not only expand their customer base but also contribute to a more sustainable insurance industry and a better world.

The role of AI and ChatGPT

In the rapidly evolving landscape of insurtech, the prominence of AI and the emergence of conversational AI and NLP, represented by technologies like ChatGPT, have become focal points of innovation and transformation. These advancements hold immense potential to shape the future of the insurance industry in profound ways. Across various facets of the insurance sector, there are roles and applications of AI and ChatGPT, from underwriting to claims processing and customer interactions.

Statistics: The impact of AI and chatbots on insurance

According to industry experts, AI has the potential to reduce claims processing time by up to 75 per cent, increasing operational efficiency and customer satisfaction.[9] AI can automate 10 per cent to 55 per cent of the work performed by major functions within insurance companies, including actuarial, claims, underwriting, finance and operations.[10]

AI in insurance is projected to reach a market value of \$35.77 billion by 2030, growing at a CAGR of 33.06 per cent during the forecast period.[11] These statistics underscore AI's position as the leading technology to tackle innovation challenges within the insurance industry.

There are numerous advantages of harnessing AI and ChatGPT within insurance:

Underwriting: AI is transforming the underwriting process by empowering insurers to conduct more informed and precise risk evaluations. Unlike traditional underwriting that heavily depended on historical data and predefined risk criteria, AI-driven underwriting harnesses extensive datasets and sophisticated algorithms to analyse a multitude of real-time variables. The outcome is notably improved risk forecasts and personalized pricing options for policyholders. For instance, AI can evaluate an individual's health, lifestyle and other pertinent factors to provide customized health insurance plans, delivering mutual benefits to insurers and policyholders alike. AI models excel at assessing intricate risk elements and swiftly rendering underwriting decisions with exceptional accuracy. This not only expedites policy issuance but also ensures that risk evaluations are more meticulous, subsequently diminishing the likelihood of costly claims.

Claims processing: AI can play a pivotal role in optimizing claims processing, resulting in faster, more efficient and error-resistant procedures. Utilizing conversational AI technologies like ChatGPT, customers can seamlessly report and track their claims. ML algorithms are adept at handling and verifying claims documents, efficiently identifying unusual or potentially fraudulent cases for subsequent human review. This not only expedites the claims settlement process but also elevates fraud detection measures, ensuring equitable compensation for valid claims. Claims processing stands as a critical facet of the insurance realm and AI has significantly streamlined this historically labour-intensive task. AI algorithms can swiftly evaluate claims, cross-referencing details with policy terms and historical data. Moreover, AI's data analytics capabilities prove invaluable in the realm of fraud detection, swiftly identifying irregular patterns and potential fraudulent claims.

Customer interaction: Conversational AI, like ChatGPT, transforms customer interactions in the insurance industry, offering 24/7 support for enquiries, policy guidance and instant quotes. This personalized and efficient experience reduces the need for complex website navigation or long hold times. AI-driven sentiment analysis helps insurers understand customer satisfaction and intervene proactively when necessary. ChatGPT redefines insurer-customer interactions by providing instant, personalized responses across various enquiries. Its natural language capabilities enable efficient support, from policy questions to claims processing, resulting in higher customer satisfaction and operational efficiency.

Risk assessment: AI can process vast datasets, including real-time data from telematics, IoT devices and external sources, to evaluate and mitigate risks effectively. For example, AI can analyse sensor data from a home security system to assess property insurance risks or monitor driving behaviour through telematics for motor insurance. This proactive approach not only minimizes risks for insurers but can also lead to more competitive premiums for customers who demonstrate safe behaviour.

Fraud detection: Advanced ML algorithms can detect patterns and anomalies in data, making it easier to spot potentially fraudulent claims or policy applications. Additionally, AI can analyse historical data to predict future fraud risks, allowing insurers to take preventive measures. This not only safeguards insurers' financial stability but also helps maintain trust within the industry.

AI and ChatGPT are catalysts of transformation in the insurance sector. They optimize underwriting, streamline claims processing, enhance customer interactions, improve risk assessment and fortify fraud detection. As insurers increasingly embrace these technologies, they not only enhance their operational efficiency but also offer more personalized and responsive services to their customers, ushering in a new era of innovation and customer-centricity in the world of insurance.

Challenges and strategies in adopting AI

While AI has the potential to shape the future of insurance, there are also challenges and risks that insurers must consider when embracing AI.

Data quality and availability: AI's effectiveness hinges on the quality of the data it uses. Insurers must ensure that the data employed for

AI training and decision-making is not only abundant but also accurate, up-to-date and complete. Poor data quality can lead to incorrect predictions, flawed underwriting decisions and unsatisfactory customer experiences. Regular data audits and cleansing processes are essential to maintain data quality.[12]

Privacy and data security: With AI's reliance on vast amounts of sensitive customer data, insurers bear the responsibility of safeguarding this information against data breaches and cyberattacks. In an era of increasing cybersecurity threats, insurers must establish robust security protocols, encryption mechanisms and data access controls. Compliance with stringent data protection regulations such as GDPR (General Data Protection Regulation) and HIPAA (Health Insurance Portability and Accountability Act) is not just a legal requirement but a moral obligation.

Bias and fairness: AI algorithms are susceptible to inheriting biases present in their training data. This risk poses a considerable ethical concern, particularly in the insurance industry, where AI decisions, such as coverage denial or premium rate setting, can profoundly impact individuals. It's imperative for insurers to proactively identify and mitigate biases within AI systems to ensure fairness in underwriting and claims processing. Addressing this challenge involves continuous monitoring, algorithmic adjustments and adherence to fairness guidelines.

Ethical concerns: Defining the ethical boundaries of AI decisions is a complex task. The line between automated decision-making and human judgement needs careful consideration. Ensuring that AI-driven processes align with ethical standards and societal values is essential. Ethical AI frameworks and interdisciplinary collaboration between technologists, ethicists and policymakers are valuable resources in this endeavour.

Regulation and compliance: The insurance industry operates within a highly regulated environment. The introduction of AI raises questions about compliance with existing laws and regulations, which can vary by region and product type. Insurers must carefully navigate this complex regulatory landscape and ensure that AI systems adhere to industry standards. Transparency and cooperation with regulatory bodies are vital aspects of compliance.

Customer trust: Building and maintaining customer trust is pivotal. Customers may perceive AI as intrusive or unfair if they do not fully understand how it influences their insurance policies. Insurers need to embark on educational initiatives to inform customers about the benefits of AI, such as more accurate risk assessment, faster claims processing and improved customer service. Addressing privacy concerns and emphasizing data protection measures is essential to reassure policyholders.

Cost management: While AI has the potential to yield significant long-term cost savings, the initial investment in AI infrastructure, technology and talent can be substantial. Insurers must carefully manage these costs while ensuring a positive return on investment. This involves robust cost-benefit analysis, budget allocation and continuous monitoring of AI-related expenses.

Talent acquisition: Implementing AI effectively requires a skilled workforce with expertise in developing, deploying and maintaining AI systems. The demand for AI talent often outpaces supply, making recruitment and retention of AI experts a notable challenge. Insurers must invest in training and professional development to nurture AI talent internally or explore partnerships with AI-focused educational institutions.

Legacy system integration: Many insurers operate with legacy IT systems that may not seamlessly integrate with cutting-edge AI technologies. Ensuring a smooth integration process without disrupting existing operations requires meticulous planning, testing and potential system updates or replacements. Interoperability solutions are essential to maximize the benefits of AI while preserving legacy infrastructure.

Continuous improvement: AI models can become outdated relatively quickly due to the rapid pace of technological advancement. To maintain a competitive edge, insurers need strategies for continuously updating and improving their AI systems. This includes staying informed about emerging AI trends, evaluating the performance of existing models and embracing advancements in AI technology.

Effectively addressing these multifaceted challenges and risks is essential for insurers seeking to harness the transformative potential of AI. By doing so, insurers can not only optimize their operations but also deliver enhanced customer experiences, meet evolving regulatory requirements and maintain their competitive position in the dynamic insurance industry.

The future role of blockchain and smart contracts

As we look at the future of the insurance industry, one cannot help but be captivated by the remarkable promise that blockchain and smart contracts hold. These two technologies have garnered immense attention for their potential to reshape the insurance landscape, promising heightened efficiency, security, transparency and customer satisfaction.

Blockchain, a distributed ledger, has the remarkable ability to record transactions in a secure, immutable and transparent manner. Complementing this, smart contracts are self-executing programs that operate atop the blockchain, diligently enforcing contractual terms between parties sans the need for intermediaries. Together, this duo can empower insurance companies to create smart contracts that not only track insurance claims but also automate archaic paperwork processes, while fortifying the safeguarding of sensitive data.

The advantages of harnessing blockchain and smart contracts within the insurance realm are manifold:

Streamlining information exchange and payments: By leveraging blockchain, insurers can input crucial data into smart contracts on a shared blockchain database. This facilitates rapid real-time access to information for reinsurers, retrocessionaires and regulators, who can conveniently extract data for diverse purposes, including audits and compliance checks. This streamlined exchange of information promises to enhance the industry's operational efficiency.[13]

Automating claims processing: Blockchain's automation capabilities can revolutionize the insurance claims process. With predefined rules or claim events triggered upon the receipt of matching information from reliable data sources, settlements can be executed instantly upon the occurrence of predefined and objective events (such as temperature fluctuations, wind speeds, earthquakes or flight delays). This not only reduces settlement times but also curtails costs and, most importantly, augments customer satisfaction.

Facilitating client onboarding: Blockchain steps in as a trusty ally during the client onboarding process. It helps verify the identities and credentials of clients and agents through the application of digital signatures and encryption. This not only mitigates the risk of fraud, errors and data duplication[14] but also empowers customers by granting them more control over their personal data,[15] allowing them to share it with insurers as needed.

Challenges and strategies in adopting blockchain and smart contracts

Yet, amid these promising prospects, it's important to acknowledge the challenges and unresolved issues that must be navigated to fully unlock the potential of blockchain and smart contracts in insurance:

Security and legal complexities: Blockchain and smart contracts, like any technology, are susceptible to security threats, vulnerabilities, cyberattacks, hacking and human errors. Furthermore, the legal validity, enforceability and liability of smart contracts remain ambiguous in various jurisdictions. Ethical and social considerations, including trust, accountability, responsibility and fairness, also loom large.[16]

One key strategy to address these challenges is to implement robust security measures, encryption and regular audits to mitigate security threats. Additionally, insurers can collaborate with legal experts and regulators to establish clear legal frameworks for blockchain and smart contracts.

Scalability, interoperability, privacy and governance: Technical challenges, such as scalability (the ability to handle high transaction volumes), interoperability (the capacity to communicate with other systems), privacy (the safeguarding of sensitive data) and governance (the management of network rules and participants), pose significant hurdles. These challenges bear direct implications for the performance and usability of blockchain-driven smart contracts.[17]

To overcome these challenges, insurers can employ various strategies. One effective approach is to invest in research and development to address technical challenges related to scalability and interoperability. Additionally, insurers can focus on developing privacy-preserving mechanisms to protect sensitive data within the blockchain. Furthermore, it's crucial to establish transparent governance structures to effectively manage network rules and participants, ensuring a smoother adoption process for blockchain and smart contracts.

Regulatory and legal frameworks: Blockchain and smart contracts are still emerging technologies and regulatory and legal frameworks remain inconsistent across countries and regions. This creates a complex and uncertain landscape for insurers keen on embracing these innovations.

In order to address these challenges and cultivate an environment conducive to innovation, insurers can explore several strategies. Firstly, they can implement robust security measures, encryption protocols and conduct regular audits to mitigate security threats related to blockchain and smart contracts. Moreover, fostering collaboration among regulators, policymakers, insurers and stakeholders is crucial to establish coherent and standardized legal frameworks for the adoption of smart contracts within the insurance sector. This collaborative effort promotes the seamless integration of these technologies and guarantees compliance with evolving legal standards.

The future of blockchain and smart contracts in insurance remains shrouded in uncertainty, contingent upon their adaptation to evolving user needs, expectations and the development of supportive regulatory and legal frameworks. However, one thing is undeniable: these technologies are poised to exert a profound influence on various facets of the insurance industry in the years to come. As we embark on this journey into uncharted territory, we do so with a sense of awe and anticipation, acutely aware of the transformative potential that lies ahead.

The future of IoT and telematics in insurance

Between 2019 and 2024, the IoT insurance market is expected to grow by 60 per cent, as reported by Insurance Thought Leadership in 2021.[18] Alongside this rapid expansion, the realm of insurance is witnessing a surge in IoT device applications. Year after year, an increasing array of electronic devices is entering both consumer and business markets.

This exponential growth in the IoT landscape paints an exciting future for insurance. It's a future where the convergence of IoT and telematics promises innovation and transformation. These two complementary technologies provide insurers with the tools to collect, dissect and harness data originating from interconnected devices – spanning cars, homes, health monitors and industrial equipment. Together, they have the potential to reshape the insurance landscape by enhancing product portfolios, service delivery and customer interactions to new levels of excellence.

IoT and telematics are set to bestow several benefits upon the insurance industry, including:

Enhancing customer engagement and loyalty: Through IoT and telematics, insurers can establish more frequent and personalized interactions with their clientele. By offering tailored, value-added services aligned with individual needs and preferences, insurers can foster deeper customer engagement. For instance, insurers can incentivize safe driving or regular exercise by providing feedback, rewards or discounts to customers who exhibit such behaviours.[19] Furthermore, they can introduce on-demand or usage-based insurance products[20] that dynamically adjust premiums based on actual risk exposure.

Improving risk assessment and pricing: The real-time and granular data accessible via IoT and telematics enable insurers to gain unprecedented insights into the behaviour, usage and condition of insured assets or individuals. Armed with this data, insurers can better comprehend and predict their customers' risk profiles, resulting in more accurate and equitable pricing. For instance, data from sensors or cameras in vehicles or homes can inform insurers about driving habits or security measures.[21] Similarly, health monitors or wearables can provide insights into the health status and lifestyle choices of policyholders.[22]

Streamlining claims management and fraud prevention: IoT and telematics bring automation to the claims process, streamlining data collection, verification and settlement. This not only reduces costs but also minimizes errors and delays for both insurers and customers. Telematics devices or smart home systems can automatically detect accidents or damages, initiating claims processes promptly. Additionally, IoT data can be leveraged to verify claim validity and severity, preventing fraudulent activities.

Challenges and strategies in adopting IoT and telematics

IoT and telematics technologies offer immense potential for the insurance industry by enabling the collection and analysis of data from various devices and sensors, such as vehicles, equipment and assets. These technologies can provide valuable insights for improving efficiency, safety, security and customer satisfaction in the insurance sector. However, embracing IoT and telematics in insurance also presents several significant challenges:

Compatibility and longevity: IoT and telematics solutions often involve integrating components from different vendors, leading to potential compatibility issues. Additionally, devices and sensors may have varying firmware and operating systems that can become outdated or unsupported over time. To address this challenge, insurers should prioritize choosing compatible and standardized components from reputable vendors, ensuring regular updates and implementing maintenance practices.[23]

Security concerns: IoT and telematics solutions entail the transmission and storage of sensitive data, including location, behaviour and performance information. This data is susceptible to cyberattacks, data breaches or unauthorized access, posing risks to user privacy and trust. To mitigate security risks, insurers should implement robust security measures such as encryption, authentication, authorization and monitoring. Compliance with relevant regulations and standards is also essential.[24]

Data storage capacity: IoT and telematics generate vast amounts of data, potentially exceeding existing infrastructure or cloud service capacities. This can result in increased costs, reduced performance or even data loss. To overcome this challenge, insurers can optimize data storage and transmission by employing techniques such as data compression, edge computing or selective data transfer. Choosing the appropriate cloud service provider is crucial.

Power management: IoT and telematics devices and sensors rely on batteries or external power sources, which may be unreliable or unavailable in remote or harsh environments. Insufficient power can impact device functionality and durability. To address this issue, insurers can focus on improving power efficiency and management through strategies like using low-power communication protocols, solar panels or wireless charging.

Unstructured data processing: IoT and telematics data can be unstructured, incomplete, noisy or inaccurate, requiring extensive data cleaning and preprocessing before analysis. This complexity can significantly extend data processing time and effort. To streamline this process, insurers should implement data quality and validation techniques such as filtering, imputation or anomaly detection. Standardized data formats and protocols can also aid in data handling.

Analytics challenges: IoT and Telematics data often exhibit diversity, dynamics and multidimensionality, demanding advanced analytics techniques and tools for meaningful insights. Meeting this challenge may necessitate specialized skills, knowledge and resources. Insurers can address this by leveraging advanced analytics tools and platforms, including ML, AI or foundation models. They can also invest in hiring or training qualified data analysts and scientists.

By acknowledging these challenges and implementing the corresponding strategies, insurers can navigate the complexities of IoT and telematics in the insurance industry. Effectively addressing these hurdles will not only optimize operations but also enhance customer experiences, facilitate compliance with evolving regulations and position insurers for continued success in an increasingly data-driven landscape.

The future of AR (Augmented Reality) and VR (Virtual Reality) in insurance

AR and VR are two technologies that hold the potential to revolutionize the insurance industry, offering immersive and interactive experiences for users. AR overlays digital information or objects onto the real world, while VR creates simulated environments for user exploration and interaction.

The impact of AR and VR in the insurance industry is underscored by the fact that Mazer reports that these technologies can yield a substantial 30 per cent reduction in insurance costs while simultaneously elevating customer satisfaction by an impressive 50 per cent.[25]

Additionally, findings from Kommando Tech's survey reveal that 70 per cent of consumers perceive AR as a means to gain benefits such as a deeper understanding of insurance products, expedited claims processing and enhanced safety measures. Statista's projections signal significant growth in the healthcare AR and VR market, with anticipated expansion from $2.1 billion in 2020 to a substantial $23.6 billion by 2025. These applications extend to physician training, patient treatments and hospital management.

These statistics and use cases paint a compelling picture of the transformative potential of AR and VR in insurance. These technologies are poised to redefine customer experiences, improve risk assessment and streamline operations, making them central to the future of the insurance industry and offering substantial benefits to insurers and customers alike.

AR and VR offer the capacity to reshape insurance across multiple dimensions

AR and VR offer significant opportunities for the insurance industry, transforming various aspects of operations, customer engagement and risk assessment. Here are some key opportunities:

Training and education: AR/VR can be instrumental in training and educating insurance professionals and customers on various insurance facets, including policies, claims, risks and scenarios. For instance, Allianz has leveraged AR to construct an interactive house filled with hidden dangers, enabling customers to explore and identify risks using their mobile devices.[26]

Marketing and sales: These technologies provide a compelling avenue for marketing and selling insurance products and services. They can simulate real-life situations, effectively demonstrating the value and advantages of different insurance plans. AXA, for instance, employed VR gaming through Ingress to boost brand awareness and attract new customers.[27]

Risk assessment and mitigation: AR enhances the efficiency of insurance adjusters by allowing them to remotely assess damaged objects. Using photos of the damage, AR constructs 3D models, aiding in precise damage evaluation. AR enables technical specialists to overlay pre- and post-accident object images, accurately gauging damage volume. Adjusters can measure dimensions and calculate repair costs based on processed data. In inspection apps, AR empowers inspectors to thoroughly assess concealed areas, such as behind walls, locating gas lines or fire epicentres.[28]

Claims management and settlement: AR/VR can streamline claims management and settlement processes by facilitating remote inspection, damage estimation and evidence collection. For instance, USAA introduced AR functionality that allows customers to use their smartphone cameras to scan their damaged vehicles and receive instant estimates for repair costs.

These technologies hold the potential to revolutionize various aspects of the insurance industry, enhancing training, marketing, risk management and claims processing. As insurers continue to explore and adopt AR/VR solutions, they are likely to find innovative ways to improve customer experiences and operational efficiency.

Challenges and strategies in adopting AR and VR

AR and VR present promising opportunities in the insurance industry. However, their implementation also poses challenges, particularly in hardware, limited use cases and security. These challenges necessitate strategic solutions.

Limited user experience: AR/VR devices often face issues related to field of view, display quality, battery life and user comfort. To enhance the user experience, developers must focus on designing more ergonomic and immersive devices while optimizing software and hardware performance. Also AR/VR applications are predominantly concentrated in entertainment and gaming, which may not cater to a broader audience. To expand adoption, developers need to explore AR/VR's potential in various domains like education, healthcare and marketing, creating content that appeals to diverse audiences.[29]

Network security issues: AR/VR devices handle substantial amounts of personal and sensitive data, making them susceptible to security threats. To ensure network security, developers must implement robust security measures, including encryption, authentication and authorization techniques and comply with data protection and privacy regulations.

Malware and unauthorized apps: AR/VR devices, particularly wearables, confront the risk of infiltration by malware and unsanctioned applications that evade recording restrictions. In response to this threat, manufacturers must establish and uphold robust security protocols to bolster defences against malware and unsanctioned apps. These safeguards are pivotal in preserving the devices' integrity and ensuring user safety.[30]

Incompatibility and health problems: AR/VR devices may lack compatibility with existing platforms and may cause health problems such as nausea, eye strain and fatigue. Developers should work on establishing common frameworks and guidelines for compatibility and conduct thorough testing to ensure device safety and usability.

Not meeting consumer expectations: AR/VR devices may disappoint users in terms of quality and functionality and they may also pose ethical and social challenges. Developers must provide accurate and transparent information about their products and address ethical and social implications through responsible design and usage guidelines to meet consumer expectations and build trust.

By strategically addressing these challenges, the insurance industry can leverage the potential of AR and VR to enhance customer experiences, streamline processes and improve risk assessment.

The future of drones and aerial imagery in insurance

Drones and aerial imagery are poised to become game-changers for the insurance industry, offering invaluable data and insights across multiple domains such as risk assessment, claims management, customer service and product innovation.

As these small yet powerful devices prepare to revolutionize various facets of insurance operations, it's worth noting that the US's Federal Aviation Administration (FAA) anticipates a sky filled with an estimated 2.85 million small drones by 2022.[31] These statistics highlight the significant growth potential of drones and aerial imagery in the commercial sector, with the global drone market valuation reaching $43 billion in 2022.[32]

Here's a glimpse of the potential trends and opportunities these technologies bring to the world of insurance:

Risk assessment: Drones and aerial imagery have emerged as invaluable assets for insurers seeking to enhance their risk management practices. These technologies enable insurers to gather highly accurate and comprehensive data regarding the properties and assets they cover, as well as potential hazards and exposures. Such precise data empowers insurers to perform a more in-depth assessment of their customers' risk profiles. Consequently, insurers can offer more personalized and competitive pricing and coverage options. For instance, drones are adept at inspecting areas that are challenging or costly to access through traditional means, such as roofs, buildings, crops or equipment.[33,34]

Claims management: These technologies expedite and enhance claims processing. Drones offer swift and safe access to hard-to-reach or hazardous areas, such as storm-damaged rooftops or flooded zones.[35] Aerial imagery provides before-and-after views of properties, facilitating precise assessment of loss extent and cause.[36]

Customer service: Drones and aerial imagery empower insurers to provide customers with a more convenient and engaging experience. These technologies facilitate the delivery of value-added services, such as preventive maintenance, risk mitigation and loss prevention. Drones can continuously monitor the condition of insured properties or assets, promptly notifying customers of potential issues or risks.[37,38] Additionally, drones can undertake unconventional tasks, like delivering packages or documents to customers in remote or challenging-to-access locations.[39]

The adoption of drones and aerial imagery in insurance is poised for further growth and innovation. As technology continues to advance and becomes increasingly accessible, several exciting trends are expected to emerge:

More sophisticated drones: Future drones are likely to boast enhanced capabilities and versatility, potentially featuring longer battery life, greater payload capacity, improved navigation systems, advanced sensors and even autonomous flight capabilities. These advancements will enable drones to tackle an even broader array of complex tasks, such as thermal imaging, 3D mapping or real-time video streaming.[40,41]

Integration of data sources: The future of insurance will likely witness the integration of drone and aerial imagery data with other valuable data sources, including satellite imagery, geospatial data, weather information and social media insights. This holistic approach will provide insurers with a more dynamic and comprehensive view of the insured environment, enabling deeper insights into customer needs, preferences, behaviours and risks.[42,43]

Collaborative ecosystems: Drones and aerial imagery may give rise to collaborative ecosystems involving various stakeholders within the insurance industry, including insurers, reinsurers, brokers, adjusters, regulators and customers. These collaborative platforms will facilitate the sharing and exchange of data, creating a transparent and efficient environment that fosters innovation, cooperation and trust.[44,45]

Challenges and strategies in adopting drones and aerial imagery in insurance

While the potential benefits are promising, insurers must also grapple with significant challenges and risks when it comes to incorporating drones and aerial imagery into their insurance operations. These hurdles include:

Stringent regulatory compliance: Drones and aerial imagery operations are subject to a multitude of regulations imposed by entities like the FAA and other relevant authorities. These regulations impose various limitations, including drone weight restrictions (less than 55 pounds), requirements for visual line-of-sight flight, altitude constraints (at or below 400 feet above ground level),[46] daylight or civil twilight flying and maximum speed limits (at or under 100 mph). Furthermore, drones necessitate certification and registration with the FAA.[47] These stringent regulations can create complexities for insurers seeking to deploy drones and aerial imagery for diverse applications across different geographical areas.

High implementation costs: Employing drones and aerial imagery demands a substantial financial commitment. Drones themselves represent a significant upfront investment and ongoing expenses may be incurred for maintenance, repairs resulting from wear and tear or unexpected accidents. Additionally, effectively harnessing aerial imagery requires sophisticated software and hardware infrastructure for data processing, storage and analysis. Insurers may also need to consider the recruitment and training of personnel to manage drone and aerial imagery systems or explore the possibility of outsourcing these services to third-party providers.[48]

Legal liabilities and the threat of lawsuits: The utilization of drones and aerial imagery exposes insurers to a range of potential legal risks and liabilities. These include concerns such as invasion of privacy, trespassing, property damage and personal injury. Drones have the capability to capture sensitive or personal information about individuals or properties without their explicit consent or knowledge, potentially violating privacy rights. Furthermore, drones may unintentionally cause damage or injury to other aircraft, structures, vehicles, wildlife or individuals in the event of malfunctions or collisions. This leaves insurers susceptible to lawsuits or claims from affected parties, as well as potential enforcement actions by regulatory bodies responsible for overseeing the laws and regulations governing drones and aerial imagery operations.[49,50]

In conclusion, the incorporation of drones and aerial imagery stands poised to usher in a transformative era for the insurance industry, promising advancements in risk assessment, cost reduction and enriched customer interactions. However, it's imperative to acknowledge the hurdles that insurers must navigate, including stringent regulatory frameworks, substantial set-up expenses and the looming spectre of potential legal liabilities such as invasion of privacy, trespassing, property damage or personal injury. To fully unlock the potential of drones and aerial imagery in the insurance sector, insurers must adopt a strategic approach that carefully balances the advantages and risks inherent in their utilization.

The future of quantum computing in insurance

Quantum computing stands as a rapidly evolving field with the potential to revolutionize the insurance industry in several ways. To underscore the significance of quantum computing in this context, let's begin by examining some statistics regarding the monumental influx of big data originating from IoT devices, wearables and cloud computing.

By the year 2025, an astounding 41.6 billion IoT devices will be active worldwide, with the capability to generate an astonishing 79.4 zettabytes (ZB) of data.[51] To grasp the sheer scale, envision a single zettabyte as an astronomical 1 trillion gigabytes or 1 billion terabytes.[52] Wearables, which include smartwatches, fitness trackers and smart clothing, were valued at $61.30 billion in 2022 and are anticipated to experience robust growth at a compound annual growth rate (CAGR) of 14.6 per cent from 2023 to 2030.[53]

Cloud computing serves as the cornerstone, supplying the essential infrastructure that bolsters IoT and big data applications in the insurance sector. It offers vital features like storage capacity, scalability and swift data retrieval, all of which are fundamental for robust data processing and analytics. As of 2022, the global cloud computing market is valued at $569.31 billion and it is anticipated to experience substantial growth, with projections reaching $2,432.87 billion by 2030, boasting a remarkable Compound Annual Growth Rate (CAGR) of 20 per cent throughout the forecast period.[54]

These statistics bear witness to the immense volume of big data generated, driven by the widespread adoption of IoT devices, wearables and cloud computing. This reservoir of data holds vast potential, offering diverse applications within the insurance sector, while also acting as a catalyst for expediting the advancement of quantum computing.

Let's explore some of the key applications and impacts of quantum computing on insurance:

Enhanced risk assessment and pricing: Quantum computing can perform complex algorithms and simulations that classical computers cannot handle. This enables insurers to offer faster and more accurate risk assessment and pricing strategies.[55]

Quantum computing offers unique capabilities that traditional AI, processed on classical computers, cannot match. Quantum computers, based on the principles of quantum mechanics, can handle complex algorithms and simulations far beyond the capacity of the most advanced classical computers. For instance, they can efficiently perform Monte Carlo simulations, which are essential in optimizing dynamic portfolios and managing market fluctuations. This superior computational power of quantum computing will enable insurers to provide much faster and accurate risk assessments and develop more sophisticated pricing strategies.

Unlike AI, which is a method or process often run on classical computers, quantum computing represents a significant leap in processing capabilities. While AI on classical computers is limited by processing speed and complexity, quantum computers, estimated to be over 58 million times faster, can solve problems that are currently intractable for AI due to the computational limitations of classical computers.[56]

Furthermore, quantum computing could potentially address one of AI's major challenges: bias. AI systems can exhibit bias due to limited or flawed data sets. Quantum computers, with their massive processing capabilities and ability to process a substantially larger volume of inputs, could reduce or correct these biases, leading to safer and more effective AI applications. While AI is a software process, quantum computing provides the advanced hardware platform to elevate AI's capabilities significantly. As both fields progress, their convergence will likely lead to ground-breaking advancements in various sectors, including insurance.

Improved catastrophe and weather-related loss management: Quantum computing allows for precise simulation of weather systems and climate change scenarios. Insurers can gain better insights into the frequency and severity of natural disasters, allowing them to adjust premiums and reserves accordingly. This helps in managing catastrophe and weather-related losses more effectively.[57]

Advanced data security and privacy: Quantum computing introduces quantum encryption algorithms that are highly resistant to hacking by classical or quantum computers. This enhances the security and privacy of insurance data, protecting both insurers and customers from cyberattacks and data breaches.[58]

Hyper-personalization and customer insights: Quantum computing enables insurers to offer hyper-personalized offerings to customers by tailoring policies, discounts and rewards based on individual preferences and behaviours. It also enables insurers to leverage new data sources like wearables, IoT devices and social media for deeper insights into customer needs and expectations. In an era marked by the explosion of IoT, wearables, telematics and cloud computing, which generate millions of data points, quantum computing plays a pivotal role.[59]

Challenges and strategies in adopting quantum computing in insurance

While the potential benefits of quantum computing in insurance are substantial, there are also significant challenges to overcome:

Technical expertise and specialized hardware: Quantum computing demands a high level of technical expertise and specialized hardware that are not yet widely accessible. Insurers will need to invest in quantum education, training and partnerships with quantum service providers to leverage these capabilities.[60]

Data security risks: Quantum computing poses a threat to classical data encryption methods. Insurers must adopt quantum-resistant encryption techniques and protocols to safeguard data. They should also monitor and mitigate cyber risks associated with potential quantum attacks.[61,62]

Market uncertainty and complexity: The introduction of quantum computing can lead to new products, services and business models that may not be well understood or regulated. Insurers must adapt to changing customer expectations, competitive landscapes and emerging ethical and legal frameworks related to quantum computing.

In conclusion, quantum computing holds immense promise for the insurance industry. It can bring faster and more accurate risk assessment, improved loss management, enhanced data security and innovative customer offerings. However, insurers need to prepare for the challenges it presents, including the need for technical expertise, data security concerns and the evolving market landscape. By doing so, they can position themselves to harness the power of quantum computing when it becomes a reality.

Conclusion: Navigating the future of insurtech

Throughout this chapter, we've embarked on a journey to explore the future of insurtech. We've dissected the fundamental drivers of change and emerging trends that are reshaping the insurance landscape. Our deep dive has taken us into the realms of AI, blockchain, IoT, AR/VR, drones, quantum computing and the growing prominence of ESG principles within the insurance sphere.

In summary, the future of insurtech holds the promise of relentless innovation and heightened efficiency. Challenges are not roadblocks but stepping stones, as the industry continually devises strategic solutions. It is evolving to meet the evolving needs of policyholders and aligning with broader societal demands. As we progress, insurtech is poised to thrive in an increasingly dynamic and interconnected world.

In this ever-evolving landscape, insurtech stands as a testament to the insurance industry's resilience, adaptability and unwavering commitment to ushering in a future that benefits all stakeholders. With innovation as its compass, insurtech continues to chart new territories, making insurance more accessible, responsive and relevant in the years to come.

Notes

1 '12 Insurtech Trends Leading Market Disruption in 2023', Insurtech Insights. www.insurtechinsights.com/12-insurtech-trends-leading-market-disruption-in-2023/ (archived at https://perma.cc/M3PQ-29YD).

2 'Trōv – World's First On-Demand Insurance for Things You Own', The Digital Insurer. www.the-digital-insurer.com/dia/trov-worlds-first-demand-insurance-things/ (archived at https://perma.cc/XY8Y-3DJS).

3 'How Top Tech Trends Will Transform Insurance', McKinsey, 30 Sep. 2021. www.mckinsey.com/industries/financial-services/our-insights/how-top-tech-trends-will-transform-insurance (archived at https://perma.cc/VR3D-FBDQ).

4 'Love at First Chat, with Lemonade's AI Chatbot Maya', Medium, 1 Dec. 2019. medium.com/marketing-in-the-age-of-digital/love-at-first-chat-with-lemonades-ai-chatbot-maya-7b4a105824bd (archived at https://perma.cc/SV7S-VVYX).

5 'How Top Tech Trends Will Transform Insurance', McKinsey, 30 Sep. 2021. www.mckinsey.com/industries/financial-services/our-insights/how-top-tech-trends-will-transform-insurance (archived at https://perma.cc/29KF-HYN5).

6 'Civic Pass – Identity and Access Management (IAM) for Distributed Ledger Technology', Civic. www.civic.com/ (archived at https://perma.cc/5TUA-DZHB).

7 'The Importance of Insurance Companies for Financial Stability', ECB. www.ecb.europa.eu/pub/pdf/fsr/art/ecb.fsrart200912en_05.pdf (archived at https://perma.cc/7TJP-BEMN).

8 'Next in Insurance 2023', PwC. www.pwc.com/us/en/industries/financial-services/library/insurance-industry-trends.html (archived at https://perma.cc/7E5P-B5WH).

9 'How AI in Insurance is Poised to Transform the Industry?', Appinventiv. appinventiv.com/blog/ai-in-insurance/ (archived at https://perma.cc/RR8M-69SG).

10 'The Need for Data and AI Skills in the Insurance Industry', Emeritus, 15 Dec. 2021. emeritus.org/blog/data-science-ai-in-insurance/ (archived at https://perma.cc/6MH5-S2TG).

11 'AI in Insurance Market Size, Share and Industry Forecast – 2031', Allied Market Research. www.alliedmarketresearch.com/ai-in-insurance-market-A11615 (archived at https://perma.cc/LA3Z-3NSK).

12 'Artificial Intelligence and the Insurance Industry', Deloitte UK, 18 Oct. 2021. www2.deloitte.com/uk/en/blog/auditandassurance/2021/artificial-intelligence-and-the-insurance-industry.html (archived at https://perma.cc/T2PN-PQDP).

13 'Blockchain and Smart Contracts in Insurance', Clifford Chance, 1 Jun. 2021. www.cliffordchance.com/content/dam/cliffordchance/briefings/2021/06/blockchain-and-smart-contracts-in-insurance-briefing.pdf (archived at https://perma.cc/2GMM-WGDM).

14 '10 Blockchain Insurance Examples to Know', Built In. builtin.com/
blockchain/blockchain-insurance-companies (archived at https://perma.cc/
ER9H-NELN).

15 'Blockchain Applications in Insurance', Deloitte. www2.deloitte.com/content/
dam/Deloitte/ch/Documents/innovation/ch-en-innovation-deloitte-blockchain-
app-in-insurance.pdf (archived at https://perma.cc/EKB5-LANW).

16 'Secured Insurance Framework Using Blockchain and Smart Contract',
Scientific Programming, vol. 2021. www.hindawi.com/journals/sp/
2021/6787406/ (archived at https://perma.cc/V7VH-JR3A).

17 'Secured Insurance Framework Using Blockchain and Smart Contract',
Scientific Programming, vol. 2021. www.hindawi.com/journals/sp/
2021/6787406/ (archived at https://perma.cc/TKA7-BLZB).

18 'Insurance and IoT: The Perfect Match', Insurance Thought Leadership,
10 Jun. 2021. www.insurancethoughtleadership.com/going-digital/insurance-
and-iot-perfect-match (archived at https://perma.cc/S38Y-LXKG).

19 'How IoT is Driving Insurance Digital Transformation', Digital Insurance,
17 Aug. 2021. www.dig-in.com/opinion/telematics-smart-housing-drive-
insurance-transformation (archived at https://perma.cc/VM59-2TNG).

20 '6 Ways IoT will Change the Insurance Sector in 2023', AIMultiple. research.
aimultiple.com/insurance-iot/ (archived at https://perma.cc/T657-8KW6).

21 'The Power of the Internet of Things in Commercial Insurance', BCG, 4 Oct.
2021. www.bcg.com/publications/2021/commercial-insurance-should-start-
testing-the-power-of-the-internet-of-things (archived at https://perma.cc/
6WH3-XYG8).

22 'Insurance and IoT: The Perfect Match', Insurance Thought Leadership,
10 Jun. 2021. www.insurancethoughtleadership.com/going-digital/insurance-
and-iot-perfect-match (archived at https://perma.cc/773U-KUF3).

23 'IoT Implementation: Steps, Challenges, Best Practices in 2023', AIMultiple,
13 Jan. 2023. research.aimultiple.com/iot-implementation/ (archived at https://
perma.cc/UAV4-KCRR).

24 '7 Challenges in IoT and How to Overcome Them', Hologram.io, 9 Sep. 2021,
www.hologram.io/blog/challenges-in-iot/ (archived at https://perma.cc/6CGA-
GHTR).

25 'Augumented and Virtual Reality in the Insurance Industry', Mazer, 21 Mar.
2022. mazerspace.com/augmented-and-virtual-reality-in-the-insurance-
industry/ (archived at https://perma.cc/988M-H38E).

26 'How Augmented Reality Impacts the Insurance Industry', Jasoren. jasoren.
com/how-augmented-reality-impacts-the-insurance-industry-7-use-cases-of-
ar-applications/ (archived at https://perma.cc/C75Q-AD5J).

27 'How Augmented Reality Impacts the Insurance Industry', Jasoren. jasoren.
com/how-augmented-reality-impacts-the-insurance-industry-7-use-cases-of-
ar-applications/ (archived at https://perma.cc/MG6Z-JUJW).

28 'How Augmented Reality Impacts the Insurance Industry', Jasoren. jasoren. com/how-augmented-reality-impacts-the-insurance-industry-7-use-cases-of-ar-applications/ (archived at https://perma.cc/S7G8-UDY9).

29 '6 Major Challenges Preventing Augmented and Virtual Reality Growth', Swiss Cognitive, 27 Jul. 2021. swisscognitive.ch/2021/07/27/6-ar-vr-challenges-in-2021/ (archived at https://perma.cc/6K63-AXDG).

30 'The Increased Adoption of Augmented and Virtual Reality and its Challenges', American Action Forum, 17 Aug. 2021. www.americanactionforum.org/insight/the-increased-adoption-of-augmented-and-virtual-reality-and-its-challenges-a-primer/ (archived at https://perma.cc/RN3H-SZRS).

31 'Insurance Industry Drone Use Is Flying Higher and Farther', Deloitte. www2.deloitte.com/us/en/pages/financial-services/articles/infocus-drone-use-by-insurance-industry-flying-higher-farther.html (archived at https://perma.cc/QHH6-D9H5).

32 '53 Drone Statistics & Facts (2023 Edition)', DroneSourced, 27 May 2023. dronesourced.com/industry/drone-statistics/ (archived at https://perma.cc/44NC-ARLF).

33 'Drones for Insurance Inspections: The Future of Claims Adjudication', Matt Gardner. matgardner.com/drones-for-insurance-inspections (archived at https://perma.cc/PK34-N8S8).

34 'Insurance Industry Drone Use Is Flying Higher and Farther', Deloitte. www2.deloitte.com/us/en/pages/financial-services/articles/infocus-drone-use-by-insurance-industry-flying-higher-farther.html (archived at https://perma.cc/DDC9-LKSF).

35 'Drones for Insurance Inspections: The Future of Claims Adjudication', Matt Gardner. matgardner.com/drones-for-insurance-inspections (archived at https://perma.cc/G36U-6J4N).

36 'MapSavvy Provides Powerful, Affordable Aerial Imagery for Insurance', MapSavvy, 1 Sep. 2019. www.mapsavvy.com/aerial-imagery-for-insurance/ (archived at https://perma.cc/VSE9-ZWB9).

37 'Drones for Insurance Inspections: The Future of Claims Adjudication', Matt Gardner. matgardner.com/drones-for-insurance-inspections (archived at https://perma.cc/2QPZ-FVYV).

38 'Aerial Imagery Maps the Future', Insurance Thought Leadership, 16 Mar. 2023. www.insurancethoughtleadership.com/underwriting/aerial-imagery-maps-future (archived at https://perma.cc/XQH7-5BDZ).

39 'Insurance Industry Drone Use Is Flying Higher and Farther', Deloitte. www2.deloitte.com/us/en/pages/financial-services/articles/infocus-drone-use-by-insurance-industry-flying-higher-farther.html (archived at https://perma.cc/5KEF-PXN2).

40 'Drones for Insurance Inspections: The Future of Claims Adjudication', Matt Gardner. matgardner.com/drones-for-insurance-inspections (archived at https://perma.cc/C5JM-KK86).

41 'Insurance Industry Drone Use Is Flying Higher and Farther', Deloitte. www2.deloitte.com/us/en/pages/financial-services/articles/infocus-drone-use-by-insurance-industry-flying-higher-farther.html (archived at https://perma.cc/8BUA-NF4W).

42 'Insurance Industry Drone Use Is Flying Higher and Farther', Deloitte. www2.deloitte.com/us/en/pages/financial-services/articles/infocus-drone-use-by-insurance-industry-flying-higher-farther.html (archived at https://perma.cc/M6GA-PNXD).

43 'Aerial Imagery Maps the Future', Insurance Thought Leadership, 16 Mar. 2023. www.insurancethoughtleadership.com/underwriting/aerial-imagery-maps-future (archived at https://perma.cc/XV7M-5NDM).

44 'Insurance Industry Drone Use Is Flying Higher and Farther', Deloitte. www2.deloitte.com/us/en/pages/financial-services/articles/infocus-drone-use-by-insurance-industry-flying-higher-farther.html (archived at https://perma.cc/94JF-4MYX).

45 'Aerial Imagery Maps the Future', Insurance Thought Leadership, 16 Mar. 2023. www.insurancethoughtleadership.com/underwriting/aerial-imagery-maps-future (archived at https://perma.cc/Q6MT-K55R).

46 'Everything You Need to Know About Drones in Insurance Today', IntellectSoft, 21 Sep. 2020. www.intellectsoft.net/blog/drones-in-insurance-all-you-need-to-know/ (archived at https://perma.cc/B65F-27FJ).

47 'Drones Offer Risks, Underwriting Challenges', Risk & Insurance. riskandinsurance.com/drones-offer-risks-underwriting-challenges/ (archived at https://perma.cc/8PEP-D5ZZ).

48 'Everything You Need to Know About Drones in Insurance Today', IntellectSoft, 21 Sep. 2020. www.intellectsoft.net/blog/drones-in-insurance-all-you-need-to-know/ (archived at https://perma.cc/3X5W-8YSJ).

49 'Everything You Need to Know About Drones in Insurance Today', IntellectSoft, 21 Sep. 2020. www.intellectsoft.net/blog/drones-in-insurance-all-you-need-to-know/ (archived at https://perma.cc/V2S5-BQ8S).

50 'Insurance Industry Drone Use Is Flying Higher and Farther', Deloitte. www2.deloitte.com/us/en/pages/financial-services/articles/infocus-drone-use-by-insurance-industry-flying-higher-farther.html (archived at https://perma.cc/NSG6-V8J6).

51 'The Growth in Connected IoT Devices is Expected to Generate 79.4ZB of Data in 2025', Business Wire, 18 Jun. 2019. www.businesswire.com/news/home/20190618005012/en/The-Growth-in-Connected-IoT-Devices-is-Expected-to-Generate-79.4ZB-of-Data-in-2025-According-to-a-New-IDC-Forecast (archived at https://perma.cc/G8H7-7ZAC).

52 'How Do Wearables Fuel Big Data', Ignitec. www.ignitec.com/insights/how-do-wearables-fuel-big-data/ (archived at https://perma.cc/RD9H-BT4U).

53 'Wearable Technology Market Share & Trends Report, 2030', Grand View Research. www.grandviewresearch.com/industry-analysis/wearable-technology-market (archived at https://perma.cc/VG4Y-QKGX).

54 'Cloud Computing Market Size, Growth', Trends Analysis [2030]. www.fortunebusinessinsights.com/cloud-computing-market-102697 (archived at https://perma.cc/RF8J-N5FK).

55 'Lloyd's: Impacts of Quantum Computing on Insurance', Finadium, 11 Feb. 2021. finadium.com/lloyds-impacts-of-quantum-computing-on-insurance/ (archived at https://perma.cc/Q9ZN-5TCW).

56 'AI vs Quantum Computing, No They Are Not The Same Thing', LinkedIn, 28 Aug. 2023. www.linkedin.com/pulse/ai-vs-quantum-computing-same-thing-rita-gatt (archived at https://perma.cc/4G9U-BZRA).

57 'Lloyd's: Impacts of Quantum Computing on Insurance', Finadium, 11 Feb. 2021. finadium.com/lloyds-impacts-of-quantum-computing-on-insurance/ (archived at https://perma.cc/MS79-6WLQ).

58 'Quantum Computing in Insurance: Opportunities and Threats', Sydney Quantum Academy, 14 Oct. 2021. sydneyquantum.org/news/quantum-computing-in-insurance-opportunities-and-threats/ (archived at https://perma.cc/9Q2T-LCPM).

59 'What Quantum Computing Means for Insurance', Accenture, 26 Jul. 2022. insuranceblog.accenture.com/quantum-computing-insurance (archived at https://perma.cc/S5B2-ZYE5).

60 'What Quantum Computing Means for Insurance', Accenture, 26 Jul. 2022, insuranceblog.accenture.com/quantum-computing-insurance (archived at https://perma.cc/4PGY-BNGU).

61 'Quantum Computing in Insurance: Opportunities and Threats', Sydney Quantum Academy, 14 Oct. 2021. sydneyquantum.org/news/quantum-computing-in-insurance-opportunities-and-threats/ (archived at https://perma.cc/JZ5M-DEMN).

62 'Emerging Risks: Quantum Computing, Lower Construction Quality, Legal Tech etc.', Insurance Journal, 24 Jun. 2022. www.insurancejournal.com/news/international/2022/06/24/673320.htm (archived at https://perma.cc/HGB5-6ZL6).

Conclusion

As we bring our journey through *Navigating Insurtech* to a close, it's an opportune moment to reflect on the significant insights and key themes that have been highlighted throughout this comprehensive exploration. This book has not only provided a detailed chronicle of the evolution of insurtech but has also shone a light on its substantial impact on the insurance industry, driven by a wave of technological innovation and shifts in market dynamics.

Throughout our exploration, we've explored the historical roots of insurtech, set against the backdrop of the insurance industry's rich legacy, to the transformative effects of the digital age. We have journeyed through the industry's transformation, observing the pivotal role of emerging technologies such as AI, blockchain and IoT, and how they have seamlessly woven into the fabric of modern insurance practices.

In traversing this dynamic landscape, *Navigating Insurtech* has revealed the industry at a crossroads of innovation and challenges. The book's pages have encapsulated the current state of insurtech as a beacon of innovation, marked by agility, customer-centricity and technological prowess. Looking ahead, we suggested a future for insurtech marked by continuous innovation, with emerging technologies likely playing a crucial role in reshaping various aspects of the industry.

As this exploration draws to a close, we've reflected on the transformative journey of the insurance industry, showcasing the significant strides made and the exciting possibilities that lie ahead.

Simply put, the insurtech story is far from over, with many more chapters yet to be written in this ever-evolving narrative.

Reflection on the evolution of insurtech

Our narrative commenced by charting the early roots of insurtech, meticulously tracing its development within the historical context of the insurance industry. The journey navigated through significant milestones, including the establishment of Lloyd's of London and the remarkable transformations in the 20th century, leading to the digital age's disruptive impact.

As we reflect on the evolution of insurtech, it becomes clear that this journey is not just a chronicle of technological advancements but a story of how these innovations have reshaped the very fabric of the insurance industry. Our narrative commenced with an exploration of insurtech's early roots, placing its emergence within the historical context of the insurance sector.

Delving into the insurtech landscape, we explored various facets shaping its evolution. The birth of peer-to-peer (P2P) insurance and the rise of digital distribution platforms marked a significant shift in how insurance services are delivered and consumed. The emergence of digital ecosystems introduced a new paradigm for value creation in insurance, with telematics and usage-based insurance models redefining risk assessment and pricing strategies.

The role of emerging technologies in insurtech has been profound. Blockchain technology revolutionized trust and transparency in insurance transactions, while the Internet of Things (IoT) provided data-driven insights, transforming policy customization and risk management. Artificial intelligence (AI) and machine learning (ML) introduced automation, insight and predictive precision into various insurance processes. We observed real-world applications of these technologies in cases like Progressive's Snapshot program and the AI-driven operational changes in Japanese insurance firms.

Looking towards the future, Chapter 8, 'The Future of Insurtech', provided insights into the key drivers of change and anticipated trends in the insurtech sector. The influence of advanced technology, such as the future role of blockchain, smart contracts and the growing importance of AI and ChatGPT in insurance, was underscored. The chapter also highlighted the potential of augmented reality (AR), virtual reality (VR), drones and aerial imagery in revolutionizing the insurance landscape, along with the emerging role of quantum computing in insurance.

I hope this book illuminates the challenges and opportunities that lie ahead for insurtech. We have emphasized the importance of meeting the needs of emerging markets and addressed the critical role of environmental, social and governance (ESG) considerations in shaping the future of insurtech. The narrative also shed light on the regulatory challenges and the need for global cooperation in navigating the insurtech revolution.

The evolution of insurtech as detailed across the book is a testament to the dynamic interplay between technology and the traditional insurance industry. It's a narrative of transformation, innovation and anticipation, as the industry continues to adapt and evolve in response to technological advancements and changing market needs. This reflection not only honours the journey thus far but also sets the stage for the ongoing evolution of insurtech in the years to come.

In-depth analysis of insurtech developments

In *Navigating Insurtech*, we embarked on an extensive exploration of the diverse facets of the insurtech landscape, uncovering how this sector is reshaping the insurance industry from its core. The book provided a deep dive into the emergence and impact of P2P insurance models and digital distribution platforms, highlighting their role in revolutionizing the way insurance products are accessed and experienced by customers.

The narrative unfolded the rise of digital ecosystems in insurance, illustrating how they create new paradigms for value creation and service delivery. We analysed the transformative influence of telematics and IoT, which have brought unprecedented precision and personalization to risk assessment and management. The concept of perfect information, a visionary idea in risk management, was dissected, showing how insurtech strives to achieve this ideal through advanced data analytics.

A significant portion of the book was dedicated to illustrating how insurtech, with the aid of data analytics, AI and ML, is revolutionizing risk assessment and transforming the underwriting process. We saw how predictive analytics is being leveraged to create more accurate and tailored insurance policies, and how IoT's capabilities extend beyond just monitoring to actively mitigating risks in areas like home security, health and environmental monitoring.

Chapter 4, 'Insurtech and Customer Experience', provided a thorough examination of how insurtech is enhancing the customer experience. From streamlining processes and communication to improving the speed and efficiency of claims processes, the book highlighted the role of digital tools in policy management and customer-insurer communication. It emphasized how insurtech fosters a new era of customer service marked by personalization, transparency and responsiveness.

Insurtech's role in empowering customers in their insurance decision-making was explored, with a focus on how digital tools and data analytics are being used to boost customer retention and loyalty. The book addressed the critical aspect of handling customer data and privacy, underscoring the need for robust mechanisms to safeguard sensitive information.

We also delved into the regulatory considerations and challenges in the insurtech space, discussing the future trends in risk assessment and the growing importance of incorporating ESG considerations into insurtech operations. The role of AI in fraud detection and the transformative impact of blockchain technology in ensuring transparency and trust in insurance transactions were also highlighted.

Chapter 7, 'Investing in insurtech', shed light on the financial aspects and investment dynamics within the insurtech sector. It provided insights into the global tapestry of insurtech investments, unravelling regional nuances and discussing the key factors influencing investment decisions. The importance of diversity, equity and inclusion (DEI) and the role of founder qualifications in insurtech investments were also discussed, emphasizing the changing landscape of insurtech investment.

Navigating Insurtech has offered a comprehensive and multi-dimensional analysis of the insurtech sector, highlighting its revolutionary impact on the insurance industry. From technological innovations to customer-centric approaches and investment dynamics, the book has painted a vivid picture of an industry undergoing a significant transformation, driven by the relentless march of technology and changing consumer needs.

As we conclude, insurtech is observed standing at a juncture of exponential growth, grappling with potential challenges. The field today epitomizes innovation, marked by agile, customer-focused and technologically advanced practices. The surge in digital platforms and emphasis on data-driven decision-making underscore this evolution.

The future landscape of insurtech

In its forward-looking analysis, *Navigating Insurtech* paints a vivid picture of the future landscape of the insurtech sector, characterized by continuous innovation and transformation. The book identifies emerging technologies as pivotal in shaping this future, with quantum computing poised to join the ranks of AI and ML in revolutionizing the insurance industry.

The future of insurtech, as outlined in the book, will be significantly influenced by advanced technologies. Quantum computing is expected to bring a new dimension to data processing and risk analysis, offering the potential to dramatically reshape risk assessment and policy customization. Alongside this, the roles of AI and advanced algorithms, like those embodied in ChatGPT, will become increasingly central in automating and enhancing decision-making processes within the industry.

The book anticipates a significant role for blockchain technology and smart contracts in the future of insurtech. These technologies are expected to introduce new levels of transparency, efficiency and security to insurance transactions, enhancing trust and streamlining operations.

The integration of IoT and telematics in insurance is set to deepen, with these technologies providing more granular and real-time data for risk assessment and policy pricing. AR and VR are also predicted to play a transformative role, particularly in claims processing and customer engagement. Additionally, the use of drones and aerial imagery is expected to become more prevalent, especially in assessing damages for claims and in risk monitoring.

The book recognizes that the path forward for insurtech will encompass both challenges and opportunities. It underscores the importance of meeting the needs of emerging markets and adapting to their unique requirements. The influence of ESG factors will also be critical, as the industry moves towards more sustainable and socially responsible practices.

An evolving regulatory landscape is anticipated to play a crucial role in shaping the future of insurtech. The book highlights the need for adaptive regulatory frameworks that can keep pace with technological advancements while ensuring consumer protection and market stability. Furthermore, it emphasizes the importance of global collaboration in fostering an environment conducive to innovation and growth in the insurtech sector.

Navigating Insurtech projects a future where the insurance industry is increasingly driven by technological advancements, with a focus on innovation, adaptability and global cooperation. This future landscape is one where insurtech not only addresses current market needs but also anticipates and shapes future trends, creating a more efficient, transparent and customer-focused insurance ecosystem.

Stakeholder dynamics and recommendations

In its exploration of the insurtech ecosystem, *Navigating Insurtech* offers crucial insights into the dynamics of various stakeholders, including insurers, start-ups and regulatory bodies. The book underscores the vital importance of adaptability and strategic foresight for these key players in the evolving landscape of insurtech.

Insurers are encouraged to embrace the wave of digital transformation wholeheartedly. The book suggests that insurers should not only adopt new technologies but also integrate them deeply into their operational models. This involves a cultural shift towards innovation, a willingness to experiment and an openness to redefining traditional business processes. By fully embracing digital transformation, insurers can enhance their efficiency, improve customer engagement and stay competitive in a rapidly changing market.

Start-ups are positioned as the catalysts of change in the insurtech sector. The book advises these emerging entities to maintain a relentless focus on innovation. It calls for start-ups to continually push the boundaries of technology and creatively address the pain points in the insurance industry. The emphasis is on fostering a culture of continuous learning and adaptation, enabling start-ups to navigate the challenges of the industry and contribute to its evolution.

For regulatory bodies, the book highlights the critical role of balancing the encouragement of innovation with the protection of consumers. Regulators are advised to develop frameworks that are flexible enough to accommodate new technologies and business models, yet robust enough to ensure consumer safety and market stability. The goal is to create an environment where innovation can thrive without compromising the integrity and security of the insurance market.

In summary, *Navigating Insurtech* provides a nuanced view of the roles and responsibilities of different stakeholders within the insurtech ecosystem. It advocates for a collaborative approach where insurers, start-ups and regulators work together to foster an environment conducive to innovation, consumer protection and sustainable growth in the insurtech sector.

Navigating investment and regulatory challenges

In *Navigating Insurtech*, considerable attention is devoted to dissecting the complexities involved in insurtech investment and regulatory landscapes. The narrative delves into the cultural and regional differences that shape investment strategies across key areas like North America, Europe and Asia-Pacific. These discussions bring to the forefront the varied investment climates and market dynamics that define these regions, offering valuable insights for potential investors.

The book places a strong emphasis on the significance of DEI in the realm of insurtech investments. It argues that incorporating DEI principles is not just a moral imperative but also a strategic advantage, as it leads to more diverse perspectives and innovative solutions in the industry. The narrative encourages investors to consider DEI factors as integral to their investment decision-making processes.

Alongside DEI, ESG considerations are highlighted as crucial for insurtech investments. The book underscores the growing importance of ESG criteria in evaluating investment opportunities, stressing that sustainable and socially responsible practices can lead to long-term success and resilience in the insurtech sector.

Navigating Insurtech offers strategic advice for manoeuvring through the complex investment landscapes in insurtech. This includes understanding the unique challenges and opportunities presented by different regional markets and aligning investment strategies with the evolving trends in technology and consumer behaviour. The book suggests that a nuanced understanding of these aspects is essential for making informed and effective investment decisions in the dynamic world of insurtech.

In essence, the book provides a comprehensive overview of the investment and regulatory challenges in the insurtech industry, equipping stakeholders with the knowledge and tools needed to navigate this evolving sector successfully. It advocates for an approach that balances financial goals with ethical considerations, ultimately contributing to the sustainable growth of the insurtech ecosystem.

Addressing claims, fraud detection and cybersecurity

Navigating Insurtech offers an in-depth exploration of the significant advancements in claims processing, fraud detection and cybersecurity within the insurtech sector. The book delves into how technology has revolutionized these critical areas, highlighting the shift from traditional methods to more efficient, data-driven approaches.

The narrative examines the evolution of claims processing, moving from conventional methods to innovative, technology-driven approaches. It discusses how insurtech has streamlined the claims process by incorporating automation and AI, significantly reducing the time and resources required to manage claims. The integration of mobile applications in claims processing is also highlighted, emphasizing their role in enhancing customer experiences and improving accessibility.

A key focus of the book is on the utilization of AI and data analytics in fraud detection and prevention. These technologies have equipped insurers with sophisticated tools to identify and mitigate fraudulent activities more effectively. The use of predictive analytics and pattern recognition algorithms has transformed the way insurers approach fraud detection, making the process more proactive rather than reactive.

In the realm of cybersecurity, *Navigating Insurtech* underscores the critical importance of robust mechanisms to protect sensitive data. With the increasing reliance on digital platforms and IoT in insurance operations, safeguarding customer data and maintaining privacy have become paramount. The book discusses the implementation of advanced security protocols and the adoption of blockchain technology to enhance transparency and data integrity in insurance transactions.

The book also explores the broader context of risk management in insurtech, detailing how technologies like telematics, IoT and AI are utilized in monitoring various risk factors, from driving behaviour to environmental monitoring. These advancements not only aid in risk mitigation but also contribute to more accurate and personalized insurance offerings.

Additionally, the book addresses the regulatory challenges in the insurtech sector, acknowledging the need for regulatory frameworks that can adapt to the fast-paced changes in technology while ensuring consumer protection and market stability.

In conclusion, *Navigating Insurtech* provides a comprehensive overview of how technological innovations are transforming claims processing, enhancing fraud detection capabilities and reinforcing cybersecurity in the insurance industry. By embracing these technological advancements, the insurtech sector is set to continue its trajectory of growth, efficiency and increased customer satisfaction, all while navigating the challenges and complexities of an increasingly digital world.

Acknowledgement of limitations and continuous evolution

In its comprehensive coverage of the insurtech sector, *Navigating Insurtech* recognizes that the swift pace of technological advancements might give rise to emerging trends and unforeseen challenges that extend beyond the scope of the book. The insurtech landscape is acknowledged as a rapidly evolving one, where new developments and innovations continuously reshape the industry.

This dynamic nature of insurtech underscores the importance of ongoing learning and the need for stakeholders to remain adaptable. As the sector progresses, staying abreast of the latest technological breakthroughs and understanding their implications becomes crucial for anyone involved in insurtech.

Therefore, while *Navigating Insurtech* lays a solid foundation of understanding, it also serves as a reminder of the necessity for continuous engagement with the ever-evolving trends and practices within the insurtech ecosystem.

Call to action and recommendations

Navigating Insurtech emphasizes the need for a proactive and dynamic approach in the rapidly evolving field of insurtech. It calls on industry leaders and policymakers to create environments that not only drive innovation but also prioritize consumer protection and market stability.

The book advocates for the insurance industry to actively engage with emerging technologies. It urges insurers to incorporate these technologies into their business models, not merely as an add-on but as a core part of their strategy to enhance efficiency and improve customer experiences. This requires a cultural shift towards embracing change and fostering an environment of continuous innovation.

For policymakers and regulatory bodies, *Navigating Insurtech* stresses the importance of developing flexible, adaptive regulatory frameworks. These frameworks should be capable of keeping pace with technological advancements while simultaneously safeguarding consumers against the potential risks associated with new technologies.

The book recognizes its limitations, acknowledging that the swift pace of change in insurtech might mean that some emerging trends and developments have not been fully covered. This acknowledgement highlights the need for ongoing vigilance and adaptability in the face of new innovations and shifts within the sector.

Personal reflections in the book reveal the profound impact of technology on the insurance sector, illustrating that technology serves not just as a facilitator but as a catalyst for fundamental change in the essence of insurance.

As it concludes, *Navigating Insurtech* is not just a retrospective of past developments but a call to action for continued engagement and adaptation in the insurtech arena. It encourages continuous learning and strategic evolution for all stakeholders in the field. Insurers, start-ups and regulators are all advised to embrace adaptability and foresight. Insurers need to fully commit to digital transformation, start-ups are encouraged to continually innovate and challenge the status quo and regulators are tasked with balancing the promotion of innovation with the necessity of consumer protection.

Final thoughts on *Navigating Insurtech*

As we reach the end of *Navigating Insurtech*, it becomes clear that this book is more than a chronicle of the sector's evolution; it is a beacon for the ongoing journey within the dynamic realm of insurtech.

The book extends an invitation to readers, industry professionals and enthusiasts to actively participate, innovate and adapt to the continuously shifting landscape of insurtech.

This work does not merely recount the history of insurtech but also illuminates a path forward, guiding stakeholders through the present complexities and into the future possibilities of the industry. It stands as a comprehensive resource and a forward-thinking vision, seamlessly connecting the historical development, current state and potential future of the insurtech industry.

In essence, *Navigating Insurtech* is a tribute to the transformative impact of technological innovation on the world of insurance. It envisages a future where the insurance industry is not only more efficient and effective but also more attuned to the evolving demands of a digitally advanced society. A forward-looking perspective, highlighting the synergies between insurance and technology. It stands as a testament to the transformative power of innovation, signalling a future where insurance is more accessible, efficient and tailored to the needs of an ever-evolving society.

GLOSSARY

Discover the Glossary below. It's your book dictionary, clarifying industry-specific terminology and concepts in alphabetical order. Whether you're new to this subject or need clear explanations, the Glossary is here to enhance your reading experience.

5G or fifth-generation wireless technology   5G is the latest generation of cellular network technology that provides faster and more reliable wireless communication compared to previous generations (such as 4G or LTE). It offers significantly higher data speeds, lower latency (response time) and the ability to connect a vast number of devices simultaneously. 5G technology is expected to revolutionize various industries, including telecommunications, healthcare, transportation and more, by enabling new applications and services that rely on ultra-fast and low-latency wireless connections.

Actuaries   Actuaries use mathematical and statistical models to analyse data and calculate insurance premium rates, policy reserves and financial projections. They help insurers make informed decisions about pricing, risk management and product development. Much like underwriters, actuaries hold a pivotal role not only within insurance firms but also within organizations such as MGAs (managing general agents) and service providers that provide actuarial consultancy services.

Application programming interface (API)   API is a set of rules and protocols that allows different software applications to communicate and interact with each other. APIs define the methods and data formats that developers can use to request and exchange information between applications, making it easier to integrate and connect different systems.

APIs play a crucial role in modern software development by enabling developers to access the functionality of other software components, services or platforms without needing to understand their internal workings. They are commonly used to enable third-party developers to build applications or services that can interact with existing platforms, such as social media networks, payment gateways or cloud services.

For example, a weather application on your smartphone might use an API to fetch weather data from a remote server. Similarly, when you log in to a website using your Google or Facebook account, you are using APIs to authenticate and access your information. APIs are essential for creating interoperability and flexibility in software systems, allowing developers to build on top of existing technologies and create more powerful and feature-rich applications.

Artificial intelligence (AI)   AI refers to the simulation of human intelligence in machines or computer systems. It involves the development of algorithms and computer programs that enable machines to perform tasks typically requiring human intelligence, such as understanding natural language, recognizing patterns, learning from experience, making decisions and solving problems.

Augmented reality (AR)   AR is a technology that combines computer-generated elements, such as images, videos or 3D models, with the real-world environment to create an augmented or enhanced view of reality. Unlike virtual reality (VR), which immerses users in a completely computer-generated environment, AR enhances the real world by overlaying digital content onto it.

AR is often experienced through devices like smartphones, tablets or AR glasses, which use cameras and sensors to capture the real-world surroundings and then superimpose computer-generated graphics or information onto the user's view. These digital elements can be interactive and contextually relevant to the physical environment.

Augmented reality has a wide range of applications across various industries, including gaming, education, healthcare, retail and manufacturing. For example, in gaming, AR games like Pokémon GO use the smartphone's camera and GPS to place virtual creatures in the real world, allowing players to interact with them as if they were physically present. In education, AR can provide immersive learning experiences by overlaying educational content onto textbooks or physical objects. In healthcare, AR can assist surgeons with real-time data and guidance during surgeries.

Big data   Big data refers to extremely large and complex datasets that are too large to be effectively managed, processed and analysed using traditional data processing tools and methods. Big data is characterized by its volume, velocity, variety and sometimes veracity, which are often referred to as the '4 Vs' of big data:

Volume: Big data involves vast amounts of data. This can range from terabytes to petabytes or even exabytes of information. It includes both structured data (e.g. databases) and unstructured data (e.g. text, images, videos, social media posts).

Velocity: Big data is generated and collected at a high speed. It flows into organizations rapidly, often in real-time or near-real-time. Examples include social media updates, sensor data from IoT devices and financial transactions.

Variety: Big data comes in various formats and types. It includes structured data (e.g. databases and spreadsheets) and unstructured data (e.g. text documents, images, videos). The diversity of data sources and formats adds complexity.

Veracity: Veracity refers to the trustworthiness and quality of the data. Big data can include noisy, incomplete or inconsistent data, which makes it challenging to ensure data accuracy.

To handle big data organizations use specialized tools and technologies, including distributed computing frameworks like Apache Hadoop and Apache Spark, NoSQL databases, data lakes and advanced analytics techniques. These technologies allow organizations to store, process and analyse big data to extract valuable insights, make data-driven decisions and gain a competitive advantage.

Blockchain   Blockchain is a distributed ledger technology that enables secure and transparent recording of transactions across a network of computers. It was originally created to support the digital cryptocurrency bitcoin, but its applications have since expanded far beyond digital currencies. Blockchain is often described as a decentralized and immutable digital ledger.

Key characteristics of blockchain technology include:

Decentralization: Blockchain operates on a decentralized network of computers (nodes) rather than relying on a central authority like a bank or government. This means no single entity has complete control over the network, making it resistant to censorship and tampering.

Distributed ledger: Each participant in the blockchain network maintains a copy of the entire ledger. This distributed ledger is continually updated with new transactions in a chronological order, creating a permanent and tamper-resistant record.

Transparency: Transactions recorded on a blockchain are typically visible to all participants in the network. This transparency can enhance trust among participants and reduce the risk of fraud.

Immutability: Once a transaction is added to the blockchain, it becomes nearly impossible to alter or delete. This immutability ensures the integrity of the ledger.

Security: Blockchain uses cryptographic techniques to secure transactions and control access to the network. Public and private keys are used to sign and verify transactions, adding a layer of security.

Smart contracts: Smart contracts are self-executing contracts with the terms of the agreement directly written into code. They automatically execute when predefined conditions are met, eliminating the need for intermediaries.

Blockchain technology has a wide range of applications, including:

Cryptocurrencies: Bitcoin and other cryptocurrencies use blockchain technology for peer-to-peer transactions and as a store of value.

Supply chain management: Blockchain can track the provenance and movement of goods, enhancing transparency and reducing fraud in supply chains.

Financial services: It's used for cross-border payments, remittances and trade finance to improve efficiency and reduce costs.

Healthcare: Blockchain can securely manage patient records, ensuring data integrity and facilitating interoperability among healthcare providers.

Voting systems: Some countries are exploring blockchain for secure and transparent voting systems.

Real estate: Blockchain can streamline property transactions, reducing the need for intermediaries.

Blockchain technology continues to evolve and its potential applications are still being explored across various industries. It has the potential to disrupt traditional business models and revolutionize how transactions and data are managed and secured.

Broker   A broker is a financial intermediary or agent who facilitates transactions between buyers and sellers. Brokers play a crucial role in various industries, including finance, insurance, real estate and commodities trading. Their primary function is to act as intermediaries, connecting individuals or entities who want to buy or sell specific assets or services. Here are some common types of brokers and their roles:

Stockbroker: A stockbroker facilitates the buying and selling of stocks and other securities on behalf of investors. They execute orders on stock exchanges and provide investment advice.

Real estate broker: Real estate brokers help individuals buy, sell or rent properties. They assist with property listings, negotiations and legal documentation, often working alongside real estate agents.

Insurance broker: Insurance brokers work on behalf of clients to help them find suitable insurance coverage. They assess clients' needs, provide policy options from various insurers and assist in the purchasing process.

Commodity broker: Commodity brokers facilitate the trading of commodities such as oil, gold, agricultural products and more. They connect buyers and sellers in commodity markets and execute trades.

Forex broker: Forex (foreign exchange) brokers enable individuals and institutions to trade currencies in the foreign exchange market. They provide trading platforms and access to currency pairs.

Mortgage broker: Mortgage brokers help individuals and businesses secure loans for real estate purchases. They connect borrowers with lenders and assist in the loan application process.

Business broker: Business brokers specialize in the buying and selling of businesses. They help business owners find suitable buyers and guide prospective buyers through the acquisition process.

Freight broker: Freight brokers facilitate the transportation of goods by connecting shippers with carriers. They negotiate shipping rates and ensure the smooth movement of cargo.

Customs broker: Customs brokers assist importers and exporters in navigating customs regulations and clearance processes for international shipments.

Investment broker: Investment brokers offer a range of financial services, including investment advisory, portfolio management and trading of various financial instruments.

Brokers typically earn commissions or fees for their services and their compensation may vary depending on the type of transactions they handle. They are expected to act in the best interests of their clients and provide expertise in their respective fields to help clients make informed decisions. It's important to choose a reputable broker who is licensed and regulated in their industry to ensure transparency and compliance with relevant laws and regulations.

Claims adjuster   Claims adjusters, often referred to as insurance claims examiners or claims investigators, work on behalf of insurance companies. They assess insurance claims, investigate the extent of an insurance company's liability and help determine the validity of claims. They evaluate the damage or loss, determine coverage and negotiate settlements with policyholders or claimants. Claims adjusters ensure that claims are settled fairly and in accordance with the terms and conditions of insurance policies.

Cloud computing   Cloud computing refers to the delivery of various computing services, including servers, storage, databases, networking, software, analytics and more, over the internet. Instead of owning and maintaining physical hardware and software, users and organizations can access these resources on a pay-as-you-go basis from cloud service providers.

Key characteristics of cloud computing include:

On-demand self-service: Users can provision and manage computing resources as needed, without requiring human intervention from the service provider.

Broad network access: Cloud services are accessible over the internet from a variety of devices, such as computers, smartphones and tablets.

Resource pooling: Cloud providers use multi-tenant models to serve multiple customers from a shared pool of computing resources. Resources are dynamically allocated and reassigned as needed.

Rapid elasticity: Cloud resources can be quickly scaled up or down to accommodate changing workloads or user demands.

Measured service: Cloud usage is metered and customers are billed based on their actual resource consumption. This 'pay-as-you-go' model is cost-effective because users only pay for what they use.

Cloud computing services are typically categorized into three main service models:

Infrastructure as a service (IaaS): IaaS provides virtualized computing resources over the internet. Users can rent virtual machines, storage and networking infrastructure on a per-use basis. Examples of IaaS providers include Amazon Web Services (AWS), Microsoft Azure and Google Cloud Platform (GCP).

Platform as a service (PaaS): PaaS offers a platform that includes not only infrastructure but also development tools and services to help developers build, test and deploy applications. PaaS providers include Heroku, Google App Engine and Microsoft Azure App Service.

Software as a service (SaaS): SaaS delivers software applications over the internet on a subscription basis. Users can access the software through a web browser without the need for installation or maintenance. Common examples of SaaS include Microsoft Office 365, Salesforce and Google Workspace (formerly G Suite).

Cloud computing offers several advantages, including scalability, flexibility, cost-efficiency and accessibility. It allows organizations to focus on their core business functions while outsourcing IT infrastructure management to cloud providers. However, it also raises concerns related to security, privacy and data sovereignty, which must be addressed when adopting cloud solutions.

Cognitive diversity   Cognitive diversity represents the diversity of thoughts, encompassing differences in how individuals think, process information, approach problem-solving and generate ideas. It comprises a variety of cognitive styles, skills and perspectives that individuals contribute to a team or organization.

Diversity, equity and inclusion (DEI)   DEI are three interconnected principles that focus on promoting fairness, representation and respect for all individuals within an organization or society, regardless of their backgrounds or identities. Here's what each of these principles means:

Diversity: Diversity refers to the presence of a wide range of individual differences and identities within a group organization or community.

These differences can encompass various aspects, including but not limited to:

- Gender
- Age
- Race and ethnicity
- Sexual orientation
- Religion
- Disability status
- Socioeconomic background
- Nationality
- Cognitive diversity
- Neurodiversity

Equity: Equity involves ensuring that all individuals have equal access to opportunities, resources and treatment, regardless of their differences or identities. It aims to level the playing field and rectify historical and systemic disparities that have disadvantaged certain groups. Equity recognizes that individuals may require different levels of support and accommodations to achieve equality.

Inclusion: Inclusion centres on creating a welcoming and inclusive environment where all individuals, regardless of their differences, feel valued, respected and empowered to participate fully. Inclusion promotes a sense of belonging, where everyone's perspectives and contributions are appreciated and considered.

DEI initiatives and practices aim to foster a culture that embraces and upholds these principles, ultimately leading to a more diverse, equitable and inclusive organization or society. The goal is to break down barriers, challenge biases and prejudices and create a space where everyone has an equal opportunity to thrive and contribute to their fullest potential. DEI is important not only for promoting social justice but also for driving innovation, improving decision-making and enhancing the overall performance of organizations and communities.

Drone   A drone, also known as an unmanned aerial vehicle (UAV), is an aircraft that operates without a human pilot on board. Drones are typically controlled remotely by a human operator or autono-mously by onboard computers. They have gained widespread use in various industries and applications due to their versatility and ability to perform tasks without risking human lives.

Key features and characteristics of drones include:

Remote control: Most drones are operated by remote control devices such as joysticks or specialized transmitters. The operator can control the drone's movement, altitude, speed and other functions from a distance.

Autonomous flight: Many modern drones are equipped with advanced sensors and GPS technology, allowing them to fly autonomously and follow pre-programmed flight paths or perform tasks without constant human input.

Cameras and sensors: Drones often come equipped with cameras, sensors (such as GPS, accelerometers and gyroscopes) and other imaging equipment. These sensors enable various applications, including aerial photography, videography, surveillance and data collection.

Size and types: Drones come in various sizes, from small quadcopters that can fit in the palm of your hand to larger fixed-wing aircraft. The choice of drone type depends on the specific application and requirements.

Applications: Drones have a wide range of applications across industries, including but not limited to:

- Aerial photography and videography
- Surveying and mapping
- Agriculture (crop monitoring, pesticide spraying)
- Search and rescue operations
- Environmental monitoring
- Infrastructure inspection (e.g. bridges, power lines)
- Package delivery (e.g. by companies like Amazon)
- Entertainment and racing
- Military and defence

Regulations: The use of drones is subject to regulations and laws in many countries to ensure safety and privacy. These regulations may include rules for drone registration, flight restrictions in certain areas (e.g. near airports) and licensing for commercial drone operators.

Drones have revolutionized various industries by providing cost-effective and efficient solutions to tasks that were once difficult or dangerous to perform. They continue to evolve with advancements in technology, including longer flight times, improved cameras and enhanced autonomous capabilities.

Ecosystem   In technology terms, **an ecosystem** typically refers to a complex and interconnected network of software, hardware, applications and services that collectively work together to provide a specific set of functionalities or solutions. These ecosystems are often designed to offer users a seamless and integrated experience.

For example, in the context of mobile devices, an ecosystem might include the operating system (such as iOS or Android), the hardware device itself, various pre-installed and third-party apps, cloud services for data synchronization and accessory products that all function together to provide a comprehensive user experience. Users can often move data and services seamlessly between devices and services within the same ecosystem.

Major technology companies like Apple, Google and Microsoft have created their own ecosystems, which encompass a wide range of products and services, including smartphones, tablets, desktop computers, laptops, smart home devices and more. These ecosystems are designed to create a sense of continuity and convenience for users, encouraging them to use multiple products and services from the same company.

In essence, a technology ecosystem in the tech industry refers to a comprehensive and integrated network of devices, software, applications and services that work together to deliver a unified and user-friendly experience.

GI life insurance   GI life insurance refers to life insurance policies that are issued and provided to members of the United States military, specifically those in the Armed Forces. This type of life insurance is designed to provide financial protection to military personnel and their families.

Key features of GI life insurance include:

Availability: GI life insurance is available to active-duty service members, members of the National Guard and Reserves and eligible veterans.

Low-cost coverage: GI life insurance policies typically offer coverage at lower premium rates compared to many civilian life insurance options. This affordability makes it accessible to military personnel.

Different types: There are different types of GI life insurance programmes, including:

Servicemembers' Group Life Insurance (SGLI): This is available to active-duty service members and members of the National Guard and Reserves. It provides low-cost term life insurance coverage and service members are automatically enrolled unless they decline coverage.

Veterans' Group Life Insurance (VGLI): VGLI is available to veterans who had SGLI coverage while in the military. It allows veterans to convert their SGLI coverage to a renewable term life insurance policy after leaving the service.

Family Servicemembers' Group Life Insurance (FSGLI): FSGLI provides life insurance coverage for spouses and dependent children of service members insured under SGLI. It includes coverage for the spouse and dependent children of service members.

Coverage amount: SGLI provides a maximum coverage amount and service members can choose the level of coverage they desire within those limits.

Beneficiary designation: Service members can designate beneficiaries who would receive the insurance proceeds in the event of their death.

Automatic enrolment: SGLI coverage is typically automatically provided to service members, but they have the option to adjust their coverage levels or decline the insurance if they have other coverage.

It's important for military personnel to review their GI life insurance coverage and make informed decisions regarding their life insurance needs. While GI life insurance can be a cost-effective way to provide financial protection for military families, some service members may choose to supplement it with additional civilian life insurance policies to meet their specific requirements.

Gig economy   The gig economy, also known as the 'freelance economy' or 'platform economy', refers to a labour market characterized by the prevalence of short-term, temporary or freelance jobs rather than traditional, long-term employment with a single employer. In the gig economy, individuals, often referred to as 'gig workers' or 'independent contractors', work on a project-by-project basis, taking on tasks, assignments or gigs as they become available.

Key features of the gig economy include:

Flexibility: Gig workers have the flexibility to choose when, where and how much they work. They can often set their own schedules and take on multiple gigs simultaneously.

Freelance work: Many gig workers are self-employed freelancers who offer their skills or services to clients or businesses on a contractual basis. This can include a wide range of professions, from graphic designers and writers to software developers and consultants.

Digital platforms: Digital platforms and online marketplaces play a crucial role in connecting gig workers with potential clients or customers. These platforms facilitate gig matching, payment processing and communication between parties.

Varied income sources: Gig workers often rely on multiple income sources, taking on gigs from different clients or platforms to diversify their earnings.

Independent status: Gig workers are typically considered independent contractors rather than traditional employees. This distinction can impact taxation, labour rights and access to benefits like healthcare and retirement plans.

On-demand services: The gig economy extends beyond traditional employment sectors, encompassing various on-demand services such as ride-sharing (e.g. Uber, Lyft), food delivery (e.g. DoorDash, Uber Eats) and household tasks (e.g. TaskRabbit).

Gig platforms: Prominent gig platforms include Uber, Lyft, Airbnb, Upwork, Fiverr and many others, each catering to different types of gig work.

While the gig economy offers flexibility and opportunities for income generation, it also raises important questions and challenges. Gig workers often lack the job security, benefits and labour protections enjoyed by traditional employees. As a result, debates surrounding workers' rights, employment classification and social safety nets have become prominent in discussions related to the gig economy.

Health insurance   Health insurance covers medical expenses and healthcare costs. It includes individual health insurance plans, group health insurance provided by employers and government-funded healthcare programmes like Medicare and Medicaid. Health insurance helps individuals and families access necessary medical care and services while minimizing out-of-pocket expenses.

Insurance agents   Insurance agents are intermediaries between insurance companies and policyholders. They help individuals and businesses select insurance policies that best suit their needs. Insurance agents can work independently, for a specific insurance company (captive agents) or as part of an independent agency representing multiple insurance providers. Their responsibilities include explaining policy options, helping clients understand coverage and assisting in the application and claims processes. Insurance agents earn commissions or fees for their services and must often obtain licences to operate legally in their respective regions. Their goal is to ensure clients have appropriate insurance coverage to protect against various risks.

Insurance broker   Insurance brokers are professionals who act as an intermediary between individuals or businesses seeking insurance coverage and insurance companies. Unlike insurance agents, who typically represent specific insurance companies or agencies, insurance brokers work independently and have no ties to any particular insurer. Their primary role is to assess the insurance needs of their clients and then search the insurance market for policies that meet those needs. Insurance brokers are not limited to offering products from a single insurance company, which allows them to provide clients with a broader range of options and potentially better coverage at competitive prices. They assist clients in comparing policies, obtaining quotes and negotiating terms. Insurance brokers earn commissions or fees for their services.

Insurance claim   An insurance claim is a formal request made by an individual or entity to their insurance company for compensation or coverage of a specific loss, damage, injury or event that is covered by their insurance policy. When an insured event occurs, policyholders have the right to file a claim with their insurance provider to receive financial assistance or benefits according to the terms and conditions of their policy.

Here are some key points about insurance claims:

Loss or damage: Insurance claims typically arise when an insured event occurs, resulting in a financial loss, damage to property, injury or other covered events. These events can include car accidents, home damage, medical expenses, theft, fire, natural disasters and more, depending on the type of insurance coverage.

Notification: The policyholder is responsible for notifying their insurance company as soon as the covered event occurs. Timely notification is essential, as most insurance policies have specific timeframes within which claims must be filed.

Claim process: Once the insurance company is notified, they will provide guidance on how to proceed with the claims process. This may involve submitting documentation, completing claim forms, providing evidence of the loss or damage and cooperating with any investigations if necessary.

Adjustment: Insurance adjusters, who work for the insurance company, are responsible for assessing the validity and extent of the claim. They may inspect damaged property, review medical records or interview witnesses to determine the value of the claim.

Approval or denial: After reviewing all relevant information, the insurance company will either approve or deny the claim. If approved, the insurer will provide compensation or benefits to the policyholder, which can take the form of a lump sum payment, reimbursement for expenses or direct payment to a service provider (e.g. medical provider, repair shop).

Appeals: In cases where a claim is denied or if the policyholder disagrees with the settlement offer, they have the right to appeal the decision or negotiate with the insurance company. Policyholders can also seek legal assistance or mediation if disputes arise.

Policy limits: Insurance policies often have coverage limits and deductibles. Policyholders should be aware of these limits, as they can impact the amount of compensation they receive.

Insurance claims are a fundamental part of the insurance process, allowing policyholders to access the financial protection they've paid for through their insurance premiums. It's essential for policyholders to understand the terms and conditions of their insurance policy and follow the proper procedures when filing a claim to ensure a smooth and fair claims experience.

Insurance-as-a-utility Insurance-as-a-utility is a concept in the insurance industry that refers to providing insurance coverage to consumers in a manner similar to how utilities like water, electricity or gas are supplied. It involves offering insurance products and services in a more flexible, on-demand and usage-based fashion, aligning more closely with the actual needs and behaviours of policyholders.

Key characteristics of insurance-as-a-utility include:

Pay-per-use: Instead of traditional fixed-term insurance policies, this model allows policyholders to pay for insurance coverage only when they need it. For example, they might purchase coverage for a specific duration, such as a day, week or month or for a particular event or activity.

Usage-based pricing: Premiums are calculated based on actual usage or behaviour. Policyholders may be rewarded with lower premiums for safe driving, healthy living or other positive behaviours that reduce the likelihood of claims. This encourages policyholders to adopt risk-reducing habits.

Flexibility: Policyholders have the flexibility to customize their coverage to suit their specific needs. They can easily adjust their insurance plans to add or remove coverage components as circumstances change.

On-demand access: Policyholders can access insurance services and make changes to their coverage at any time and from anywhere, typically through digital platforms and mobile apps.

Personalization: Insurers leverage data and analytics to personalize insurance offerings for individual policyholders. This can include tailoring coverage limits, deductibles and pricing to match an individual's risk profile.

Seamless integration: Insurance-as-a-utility often integrates with other services and platforms, making it convenient for policyholders to access coverage when engaging in various activities or transactions. For example, travel insurance may be offered seamlessly when booking a flight or hotel.

This concept reflects the insurance industry's efforts to adapt to changing consumer expectations and technological advancements. It aims to provide insurance coverage that is more transparent, convenient and closely aligned with the needs and behaviours of modern consumers.

Insurance premium   An insurance premium is the amount of money that an individual or entity pays to an insurance company in exchange for insurance coverage. This payment is typically made on a regular basis, such as monthly, quarterly or annually, depending on the terms of the insurance policy.

The insurance premium serves several important purposes:

Coverage: The premium is the price that policyholders pay to the insurance company for the protection and coverage provided by the insurance policy. It ensures that the policyholder is financially protected against specific risks or events, as outlined in the policy terms.

Risk pooling: Insurance companies collect premiums from a large number of policyholders to create a pool of funds. These funds are used to pay for claims made by policyholders who experience covered losses. By pooling the premiums of many policyholders, insurers can effectively spread the risk.

Profit: Insurance companies use premiums to cover their operating expenses, make a profit and maintain financial stability. The difference between the total premiums collected and the claims paid out, along with other expenses, represents the insurer's profit margin.

Actuarial calculations: Premiums are calculated based on various factors, including the insured's risk profile, the type of coverage, the coverage limits, deductibles and the insurer's underwriting practices. Actuaries play a critical role in determining the appropriate premium rates by assessing the likelihood of claims and potential losses.

Policy duration: The frequency and timing of premium payments depend on the policy's duration and the payment plan chosen by the policyholder. Some policies require annual premiums, while others offer more flexible payment options.

Insurance premiums can vary widely based on the type of insurance and the specific risk factors associated with the insured individual or property. For example, motor insurance premiums are influenced by factors like the driver's age, driving history and location, while health insurance premiums may depend on factors such as age, health status and coverage options.

It's important for policyholders to pay their premiums in a timely manner to maintain their insurance coverage. Failure to pay premiums can result in a policy cancellation, which means the policyholder will no longer have the protection provided by the insurance policy.

Insurer   Insurers (insurance companies) form the bedrock of the insurance industry, providing insurance coverage to both individuals and organizations in exchange for premium payments. Their responsibilities encompass risk assessment, policy term establishment and the facilitation of claim settlements in the event of covered incidents. While numerous insurers adhere to a traditional model with a primary focus on underwriting and risk-taking, a paradigm represented by the Lloyd's of London Market, insurers operating beyond this domain often assume broader roles that encompass distribution and claims management.

In the case of larger insurers, they frequently have in-house claims departments. However, the specific approach to claims management varies based on the nature of the risks and the jurisdiction involved. Many insurers opt to outsource their claims processing to mitigate claim-related costs, making it a strategic decision.

Insurtech   Insurtech, short for 'insurance technology', refers to the use of technology innovations to enhance and streamline various aspects of the insurance industry. Insurtech companies leverage digital tools, data analytics, AI, machine learning and other cutting-edge technologies to transform traditional insurance processes, improve customer experiences and drive innovation in the sector.

Key aspects of insurtech include:

Digital distribution: Insurtech companies often provide digital platforms and apps that allow customers to easily purchase insurance policies online or through mobile devices. This simplifies the buying process and makes insurance more accessible.

Data analytics: Insurtech firms use advanced data analytics to assess risks more accurately, price policies effectively and identify potential fraud. They can analyse large volumes of data from various sources to make data-driven decisions.

AI and machine learning (ML): AI and ML algorithms are employed for tasks such as underwriting, claims processing and customer support. These technologies can automate routine tasks and improve decision-making.

Telematics: Insurtech companies often utilize telematics devices, such as sensors in vehicles, to gather real-time data on driving behaviour. This data can be used to create personalized motor insurance policies and promote safe driving habits.

Blockchain: Blockchain technology can be employed to enhance the transparency and security of insurance transactions. It can streamline processes like claims management and reduce fraud.

Peer-to-peer insurance: Some insurtech firms explore peer-to-peer insurance models, allowing individuals to pool their resources and provide coverage for each other. This can lead to cost savings and more personalized policies.

On-demand insurance: Insurtech companies may offer on-demand insurance solutions, allowing customers to activate coverage only when needed for specific activities or time periods.

Claims processing: Automation and AI-driven claims processing can expedite the settlement of claims, reducing paperwork and administrative delays.

Customer engagement: Insurtech firms often focus on improving the overall customer experience by providing easy access to policy information, quick claims filing and personalized recommendations.

Risk assessment: Advanced algorithms can analyse vast amounts of data to assess risks more accurately, allowing insurers to tailor coverage and pricing to individual policyholders.

Insurtech has the potential to make insurance more efficient, affordable and customer-centric. It also encourages traditional insurance companies to embrace digital transformation to remain competitive in a rapidly evolving industry.

Internet of Things (IoT)   IoT refers to a network of interconnected physical devices, vehicles, buildings and other objects that are embedded with sensors, software and connectivity, allowing them to collect and exchange data over the internet. These 'smart' devices can communicate with each other and with central systems to perform various tasks and provide valuable insights based on the data they collect.

Key characteristics and components of IoT include:

Sensors: IoT devices are equipped with various types of sensors (e.g. temperature, humidity, motion, light) that gather data about their surroundings.

Connectivity: IoT devices use wireless technologies such as wi-fi, cellular networks, bluetooth and low-power wide-area networks (LPWAN) to connect to the internet and communicate with other devices.

Data processing: Data collected by IoT devices is processed and analysed either locally on the device or in the cloud, depending on the device's capabilities and purpose.

Automation: IoT devices can trigger actions or responses based on the data they collect. For example, a smart thermostat can adjust the temperature based on occupancy and user preferences.

Remote control: Many IoT devices can be controlled remotely through mobile apps or web interfaces. For instance, you can remotely lock and unlock a smart door lock or adjust the settings of a smart home security camera.

Scalability: IoT networks can scale to accommodate a large number of devices, making them suitable for various applications, from smart cities to industrial automation.

IoT has a wide range of applications across industries, including:

Smart homes: IoT devices like smart thermostats, lights and appliances enhance convenience, energy efficiency and security in homes.

Healthcare: Wearable devices and medical sensors can monitor patients' vital signs and send data to healthcare providers for remote monitoring and early intervention.

Smart cities: IoT technologies are used to improve urban planning, traffic management, waste management and public safety in cities.

Agriculture: IoT sensors and drones are employed for precision agriculture, enabling farmers to monitor soil conditions, crop health and irrigation.

Manufacturing: IoT devices enhance automation and process optimization in factories, leading to improved productivity and reduced downtime.

Transportation: Connected vehicles and smart traffic management systems improve traffic flow and road safety.

Supply chain: IoT is used to track the location and condition of goods during shipping and logistics operations.

Environmental monitoring: IoT sensors collect data on air and water quality, weather conditions and wildlife behaviour for environmental conservation efforts.

While IoT offers numerous benefits in terms of efficiency, convenience and data-driven insights, it also raises concerns about data privacy, security and the potential for misuse of data. Addressing these challenges is crucial for the responsible and secure deployment of IoT technologies.

Life insurance   Life insurance provides financial protection to beneficiaries in the event of the policyholder's death. It comes in various forms, including term life insurance, whole life insurance and universal life insurance. Life insurance helps replace lost income, cover debts and provide financial security to loved ones.

Loss ratio   The insurance loss ratio is a key financial metric used in the insurance industry to assess the profitability and performance of an insurance company's underwriting operations. It represents the ratio of insurance losses incurred by the company to the premiums earned during a specific period, typically expressed as a percentage.

The formula for calculating the loss ratio is:

Loss ratio = (Total insurance losses incurred / Total premiums earned) × 100

Here's what each component means:

Total insurance losses incurred: This includes all the claims and losses paid out by the insurance company during a given period. It represents the total amount of money the insurer has to pay to policyholders for covered losses.

Total premiums earned: This represents the total amount of premium revenue generated by the insurance company from policies issued during the same period. It includes all the premiums collected from policyholders.

The loss ratio is an essential metric for insurers because it helps them evaluate the effectiveness of their underwriting practices. A loss ratio above 100 per cent indicates that the company is paying out more in claims than it is collecting in premiums, which may lead to underwriting losses. Conversely, a loss ratio below 100 per cent suggests that the company is generating an underwriting profit, as it is paying out less in claims than it is collecting in premiums.

Insurance companies often aim to maintain a loss ratio within a specific range to ensure profitability and financial stability. However, the acceptable range can vary depending on the type of insurance and the company's business strategy. High loss ratios may prompt insurers to adjust their underwriting practices, such as increasing premiums or modifying coverage terms, to improve profitability.

Machine learning (ML)   ML is a subset of AI that focuses on the development of algorithms and statistical models that enable computer systems to improve their performance on a specific task through learning and experience, without being explicitly programmed for that task. In other words, it's a field of AI that teaches computers how to learn from data and make predictions or decisions based on that learning.

Here are some key concepts and components of ML:

Data: ML relies heavily on data. Algorithms are trained using large datasets that contain examples, features and outcomes. For instance, in an ML model for image recognition, the dataset might include thousands of images of different objects, each labelled with the correct object category.

Features: Features are the characteristics or attributes extracted from data that the ML model uses to make predictions. In a spam email filter, features might include the frequency of certain words or the sender's email address.

Labels or targets: In supervised learning, a subset of ML, each example in the dataset is associated with a label or target, which represents the correct answer or outcome. For instance, in a spam email classifier, the label might be 'spam' or 'not spam'.

Algorithms: ML algorithms are mathematical models or techniques that process the data to find patterns, relationships or trends. Examples of ML algorithms include decision trees, neural networks, support vector machines and k-nearest neighbours.

Training: The process of training a ML model involves feeding it a labelled dataset and allowing it to learn from the data. During training, the model adjusts its parameters to minimize the difference between its predictions and the actual labels in the training data.

Testing and evaluation: After training, the model is tested on new, unlabelled data to assess its performance. Various evaluation metrics, such as accuracy, precision, recall and F1 score, are used to measure how well the model generalizes to unseen data.

Types of ML:

Supervised learning: The model is trained on labelled data, where it learns to map input features to output labels. It is used for tasks like classification and regression.

Unsupervised learning: The model is trained on unlabelled data to discover patterns or group similar data points together. Examples include clustering and dimensionality reduction.

Reinforcement learning: Agents learn to make sequences of decisions in an environment to maximize a reward signal. This is common in robotics and game playing.

Semi-supervised learning: It combines elements of both supervised and unsupervised learning, often using a small amount of labelled data and a larger amount of unlabelled data.

ML has a wide range of applications, including natural language processing, computer vision, recommendation systems, autonomous vehicles, fraud detection and healthcare diagnostics. It has revolutionized industries by automating tasks, making predictions and extracting valuable insights from data.

Managing general agent (MGA)   An MGA is a specialized type of insurance intermediary or agency that plays a significant role in the insurance industry. MGAs act as intermediaries between insurance companies (carriers or insurers) and insurance agents or brokers. Here are key points to understand about MGAs:

Intermediary role: MGAs serve as intermediaries between insurance carriers and insurance agents or brokers. They have the authority to underwrite and issue insurance policies on behalf of one or more insurance companies.

Underwriting authority: MGAs are granted underwriting authority by insurance companies, allowing them to assess risks, set premiums and issue policies within specified guidelines. This authority enables MGAs to make decisions regarding policy issuance without requiring direct approval from the insurance carrier.

Specialization: Many MGAs specialize in specific types of insurance, such as niche markets or unique coverage areas. They may have expertise in areas like speciality liability, high-risk policies or hard-to-place risks.

Distribution: MGAs work closely with insurance agents and brokers, who act as intermediaries between them and policyholders. Agents and brokers rely on MGAs to provide access to specialized insurance products and markets.

Risk assessment: MGAs play a crucial role in risk assessment and pricing. They evaluate the risks associated with potential policyholders and determine appropriate premium rates based on the assessed risks.

Claims handling: In addition to underwriting, some MGAs also handle claims processing and management for the insurance policies they issue. This includes investigating claims, processing claims payments and ensuring policyholders receive the coverage they are entitled to.

Regulation: MGAs are subject to regulatory oversight in many jurisdictions and they must adhere to insurance laws and regulations. Licensing requirements and regulations may vary by location.

Business relationships: MGAs often have established relationships with insurance carriers and have the authority to bind coverage on behalf of these carriers. This streamlines the underwriting process for agents and brokers.

Market access: Insurance agents and brokers rely on MGAs to access insurance markets and products that may not be readily available through direct channels.

Profit sharing: MGAs typically earn a share of the premiums they generate, as well as potential profit-sharing arrangements with the insurance carriers they work with.

Overall, MGAs serve as key players in the insurance distribution chain, providing expertise, market access and specialized underwriting capabilities. They help insurance companies reach specific markets and expand their distribution channels while assisting agents and brokers in meeting their clients' unique insurance needs.

Microinsurance   Microinsurance is affordable insurance designed for low-income individuals and communities, offering simplified coverage for specific risks like health emergencies or natural disasters. It provides financial protection to economically vulnerable populations who have limited access to traditional insurance.

Policyholder   Policyholders are individuals or entities who hold insurance policies with an insurance company. They are the customers or clients of the insurance company and have purchased insurance coverage to protect themselves or their assets against specific risks or losses.

Property and casualty (P&C) insurance   P&C insurance provides coverage for property and liability risks. It includes various types of insurance, such as homeowners' insurance, renters' insurance, motor insurance and commercial property insurance. Property insurance protects against damage or loss of physical assets like homes, cars and business properties, while casualty insurance covers liability for injuries or damage caused to others.

Quantum computing   Quantum computing is an advanced field of computing that harnesses the principles of quantum mechanics to perform calculations. Unlike classical computers that use bits to represent data as either 0 or 1, quantum computers use quantum bits or qubits. Qubits can exist in multiple states simultaneously, thanks to a phenomenon known as superposition, which allows quantum computers to explore many possible solutions to a problem simultaneously.

Key concepts and characteristics of quantum computing include:

Superposition: As mentioned, qubits can exist in multiple states at once. This property allows quantum computers to perform certain calculations exponentially faster than classical computers.

Entanglement: Qubits can become entangled, meaning the state of one qubit is linked to the state of another, even when they are physically separated. This property enables quantum computers to perform complex calculations that involve interdependent variables.

Quantum gates: Quantum computers use quantum gates to manipulate qubits. These gates can perform operations like flipping the state of a qubit or creating entanglement between qubits.

Quantum parallelism: Quantum computers can perform many calculations in parallel, thanks to superposition. This makes them well suited for specific tasks, such as factoring large numbers (important for encryption) and simulating quantum systems.

Quantum supremacy: Quantum supremacy refers to the point at which a quantum computer can solve a problem that is practically impossible for classical computers to tackle in a reasonable amount of time. Google claimed to achieve quantum supremacy in 2019.

Despite their immense potential, quantum computers are still in the early stages of development and building practical, error-resistant quantum machines remains a significant challenge. Researchers and companies are working to overcome these challenges and quantum computing is expected to play a crucial role in solving complex problems in the future.

Regulator Government regulatory authorities oversee the insurance industry to ensure compliance with laws and regulations. They set standards for financial stability, consumer protection and fair business practices within the insurance sector.

Reinsurance Reinsurance is a process where an insurance company (the reinsurer) purchases insurance from another insurer (the ceding company) to protect itself against the risk of large losses from its policyholders. In essence, reinsurance is insurance for insurance companies.

When an insurer writes policies, it takes on the risk of paying claims to policyholders. To manage this risk and ensure its financial stability, the insurer can transfer a portion of that risk to a reinsurer. In exchange for a premium paid to the reinsurer, the ceding company is indemnified for a portion of its losses, reducing its financial exposure.

Reinsurance is a crucial aspect of the insurance industry, as it allows insurers to spread their risk and protect their financial stability in the face of unforeseen events or catastrophes. It helps insurers ensure that they have the financial capacity to pay policyholders' claims, even in extreme circumstances.

Reinsurer A reinsurer is a company or entity that provides insurance coverage to other insurance companies. In essence, reinsurers offer insurance to insurers. The primary purpose of reinsurance is to help insurance companies manage their risk exposure and protect their financial stability. Here are key points to understand about reinsurers:

Risk transfer: Reinsurance allows insurance companies (often referred to as primary insurers or cedants) to transfer a portion of their risk to reinsurers. This risk transfer helps primary insurers protect their financial assets and maintain their ability to pay claims to policyholders.

Risk sharing: Reinsurance operates on the principle of risk sharing. By ceding a portion of their policies to reinsurers, primary insurers effectively share the financial burden of claims payments, especially in the case of large or catastrophic losses.

Diversification: Reinsurers often have a broad and diverse portfolio of policies covering various geographic regions and types of risks. This diversification helps spread risk across a wider spectrum, reducing the impact of localized or specific losses on primary insurers.

There are different types of reinsurance arrangements, including:

Treaty reinsurance: This is an ongoing, contractual agreement between the primary insurer and reinsurer, where the reinsurer agrees to cover a predetermined portion of the primary insurer's policies.

Facultative reinsurance: This is a case-by-case or policy-specific arrangement where the primary insurer seeks reinsurance for individual policies or specific risks. Facultative reinsurance is typically used for unique or high-risk policies.

Reinsurance premium: Primary insurers pay reinsurance premiums to reinsurers in exchange for the coverage provided. The cost of reinsurance is factored into the primary insurer's overall operating expenses.

Claims handling: In the event of a covered claim, the primary insurer is responsible for processing and paying claims to policyholders.

Reinsurers do not typically interact directly with policyholders but settle claims with the primary insurer according to the terms of the reinsurance agreement.

Regulation: Reinsurers are subject to regulatory oversight in many jurisdictions to ensure their financial stability and ability to fulfil their obligations to primary insurers.

Capital management: Reinsurance helps primary insurers manage their capital more efficiently. By offloading some of the risk to reinsurers, primary insurers can free up capital for other purposes, such as expanding their business or investing in growth opportunities.

Catastrophe coverage: Reinsurers often provide coverage for catastrophic events, such as natural disasters or large-scale accidents, where the potential losses could be overwhelming for primary insurers to handle on their own.

Global reach: Reinsurers may operate internationally and offer coverage to primary insurers around the world. This global reach allows them to provide coverage for risks in different regions.

Reinsurance plays a crucial role in the insurance industry's stability and capacity to handle unexpected or severe events. It allows primary insurers to underwrite policies with confidence, knowing that they have the support of reinsurers to share the risk and financial responsibility. The relationship between primary insurers and reinsurers is a key component of the overall risk management strategy in the insurance sector.

Robotic process automation (RPA)   RPA is a technology that uses software robots or 'bots' to automate repetitive and rule-based tasks in business processes. These bots can mimic human actions to interact with digital systems, such as entering data, processing transactions and performing calculations. RPA is often used to streamline workflows, reduce human error and increase efficiency in various industries, including finance, healthcare and customer service. It allows organizations to automate routine tasks and free up human employees to focus on more complex and value-added activities.

Service provider A service provider is a company organization or individual that offers services to clients, customers or businesses in exchange for compensation or payment. Service providers deliver a wide range of services across various industries and their offerings can include anything from professional services to technology solutions, maintenance and support. Service providers play a crucial role in various sectors by offering specialized services to meet the needs and requirements of clients and businesses. Their expertise and capabilities contribute to the growth, efficiency and success of their clients' operations.

Sharing economy The sharing economy, also known as the collaborative economy or peer-to-peer economy, is an economic model where individuals and organizations share access to resources, services or goods, often facilitated through digital platforms or apps. It enables people to rent, share or exchange assets like vehicles, accommodations, tools and more, promoting efficient use of resources and fostering community-based interactions. Notable examples include ridesharing services like Uber and Airbnb for short-term rentals.

Telematics **Telematics** refers to the technology and field of study that combines telecommunications and informatics to send, receive and store information about remote objects or vehicles via telecommunication devices. In practical terms, telematics often involves the use of GPS (global positioning system) technology to track and monitor the movements, behaviours and performance of vehicles or assets.
  Key components of telematics typically include:

GPS technology: Telematics systems use GPS or other satellite-based positioning systems to accurately determine the location of a vehicle or asset in real-time. GPS enables precise tracking and mapping of routes and movements.

Data communication: Telematics devices are equipped with communication modules (usually cellular or satellite) that allow them to transmit data to a central server or database. This data can include location information, vehicle speed, engine diagnostics and more.

Data analysis: The data collected by telematics systems is often analysed to extract valuable insights. This analysis can involve identifying patterns, trends or anomalies in vehicle behaviour, driver performance or asset utilization.

Fleet management: Telematics is commonly used in fleet management, where it helps businesses track and manage their vehicles efficiently. Fleet operators can monitor vehicle locations, optimize routes, reduce fuel consumption and ensure driver safety.

Insurance telematics: In the insurance industry, telematics is used to monitor and assess driver behaviour. Insurance companies may offer usage-based insurance (UBI) programmes that use telematics data to determine premiums based on individual driving habits, such as speed, braking and mileage.

Asset tracking: Telematics is also used for tracking valuable assets beyond vehicles, such as shipping containers, construction equipment and even personal items. Asset tracking can help prevent theft, improve security and optimize asset utilization.

Safety and security: Telematics systems can provide real-time alerts and notifications for various safety and security purposes. For example, they can alert authorities in the event of a vehicle accident or trigger anti-theft measures if unauthorized movement is detected.

Environmental monitoring: Some telematics systems are used to monitor environmental factors, such as air quality, temperature and humidity, in specific locations or vehicles.

Telematics technology has applications in various industries, including transportation, logistics, insurance, agriculture and healthcare. It enables organizations to gather data, make informed decisions, enhance operational efficiency and improve safety and security.

Third-party administrators (TPAs) TPAs are independent organizations or entities that manage various aspects of insurance claims and policy administration on behalf of insurance companies. They provide services such as claims processing, policy management, customer service and other administrative functions. TPAs serve as intermediaries between insurance companies and policyholders, help-ing streamline operations and improve efficiency in handling claims and policy-related tasks. Their role is particularly significant in managing large volumes of claims and ensuring a smooth claims process.

Underwriter Underwriters assess and evaluate insurance applica-tions to determine the level of risk associated with insuring a particular policyholder or asset. They decide whether to accept, modify or reject insurance applications and set premium rates accord-ingly. This role is integral not only within insurance companies but also in organizations such as MGAs and service providers that offer underwriting consultancy services.

Underwriting Underwriting is the process of evaluating and assess-ing the risks associated with insuring a person, property or event and determining the terms and conditions of the insurance coverage. It involves analysing various factors such as the applicant's health, age, occupation and other relevant information in the case of life or health insurance or assessing the value, condition and location of property in the case of property and casualty insurance. Based on this evalua-tion, the underwriter decides whether to accept the risk, what coverage to offer and at what premium (price). Underwriting helps insurance companies manage their risk exposure and ensure that they can meet their financial obligations to policyholders.

VA Home Loan VA Home Loan, also known as a VA Loan or Veterans Affairs Home Loan, is a mortgage loan programme in the United States specifically designed to assist eligible veterans, active-duty service members and certain members of the National Guard and Reserves in obtaining home financing. This programme is admin-istered by the US Department of Veterans Affairs (VA) and is intended to help veterans and their families achieve homeownership.

Key features of VA Home Loans include:

No down payment: One of the significant benefits of VA loans is that eligible borrowers can purchase a home without making a down payment. This feature makes homeownership more accessible, particularly for those who may not have substantial savings for a down payment.

Competitive interest rates: VA loans typically offer competitive interest rates that are comparable to or lower than those of conventional mortgage loans. This can result in lower monthly mortgage payments for veterans.

No private mortgage insurance (PMI): Unlike many conventional loans, VA loans do not require borrowers to pay PMI. This can lead to additional cost savings over time.

Flexible credit requirements: While VA loans have credit requirements, they tend to be more flexible than those of some other mortgage programmes. Veterans with less-than-perfect credit histories may still qualify for a VA loan.

Lenient qualification standards: The VA does not set strict debt-to-income ratio requirements, making it easier for veterans to qualify for these loans.

Limits on closing costs: The VA limits the amount of closing costs that veterans can be charged, reducing the financial burden associated with closing on a home.

Refinancing options: VA loan holders may be eligible for VA Interest Rate Reduction Refinance Loans (IRRRL) or 'Streamline' refinancing, which can lower their monthly mortgage payments.

To qualify for a VA Home Loan, individuals must meet specific service requirements, which can include a minimum length of service or service during certain wartime or peacetime periods. Spouses of deceased veterans may also be eligible for VA loan benefits.

It's essential for potential borrowers to work with approved VA lenders to navigate the application and approval process for VA Home Loans. These loans have played a crucial role in helping veterans and their families achieve the dream of homeownership.

Virtual reality (VR)   VR is a technology that immerses users in a computer-generated, three-dimensional environment. When a person interacts with a VR system, they are typically provided with a headset that covers their eyes and ears and often includes motion-tracking sensors. This headset creates the illusion that the user is inside a virtual world, where they can see and hear objects and events as if they were physically present.

Key features and concepts of virtual reality include:

Immersive environment: VR aims to create a sense of presence and immersion, where users feel like they are inside the virtual world, surrounded by computer-generated imagery and sounds.

Head tracking: VR headsets often include sensors that track the user's head movements, allowing them to look around and interact with the virtual environment by moving their head.

Motion controllers: Many VR systems also include handheld motion controllers that enable users to interact with objects and perform actions in the virtual world.

Stereoscopic display: VR headsets use two screens, one for each eye, to create a stereoscopic effect that mimics the way humans perceive depth in the real world.

Realistic sound: VR systems often include spatial audio technology to provide realistic 3D audio cues that match the user's perspective.

VR technology has advanced significantly in recent years, with more accessible and powerful VR headsets available to consumers. It continues to evolve, offering exciting possibilities for entertainment, education and professional applications.

INDEX

Looking for another book?

Explore our award-winning
books from global business
experts in Finance and
Banking

Scan the code to browse

www.koganpage.com/finance

Printed in the USA
CPSIA information can be obtained
at www.ICGtesting.com
JSHW071907260424
61914JS00009B/38